Feb. 1979

To Monique

with my warm wishes

for happiness

love. Max D

The Life and Lore of the Bird

The Life and Lore of the Bird
In Nature, Art, Myth, and Literature

by Edward A. Armstrong

Crown Publishers Inc. New York   A Chanticleer Press Edition

First Edition
Library of Congress Catalog Card Number 75-15261
ISBN 0-517-524341

Grateful acknowledgment is hereby made for permission to reprint selections from the following works:

Flamingo Hunt, copyright © 1953, by Paul A. Zahl, reprinted by permission of the publisher, The Bobbs-Merrill Company, Inc.
A Sand County Almanac with other essays on conservation from Round River by Aldo Leopold. Copyright © 1949, 1953, 1966 by Oxford University Press, Inc. Reprinted by permission.
Canary by Gustav Eckstein. Copyright 1936 by Gustav Eckstein. By permission of Harper & Row, Publishers, Inc.
The Yearling by Marjorie Kinnan Rawlings. Reprinted by permission of the publishers, Charles Scribner's Sons.
The Singing Wilderness by Sigurd F. Olson. Copyright © 1956 by Sigurd F. Olson. Reprinted by permission of Alfred A. Knopf, Inc.
King Solomon's Ring by Konrad Z. Lorenz. Copyright © 1952 by Konrad Z. Lorenz. Reprinted by permission of Thomas Y. Crowell, Co., Inc.

Prepared and produced by Chanticleer Press, Inc.
Staff of this book:
Publisher: Paul Steiner
Editor-in-Chief: Milton Rugoff
Project Editor: Lynne Williams
Production: Gudrun Buettner and Emma Staffelbach
Design: Roberta Savage

Printed in Japan

Contents

Introduction 6
1. The Evolution of Birds 14
2. Flight, Song, and Dance 28
3. Birds in Prophecy and Magic 50
4. Birds Fabulous and Mythical 76
5. Birds in Sport and Recreation 100
6. Birds Friendly, Decorative, and Useful 128
7. Feathers and Finery 150
8. Endangered Birds and the Struggle to Save Them 174
9. Birds in Art 200
10. Birds in Literature 230
   Appendix: A Selection of Great Writings about Birds 250
   Index 269
   Credits 272

Introduction

Men and birds have always had close relationships. This may be said of other creatures but birds have been associated with mankind in so many different ways throughout the ages that they have a special interest for most of us. In the following pages we can do no more than touch briefly on some of these relationships.

Birds are remarkable, indeed unique, in that no member of this huge group of animals has ever been a direct menace to man. Bacteria may kill us; insects may plague us and transmit disease to us; some snakes are deadly to us; and the shark, crocodile, lion, and tiger have the reputations of being, at times, man-eaters, but even the largest and most powerful birds have never been a serious threat.

On the other hand, birds have been used by man in innumerable ways. Primitive people killed them for food and other purposes, including sacrifice, and raided their nesting colonies for eggs—a convenient source of nutritious food, palatable even when uncooked. Civilized man has slaughtered them for their plumage. Birds may even have had a share in the initiation of cultural developments, such as pottery-making and weaving, although this cannot be proved; but as man is an imitative creature, it is not a wild flight of fancy to picture one of our remote ancestors watching a swallow or martin building a nest and then trying his hand at shaping clay into a bowl. When robbing a nest he may have examined the way it was woven and then tried to imitate it in weaving a mat.

Putting aside speculation, we know that from earliest times birds aroused wonder and became involved in magical or magico-religious ceremonies. However we may interpret the Old Stone Age painting in a cave at Lascaux of a bird-headed man falling backward while confronted by a wounded bison as a bird perched on a post nearby looks on, it proves that birds were viewed with interest and respect, and probably with awe, as magical or supernatural creatures. The use of feathers as headdresses from the Stone Age onward shows how ancient is man's admiration for the colors and shapes of birds. Birds have also been appreciated in many cultures, not only for what they are—bright, active, colorful, melodious—but as mysterious beings, able to mount to the heavens, to disappear for months at a time and then return from no man knows where. Our primitive ancestors may have regarded birds as better adapted to cope with the environment than they were themselves. Apart from other considerations their plumage enabled birds to adapt to changes in the weather more readily than men could. Of course, unsophisticated people have never thought of birds in the analytical way natural to us, but direct observation, wonder, and speculation made it easy to view them as numinous, otherworldly

Above *Fowling in the marshes, as shown in a painting from the Tomb of Nebamum at Thebes (c. 1400 B.C.).* Facing page *North African prehistoric rock engraving depicting ostriches. These birds are now extinct in this region.*

Below *Coin with swan from Ionia, Greece (c. 200–300 B.C.).*
Facing page *Bird drawn on a garment made of tree bark for use in ceremonial costume by the Kashinaua Indians of Brazil.*
Overleaf *Hunting scene in a thicket, a detail from a papyrus painting from the Tombs of the Nobles at Thebes (c. 1450 B.C.). The painter has shown black hunting slings hurled into the air among the birds.*

beings in league with unseen powers; and so birds had their share in stretching men's minds and enlarging their outlook to include the unseen. Thus magical and religious concepts were formulated which still influence and enrich our thinking. All over the world birds have had spiritual significance, in the broad sense that would encompass aesthetic appreciation, wonder, and reverence.

With the dawn of civilization, notions of the affinity between man and animals which had underlain totemic and related cults continued to have importance, as shown in the arts—painting, sculpture, dancing, and the wearing of bird masks and plumage. The development of agriculture led to a change in attitudes toward birds. Man realized that he was separate from his environment and could mold it in a special degree. Early literatures testify to this. Adam was given lordship over other creatures and Noah accepted responsibility for the survival of wildlife. Thus mythology emphasized the gulf between man and beast.

In the plentiful myths and legends which have come down to us we find our ancestors bringing imagination to bear on their relationship with animals, and striving to establish order in their thoughts about their surroundings, their fellows, and the unseen powers. So literature and art were born as creative efforts to convey such ideas and ideals. Some birds came to be regarded as oracular and were used in divination and other rituals. Others were spoken of as bearing gods or heroes magically from place to place, and strange stories were formulated. Some of them are beautiful, such as the Irish myth of the Children of Lir, which tells of their magical transformation into swans. Fionnuala tenderly cared for her brothers on the stormy Waters of Moyle off the Irish coast until, centuries later, they were restored to human form and were baptized before they died. Beneath the surface of such tales there is much to be explored. They mirror the activities of our own minds, usually hidden from us. Similarly, the symbolism of such birds as the eagle and the dove occurs so extensively that to study it would be not only a fascinating historical investigation but a plunge deep into man's subconscious mind.

When the countryside was gradually tamed, as in England, the attitude to birds changed and became patronizing. Some birds, such as the fowl, duck, and goose, were domesticated, and wild birds were killed for sport rather than for food, but there was also a growth of tenderness, to which our pet names for many species of birds bear witness.

From the late medieval period onward there was increasing dissatisfaction with the book lore about birds, which derived largely from the works of Aristotle and

Pliny. Emperor Frederick II, the great falconer, declared some of it to be false; the stories of Saint Francis revealed the emergence of a feeling of fellowship with birds; and artists such as Giotto studied birds carefully and depicted what they saw. The scientific outlook increasingly constrained those who wrote of birds to go into the field rather than the library.

Within this generation there have been two outstanding developments in man's relationship with birds. First, popular interest has increased, particularly in the developed countries, though some lag lamentably behind. In English-speaking lands, ornithological societies and bird clubs abound, and informed opinion is fostered by excellently illustrated books, lectures, TV films, and recordings of bird songs. A normal feature of such groups' activities is trips into the countryside. Travel firms organize visits to bird haunts far and near. Young bird-lovers are thus encouraged and helped. With greater understanding of bird life has come a realization of how birds are menaced, and interest in conservation has increased enormously. Secondly, when the older generation of bird-lovers was young, almost all wild-bird study was done by amateurs, whereas today ornithology is an established profession. An able student can look forward to studying birds as a full-time occupation, adequately remunerated. Ornithology has advanced quickly and has evolved such specializations as the study of bird song, with much time and energy devoted to the analysis of recordings, using apparatus that has improved immensely in recent years.

The amateur need not be discouraged by the realization that specialists are spending all their time in bird study. He can enjoy birds and bird-watching as most people enjoy novels without becoming novelists themselves. But for some there is special delight in having an intimate knowledge of one bird or one aspect of bird life, gained after years of study. The following pages mention some topics well worth investigating.

By reason of the opening up of previously inaccessible parts of the world and the knowledge already amassed, we are in a better position than any of our predecessors to review the role that birds, and other animals, have played in religion, magic, mythology, ritual, art, and in influencing man's response to his total environment, seen and unseen. There is an endless fascination in exploring these relationships.

Facing page A skillful rendering of birds in a Roman wall painting from the Villa of Livia (c. 38 B.C.). Below Minoan gold pendant representing what is known as the Master of the Animals motif. In it a human figure grasps animals of the same species in either hand (c. 1700–1600 B.C.).

1
The Evolution of Birds

The patient work of scientists studying fossils and scraps of bone enables us to glimpse the world as it was millions of years ago and visualize strange scenes from a time long before a human being was there to see them. The guiding principle of such experts is that there was an evolution from lower to higher forms of life, so that if enough of an animal has been preserved as a fossil, we can place it in its correct sequence. A comparison of fossils reveals that at one time no warm-blooded animals existed; they developed over an immense period of time from certain cold-blooded animals, such as snakes and frogs. Moreover, by studying fossils that occur in the same layers of rock we can determine which animals and plants lived together in the same epoch and imagine what the world was like at certain periods in the past. So let us make an imaginary excursion into such a remote period, to south Germany as it was 150 million years ago, using whatever guidelines are available. What would we see?

We are standing where the tide spreads in rhythmic wavelets over shallow lagoons and we notice that the sand is mounded up in hillocks here and there, indicating that sometimes fierce winds blow and sandstorms occur. The shells of mollusks lie around us, for snails and shellfish have inhabited the earth for a vast amount of time, and because their shells are preserved in the rocks we know a good deal about how they evolved. Peering into a clear pool we see fish darting about, and in the mud of another pool a strange-looking big crab with a spiked "tail"—a king crab, not very different from the king crabs living in warm seas today. On the shore, lizards scurry across the warm sand or bask on the stumps of spiny-leafed trees. There are no flowering plants. Insects big and little fly around.

THE FIRST BIRD—BUT NOT QUITE

Looking up we are surprised to see what appears to be a big, angular bat, with a long head and toothed jaws, floating and flapping among the trees—a flying reptile called a pterosaur or pterodactyl. (The largest known pterodactyl fossil was found recently in Texas; it had a wingspan of fifty-one feet!) Next, our attention is drawn to a brown creature about the size of a crow among the branches of a large bush nearby. It is hauling itself up with the aid not only of its strong legs and feet but of hooks or claws at the angles of its wings. As it clambers, the creature stops to push its snout into crevices, seizing insects, spiders, and other such organisms. It looks like a very odd lizard, with feathery flaps hanging down its body and extending on either side of its long tail. So it ascends until it reaches a projecting branch. There it rests for some time, then looks warily around, crouches, springs into the air, and

Above *Restoration of the fossil* Archaeopteryx. *This creature was about the size of a crow.*
Facing page *Cast of the fossil* Archaeopteryx. *Its reptilian head and unusual tail are evident.*

Facing page *Restoration of a pterosaur* (Rhamphorynchus) *in flight. Unlike a bird, it has prominent teeth.*
Below *Flamingo. Fossil remains show that there were flamingos about 50 million years ago.*

floats down to the ground with stubby wings outspread and its very long, flattened tail supporting it as it glides. Attached to a body that is in some respects so birdlike, this tail looks very peculiar. When the creature alights among some ferns, we see that although it has the head of a lizard, its wings are indeed feathered.

We have been looking at a creature named *Archaeopteryx lithographica,* meaning "the ancient winged one of the lithographic slate," after the slate quarry in which the fossil was found. The fossil remains, found in Bavaria in 1861, 1877, and 1956, tell such a clear story about its appearance that we can be confident our imagination has not led us far astray. If, during our peep into the past, we had been able to examine the animal as closely as we can inspect the slabs of slate which record its characteristics in wonderful detail, we would have noticed that it had teeth and that its tail looked strange because it had a large number of free vertebrae—twenty. In both respects it was quite unlike a bird. It was incapable of flying to the tops of tall trees, but once it had climbed some distance it could glide down, much as flying lizards and squirrels do today. Incidentally, although we think the power of flight so useful, it has been lost by members of many families of birds including grebes, cormorants, quails, ducks, parrots, and whole groups—the running birds (ratites) and penguins. Flight uses up energy very quickly, so there has been a tendency for it to deteriorate and disappear wherever an animal did not need it to escape enemies or to secure food. The dodo and the great auk, both flightless, were well adapted to their surroundings until an ingenious mammal, man, invented big seagoing boats and could invade their haunts.

The remains of *Archaeopteryx,* with its mingled reptilian and bird features, enable us to deduce that it evolved from a group of small, agile reptiles called pseudosuchians, which relied on two feet for getting around. The parts of its body were not all modified at one time during its evolution, but one after the other—as if it had to make sure that one modification worked before it tried another! The long tail and the claws were reptilian but the thumb, or "hallux," for grasping branches was not. The brain was relatively small and reptilian, implying less adaptability than birds possess. Its feathers were identical with birds' feathers today, as is confirmed by a single, beautifully preserved mineralized specimen, also found in the Bavarian quarry. Feathers played a crucial part in the advance from reptiles to birds that could fly in the fullest sense, because feathers are not only light but warm, enabling their possessors to maintain the high temperature necessary for strenuous activity. The remains of some ancient lizards with large, somewhat leaflike scales

and a striation down the center hint at the way feathers evolved.

We may venture to infer a little more concerning the behavior of this "halfway bird." Since various amphibians and reptiles can make vocal sounds, we may assume that *Archaeopteryx* could do so because it would have been advantageous for individuals whose movements were both vertical and horizontal to be able to keep in touch with one another. The projections on the wings suggest that the bushes and trees amid which *Archaeopteryx* lived were fairly dense. Today, birds frequenting thick cover, such as the jay, the nutcracker, and many rain-forest birds, including the greater bird of paradise, commonly have loud and harsh voices. Thus we may assume that *Archaeopteryx* uttered croaks, grunts, moans, or hisses, especially when courting or threatening.

The advantages of flight or gliding flight are obvious: not only may food be sought in bushes and trees as well as on the ground, but there is greater safety aloft from certain pursuers. Because it is also safer to nest off the ground—even though there were reptiles that could climb trees—*Archaeopteryx* probably did so.

The hoatzin of South America resembles *Archaeopteryx* in some respects, so its structure and behavior can throw light on the characteristics of its distant ancestor. Its plumage is brown, the young have "wing-claws" that enable them to climb about in trees, and even a quite young bird can use its wings somewhat as if they were forepaws and can grip twigs with its bill as well as its powerful feet. These adaptations are particularly valuable because the flight feathers develop late and sometimes get broken as the bird uses its wings in moving among branches. The adult flaps around rather clumsily in the foliage, using its long tail to keep its balance. Hoatzins live in flooded mangrove swamps, and when a predator approaches they dive from the nest down to the water. They utter harsh cries and tend to remain secluded during the hours of bright sunshine. *Archaeopteryx* also may have nested over water, and probably was active at dawn and dusk when it was less liable to be seized by some reptile.

OTHER PREHISTORIC BIRDS

It is very fortunate that the remains of *Archaeopteryx* were preserved because the next fossil bird about which we know anything lived some 30 million years later. It is as if, after prolonged darkness, a lightning flash had given us a vivid, momentary glimpse of this half-bird and then all was darkness again. As far as can be judged from a single thighbone, we know that the next bird in the line of fossils was apparently gooselike. Still nearer our time lived a proto-cormorant and another sea bird the size of a pigeon which may have flown around near what is now Cambridge, England. After it, fossils of several species of *Ichthyornis* (fish bird), which could fly well, were found in chalk formations in Kansas. They were about eight inches long, rather like terns, and picked fish from the water. Still another, *Hesperornis* (western bird), from the same chalk formation, was five feet in length and entirely aquatic. *Hesperornis* was streamlined for swimming but it was unable to fly and its legs were set so far back on its body that it must have been even more awkward on land than the loon, or great northern diver, which can only shuffle clumsily to where it lays its eggs only a foot or two from the water. Thus by the Cretaceous period of the Mesozoic era, some 120 million years ago, birds were well established. During this period flowering plants appeared, rendering land habitats more varied and providing a wider range of nesting sites and sources of food.

Facing page *Cast of a reconstruction of a* Diatryma, *a North American species that lived some 60 million years ago. It was flightless, carnivorous, stood seven feet high, and had a donkey-sized head.*
Below *Whale-headed stork, the modern species which most nearly resembles the powerful* Phororhacos, *which lived during the Miocene epoch, between 11 and 25 million years ago.*

Since land birds are much less likely than aquatic or wet-land species to fall into water and have their bones fossilized, we are almost completely ignorant about their evolution until the Eocene epoch, 40 million to 70 million years back, when reptiles had passed their heyday. At that point, birds succeeded in supplanting the flying reptiles known as pterosaurs, feathers enabling them to outclass the winged reptiles. Undoubtedly there were great numbers of bird species whose remains have not been preserved, but many of the Eocene fossils can be identified as belonging to bird families still represented today. Birds had by then evolved sufficiently for a modern ornithologist to have been able to recognize the affinities of most of them. By that time there had also been a relatively rapid differentiation into different forms, such as bustards, herons, cranes, storks, ducks, geese, rails, grebes, gulls, and sandpipers. Some modern birds with ancestries stretching back to this period, such as flamingoes and vultures, have what a layman might call an old-fashioned look. They evolved early to fill definite "ecological niches"—flamingoes, for example, to feed on small organisms near the surface of water, and vultures to act as scavengers.

One of the strangest of these Eocene birds, *Diatryma,* was rather like a shaggy emu, seven feet in height, flightless, and equipped with a very massive beak. Later on, in the Miocene, about 10 million years ago, a large, flightless, and ferocious-looking species, truly a nightmare of a bird, *Phororhacos,* roamed the Patagonian plains. It stood five feet high and had a skull eighteen inches in length. On its powerful legs it could run down small reptiles and mammals, and defy, disable, or kill most predators. The modern species most resembling it outwardly is the shoebill or whale-headed stork, which uses its huge bill to crush the shells of turtles.

During this period a huge sea bird, *Osteodontornis,* with a wingspread of fifteen feet, flapped and glided over the sea in the area now occupied by California. More recently—that is, from the Pleistocene epoch to recent times—there lived *Aepyornis titan,* the largest of the elephant birds of Madagascar—ten feet tall. Its eggs were big enough to hold two gallons or the contents of seven ostrich eggs, and were used by the local inhabitants as mixing bowls. It has been suggested that acquaintance with these eggs or surviving traditions about the birds may have contributed to stories here about the mythical gigantic roc.

There were plenty of smaller birds in that early era but their bones were too fragile to be preserved. Very small birds can coexist with very large birds because they occupy different foraging and breeding niches.

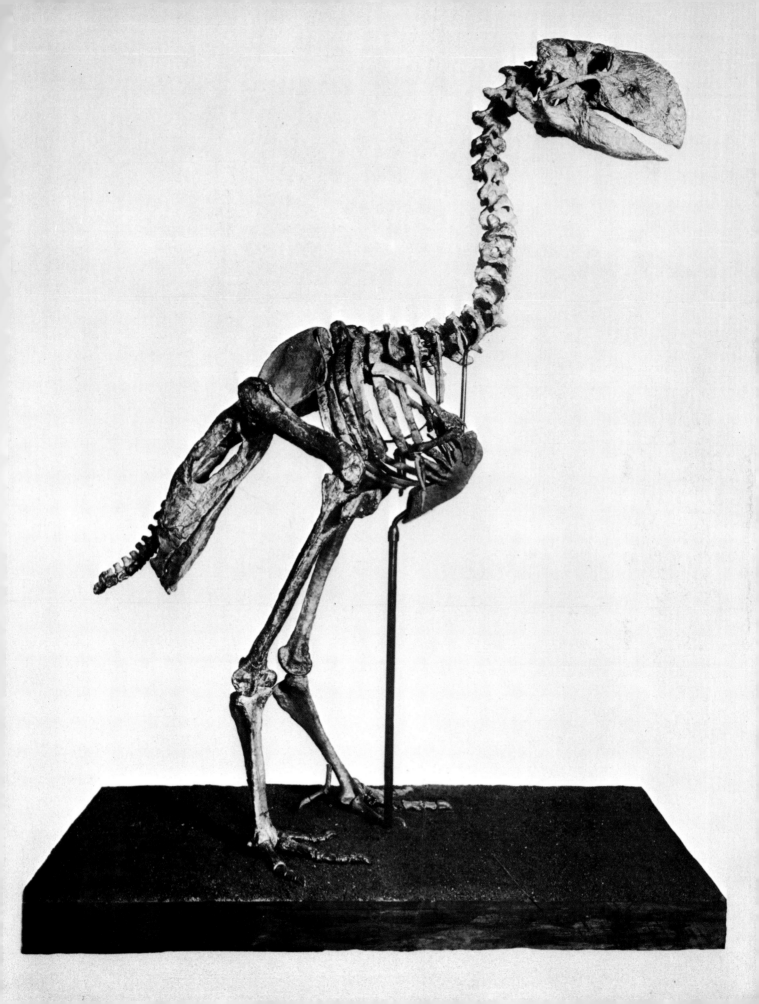

Species in the same area must not overlap too much in their requirements. A hummingbird is adapted to hover in front of flowers and suck their nectar, a pelican to catch and carry fish. This is obvious, but the principle reaches even further. Thus even closely related birds have different ways of feeding.

THE GIANTS

There is an enormous difference between the largest and the smallest bird. The scintillating hummingbird weighs only eight-hundredths of an ounce, whereas an ostrich may weigh more than three hundred pounds, so one is more than sixty-four thousand times heavier than the other. In this rapid survey we are concentrating on the large birds because, first, we are able to follow their evolution much better than that of small species, the remains of which are preserved only in exceptional circumstances. Secondly, they are important because extreme forms are useful as indicators of the environment in which they were successful; and thirdly, monsters fascinate us just because they are monstrous.

Why should some birds in the past have evolved to so large a size? They evidently could do so because they were able to secure the food, animal or vegetable, that they needed. Most outsize land mammals—witness the elephant, hippopotamus, rhinoceros, bison, tapir, giant panda—are vegetarian. Gigantism is advantageous in the animal world insofar as few predators can overcome such big birds and beasts, even though bulk is no guarantee of survival, as the extinction of many such animals shows. Huge flightless birds occurred on large islands such as Madagascar and New Zealand, mainly because there were no large carnivorous animals to attack them. The emu of Australia and Tasmania and the cassowaries of New Guinea and Queensland also have outgrown potential predators. Moreover, a cassowary can kick so viciously as to disable or kill any beast which menaces it. The rhea of South America and the African ostrich, the largest extant bird—it is eight feet in height—live on continents where large predatory animals, such as the jaguar and puma in South America, and the lion and leopard in Africa, roam; but they favor open, arid, or grassland country where their height enables them to keep a good lookout for signs of danger and their speed facilitates escape. It is reliably reported that even month-old ostrich chicks can sprint at a speed of thirty-five miles an hour.

BIRDS AND DRIFTING CONTINENTS

These flightless birds also introduce us to some extraordinary chapters in the history of our planet. It has been noted for example that the louse that lives in the

Facing page *Male ostrich. A single species survives in Africa, whereas the Arabian ostriches, a different race of the same species, have been exterminated by man.* Below *A comparison of an ostrich egg with a hummingbird egg illustrates the great range in the size of bird species.*

Facing page *Maps illustrating the "drifting" of the continental land masses, showing approximate locations from 225 million years ago* (top) *to the present* (bottom).
Below *Male rhea displaying to the female. Two species of this flightless bird occur in South America.*

plumage of the ostrich is found also in the plumage of the rhea and nowhere else. The possibility that it has been carried by man or any other creature from one continent to the other may be ruled out for a number of reasons. Only recently, through the labors of scientists in such different fields as geology and entomology, has the explanation been found.

When they first study a map of the world, children often get the impression that Europe and Africa, if pushed together, would fit into North and South America. What was once thought to be a childish fancy is now a widely accepted theory: to wit, that long ago the continents drifted apart. Briefly, there was a great southern landmass, named Gondwanaland, enormous slabs of which moved away from each other to form the continents of the Southern Hemisphere. Gondwanaland included Antarctica (which had a much milder climate then) and covered a huge area, enabling the ancestors of the big flightless birds to spread from South America to what are now Africa, Madagascar, Australia, and New Zealand. If we think in terms of a greatly accelerated film, Gondwanaland began to break up about 135 million years ago, Africa separated from Antarctica and from South America about 85 million years back, Australia moved northward from eastern Antarctica some forty million years ago, and New Zealand separated from western Antarctica. Madagascar became isolated from Africa, allowing its giant birds to evolve separately; so, too, did New Zealand with its moas.

Confirmation of this mind-stretching drama of the wandering continents is furnished by the discovery on the Azores of fragments of eggshells resembling those of ostriches or elephant birds. If there are still some people who wonder why scientists spend their lives looking into microscopes at lice or discussing why the feathers of the ostrich and cassowary differ from those of other birds, the answer is plain: such details enable us eventually to perceive the larger patterns. The physicist provides the ornithologist with radioisotope dating techniques, and the biochemist's analysis of birds' eggs helps to determine the relationships of species.

The Pliocene epoch, which preceded the Pleistocene, lasted about nine million years and saw the appearance of many groups familiar to us, such as larks, thrushes, and nuthatches. During the Pleistocene, covering the last two million years, advances and recessions of ice during the Ice Age caused great climatic changes and, consequently, great shifts in the distribution of species. Periods of very favorable climatic conditions, as well as the absence of mammalian predators to prey on them, and grazing beasts, such as sheep, to compete with

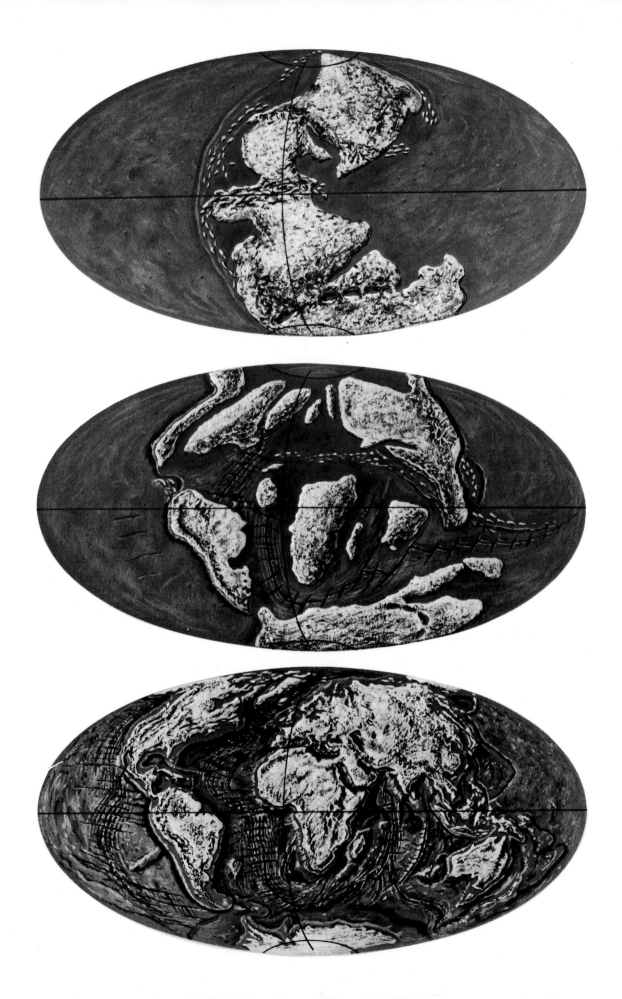

them, enabled the New Zealand moas to thrive and to differentiate into about a score of species. The largest of these attained a height of ten feet. They are now extinct, mainly because the Maoris, who invaded New Zealand in prehistoric times, exploited the birds to such an extent that the period is called the Age of the Moa Hunters. Probably moas, like the dodo and great auk, were unsuspecting and easily slaughtered.

THE FOSSIL EVIDENCE

One of the bonanzas that fossil-hunters have come upon is the many moa skeletons in a number of swamps where the birds apparently got bogged down thousands of years ago. One of these unintentional traps for birds and beasts is now a built-up area in Los Angeles, California. Unwary creatures became stuck in a tar or asphalt pit at Rancho La Brea, and from this pit scientists have unearthed or, rather, untarred the bones of a great many mammals and birds. The mammals include mastodon, mammoth, sabretooth, mountain lion, bear, horse, camel, wolf, and peccary, many of these probably attracted to an area where other beasts or birds had already been caught in the sticky mass. Amazingly, about 146 different types of birds have been found there, including the remains of a stork, a condor, and an owl that lived about 14,000 years ago and, among birds that have become extinct, two species of eagles, two species of vultures, a turkey, a goose, and a blackbird that lived, as dated by radio-carbon methods, in the period between 10,000 and 4,550 years ago. Human remains were found in a deposit contemporary with a huge condorlike vulture known as Merriam's teratorn.

Another type of site where fossils are found is caves. Thus, the remains of the largest known flying bird of this epoch, appropriately named the incredible teratorn, were found in a cave in Nevada. It had a wingspread of over sixteen feet. From these and other discoveries it has been concluded that in the broad essentials the species of birds some twenty thousand years ago—allowing for extinctions and modifications—were much the same as they are today.

Just as a small area like La Brea, in a park of twenty-five acres, can be a treasure house of extinct species, so a few larger areas such as the Hawaiian and Galapagos islands are now living museums illustrating how birds evolved. Both were colonized by a few storm-driven birds, Hawaii by honeycreepers and the Galapagos by finchlike birds, probably from Ecuador. In both groups of islands the birds in the course of time diverged from the original type and became adapted in structure and behavior to exploiting much more of the islands' resources than were the first individuals. The birds on the

Facing page *An anhinga, or snakebird, drying its wings. The stock from which these birds as well as cormorants and pelicans evolved branched off from the main stem long before the small perching birds. It often swims with only its head and neck above water.* Below *Reconstruction of the extinct bird known as the moa.*

Drawings by the American bird artist Louis Agassiz Fuertes showing the relationship between feet or bills and food-getting techniques among various birds.
Below (top to bottom) The foot of the horned grebe, whose diet includes both fish and insects, is adapted both to swimming and to foraging in marshes. Although aquatic, the common gallinule has feet better suited to land foraging than those of the grebe; its diet consists of vegetation and small organisms. The talons of the Cooper's hawk are adapted to snatching up small birds and mammals, including the young of ground-nesting game birds.

Facing page a) The curlew's long bill is suited to probing in mud or sand. b) The flattened beak of the Atlantic puffin serves to carry a number of small fish horizontally. c) The bill of the American flamingo is submerged bottom upwards and sucks in small organisms near the surface of the water; the water is then forced out through "hairs" in the bill. d) The toucan's bill is light, enabling it to reach for and accommodate berries and larger fruits. e) When feeding, the roseate spoonbill sweeps its bill from side to side, scooping up aquatic organisms. f) The beak of the white-headed eagle, adapted for tearing flesh, is typical of large birds of prey.

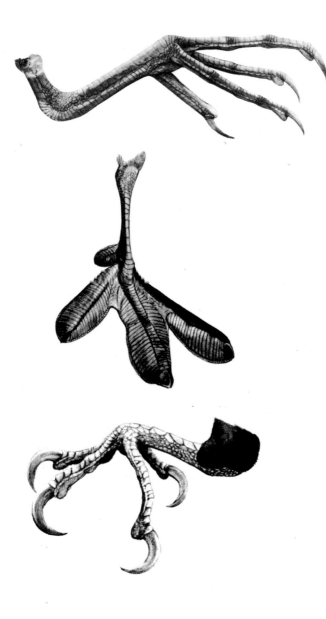

Galapagos are now known as Darwin's finches, in part because Darwin found evidence in them which led to his theory of evolution. Here it could be seen that competition and adaptation had enabled the descendants of the few immigrants—perhaps a single pair—to exploit many different resources on the islands. To do so the birds evolved into different species: some remained vegetarian, some became insectivorous, a few became warblerlike, a number adapted to feeding mainly on the ground, and still others to foraging on the islands' cacti.

Most remarkable of all is the woodpecker finch, which, like a woodpecker, climbs up and down vertical trunks and branches. Its beak is modified in the direction of the woodpecker type but, not having evolved a long tongue such as woodpeckers use to lick insects out of deep crevices, it picks up a cactus spine and pokes it into such hiding places, then drops it and seizes the insect driven out by the spine. It is as if evolution could not wait to fashion the bird fully for the job and took a shortcut, using brains rather than structure. Darwin's finches show us, in miniature, how evolution works, organisms diverging and adapting to occupy unexploited niches.

Viewed in the wide perspective of geological time we see that species are on the move. The "everlasting rocks" tell us how transitory was the stay of the creatures whose remains they preserve. It has been estimated than in the 150 million years since *Archaeopteryx* there have evolved some 1.5 million species of birds; but only between eight and nine thousand species are alive today. Nature's children come and go. An Anglo-Saxon chieftain once commented that the life of man is comparable with a bird that flutters into a council hall and flies out into the darkness. The analogy may also be applied to bird species.

a

b

c

d

e

f

Flamingo
Grassy Creek
Andros Island
May 10, 1942

young White-head
Eagle

2
Flight, Song, and Dance

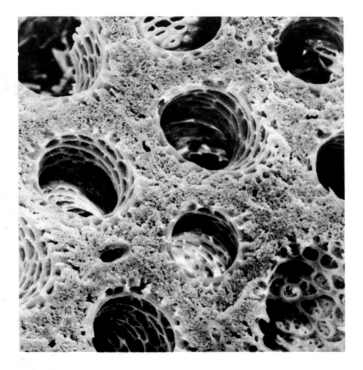

Above *Interior of a bird's lung showing the spongy structure which enables air to flow through the lung instead of in and out as in a mammal. This highly developed respiratory system contributes to the efficiency of a bird's flight.*

Facing page *A bird skeleton showing the frame that enables a bird to fly efficiently. It includes hollow bones, a deep breastbone for anchoring wing muscles, slender leg bones, and a knobby tail for controlling tail feathers.*

We have already noted that millions of years were necessary for birds to achieve flight. The whole reptilian structure from which birds evolved had to undergo many changes before true flight, as distinct from gliding, was attained. The fossil remains of *Archaeopteryx* make this clear. Whereas its feathers were like those of today's birds, its teeth and tail remained reptilian and its brain was so primitive that in itself it is proof that it could not fly. Light "pneumatized" bones and air sacs in the skull had yet to evolve. These features are characteristic of modern birds and are particularly noticeable in albatrosses, which spend much time on the wing; an exception is the flightless kiwi, which has solid bones.

The size of a bird's heart is quite as important as the flight muscles in enabling it to be active in the air. Indeed, there is a correlation between the speed a flying bird can attain and the weight of its heart in relation to the weight of its body. A bird's muscles have to sustain a higher energy output than those of mammals, and this depends on the respiratory system. Naturally, hovering requires more energy than gliding, and the relevant muscles are highly developed in such species as the kestrel, some terns, and especially in hummingbirds, whose wing-beat frequency may reach eighty per second. In contrast, owls have very large wings for their weight, they flap slowly, and their breast muscles are proportionately smaller than in any other group of birds. The wing shape and arrangement of the feathers vary according to a bird's mode of life and, particularly, its manner of foraging. The long wings of albatrosses are due to lengthy bones, whereas in the insect-eating swifts it is the primary wing feathers that are relatively long, giving the birds great maneuverability.

MIGRATION AND HOMING

The acquisition of flight gave birds new worlds to conquer, enabling them to exploit sources of food high in trees, in the air, and far out at sea. They could nest out of reach of all but other winged or arboreal predators. They could escape unfavorable climatic conditions by migrating. Bats and some insects can migrate aerially, whales and fish may travel long distances in the water, and some mammals, such as the wildebeest, migrate considerable distances overland; but, as a group, birds have perfected migration to the highest degree—even beyond what man with all his contrivances has achieved. We are unable to remove whole populations from areas threatened with famine or to transport millions to where there is a seasonal plentitude of food, but this, in effect, is what birds do.

The migratory journeys of some species are immense.

Facing page (top) *Interior of an eagle's upper "arm" bone, showing how lightness and strength are combined in the hollow structure and the reinforcing "struts." The honeycomb of spaces in a bird's bones saves weight and may also contribute to its respiratory and cooling system.*

Below *Takeoff. A swan assumes a streamlined position, flaps vigorously with its wings and paddles with its feet in order to become airborne.*

Facing page (bottom) *Coming in for a landing. A white pelican brakes with its wings and feet as it makes contact with the water.*

Banding has shown that most of the swallows which breed in Great Britain winter in South Africa. The American golden plover, which nests on the tundra in the extreme north of Canada and Alaska, migrates south over the sea by way of the Lesser Antilles some 2,360 miles to the Argentine and returns overland via western South America and the Mississippi Valley—a huge ellipse. The Arctic tern makes a round trip of some 25,000 miles from its nesting grounds in the far north to the Antarctic.

Homing experiments have revealed that some birds have an astonishing ability to return after being transported far from their nesting area. Two wrynecks carried 925 miles from their home came back; four white storks returned 1,403 miles; and two Laysan albatrosses removed 3,180 miles from a nesting colony reappeared after ten days. It is known that during daylight many birds navigate by the sun and at night they rely on the stars, and it is now thought they may orient themselves by the earth's gravitational fields, but there are aspects of how birds find their way that are still obscure.

SONG

Birds' powers of flight caused men to think of them as belonging to a different order of beings, but the similarities between birds and themselves also caught their attention. Like ourselves they are bipeds and like us they sing, display, or "show off," and build homes for themselves so we find it much easier to have a fellow-feeling for birds than for fishes or snakes. Apart from other considerations, we are happiest with creatures with which we can establish some sort of communication either by vocal or gestural language. In man the ability to detect slight nuances of spoken sounds must have developed very early. A considerable proportion of the human race, notably the Chinese, speak tonal languages in which a given sound may have totally different meanings according to the way it is inflected. We may assume that in the distant past men and even perhaps proto-men were able to detect niceties in the utterances of birds. It was in their interest to do so, for the alarm calls of birds could alert them to danger from animals or other human beings. Some tribesmen use bird calls, especially the calls of owls, as signals when on a raiding expedition. Bird calls may also indicate where a food bonanza may be obtained, for the clamor of some nesting colonies can be heard from afar. The African forest-dweller knows that by heeding the calls of a honey guide and following it he can obtain the honey he covets, leaving the wax for the bird.

Our forefathers, especially the poets among them,

Facing page (top left) *Swifts in flight. Probably the fastest birds in the world, they have been credited with astonishing speeds.*
Facing page (top right) *Arctic tern in flight.*
Facing page (bottom) *Chevron formation of migrating greylag geese in autumn.*
Below *Barn owl with vole. Owls have very large wings in proportion to their weight.*

mistakenly assumed that because human beings express joy by singing, this must also be true of birds. They failed to consider what an important role war songs and lamentations have had in many human cultures. We know so little about the emotions of birds that we are not justified in supposing that they experience the joy or sadness we feel as we listen to their songs. We must, however, avoid the opposite extreme of assuming that birds are mechanisms, without any feelings or *joie de vivre*. Ornithologists who are also musicians have made a good case for at least some birds' being "musical."

A bird's song, as popularly understood, is the utterance with which the male announces that he has secured and is defending an area for breeding. This is the territorial song. It is normally a bird's most elaborate and most informative utterance and may convey to another bird of the same species:

> Here am I, in this place,
> A cock bird
> Of such-and-such species,
> An identifiable individual
> In my territory,
> Warning off other males
> And inviting a female to join me.

Sometimes the content of the song is less significant, as, for instance, when a bird continues to sing after mating. There are also a few species in which the invitation is issued by the female. For example, the red-necked phalarope flits around low over herbage in the subarctic, making a high-pitched ripping noise with her wings which is equivalent to a song.

Thus song is not always vocal: woodpeckers "drum" with their bills on branches; Wilson's snipe dives in the air creating a throbbing, bleating sound as its outspread tail feathers flutter; the white stork clatters its mandibles; and the ruffed grouse, perched on a log, "booms" by rapidly vibrating its wings.

Although territorial or defensive song is the most familiar, there are other kinds of song. Some birds sing courtship songs when the female is close by; these are normally quieter and in some instances slower in tempo and more beautiful—at least by human standards. Such as the winter wren's invitation to the female to settle in the nest he has prepared, but he may also sing when leading the fledged brood to a roosting place, and a cock sometimes sings when leading a party of adults to a roost in winter. Moreover, the female utters a very subdued chittering song to the nestlings.

The utterances of birds constitute a language which is basically simple because it is determined by their fundamental needs and motivations, such as aggres-

Facing page *Young pelicans raise a clamor in a crowded nesting colony.*
Below *A singing European male blackbird.*

Below *A mockingbird attacking a great horned owl, which flinches and blinks its eyes.*
Facing page *Hummingbird in dodging or darting flight as it seeks nectar and insects. This type of flight, which may require 75 wingbeats per second, causes the hum that accounts for the family name.*
Overleaf *Skimmers in flight. These birds feed from the surface of the water as they fly.*

sion, attraction, keeping contact, and alarm or warning. These signals are modified according to circumstances —contact calls are used by birds leading their young, and also by some species, such as geese and cranes, on migration. The degree of urgency may be indicated by the vehemence of calls. Moreover, many species have two kinds of alarm call: one, usually short and sharp, warning of the approach of a flying predator; the other indicating the location of a slower-moving or stationary predator. When birds hear the "flying predator" alarm they immediately dash for cover. The other type of call, which is usually repetitive, may attract birds of more than one species to assemble near the suspicious object, such as a perched owl, and join in "mobbing" it (jumping from branch to branch uttering alarm calls), apparently on the principle that an enemy located can do little harm.

SONG, DAYLIGHT, AND THE ENVIRONMENT

Song and the amount of daylight are closely related. The seasonal increase in the length of day influences the development of a bird's sexual organs and consequently its songfulness. Furthermore, different species come into song in the morning at different light values so that a listener around dawn will hear them join the chorus in a definite order. This order is related to some extent to a bird's feeding behavior. For example, worm-eaters tend to sing earlier in the day than grain-eaters. Insect-eating species active at night, such as the whippoorwill, respond to decreasing light. These and other species which feed in dim light, such as owls, the woodcock, and the European robin, have relatively large eyes.

Where the rains are seasonal the breeding activities of many species are correlated with the period when insects and other animals, responding to humidity, are most abundant and available as food for the young. The calling or singing of loud-voiced birds is marked at this time, and some of these, such as a voluble cuckoo in south China, are called rain birds. Many primitive people have considered some of these birds prophetic. The birds were credited with insight into human affairs and soon certain individuals claimed to be able to interpret what such birds were prophesying. Such shamans or wise men were considered worthy of special respect.

Obviously many factors determine the character of a bird's utterances—its vocal organs, size, and other bodily characteristics—but it is less apparent that a bird's habitat and what it eats influence its calls and songs. A bird loudly proclaiming its location makes itself vulnerable; therefore, few outstanding singers

are conspicuously adorned, and many sing when they are concealed to some extent or can keep a good lookout. The corncrake, a European species which occasionally reaches the eastern seaboard of the United States, exemplifies the first type. It frequents grassland where it utters its loud, rasping *crake crake, crake crake* monotonously, but is so secretive that only once or twice in Ireland, where they were common at one time, did I manage to see one. Similarly, the nightingale, a brown bird which sings for hours at a time in woods and hedgerows, is comparatively inconspicuous. Habitat, foraging behavior, and the nature of a bird's song are closely connected. Thus relatively large songbirds which tend to sing a continuous type of song, such as is typical of thrushes and thrashers, forage on or near the ground and are often fine vocalists, whereas aerial insect-feeders, swifts, martins, and bee-eaters, which tend to nest in colonies, are mediocre singers. Fish- and carrion-eaters have at best rudimentary songs or do not sing at all.

SONG AND OTHER ADAPTATIONS

If we divide birds in a somewhat rough way into two categories, those that are most conspicuous vocally and those that are conspicuous visually, we find the following correlations:

Adaptation	Conspicuously Vocal Species	Conspicuously Visual Species
Structural	Small size and weak armament	Large size and strong armament
Plumage	Inconspicuous	Conspicuous
Habitat	Dense	Open
Territorialism	Strong	Weak
Pair bond	Short	Prolonged
Nesting	Isolated	Social
Foraging	Fixed area around nest	Extensive
Vulnerability	Vulnerable	Less vulnerable

The contrast in characteristics is most evident when comparison is made between songbirds and marine species such as gulls.

Are birds' songs "instinctive" or learned? There is no simple answer, because species differ so much; many species learn their songs to some extent, but the calls of most species appear to be innate. A number are endowed with a basic song, not precisely patterned, which becomes more typical when they hear other birds of their own kind sing. The main learning period may occur soon after the young leave the nest or the following spring when they hear their more mature neighbors

Facing page *Yellow-eyed penguins of New Zealand in courting maneuver. Among other remarkable aspects of this ritual is the way mates apparently recognize each other by voice.*
Below *Sedge-warbler. Like many notably vocal birds, the warbler is nondescript in appearance.*

sing, and imitate them. Thus in a given community the songs tend to resemble each other, conforming to a community pattern. "Dialects" arise when communities are isolated over long periods of time and divergences from the ancestral norm become accentuated. Thus the European wren (the same species as the American winter wren) sings somewhat differently on the isolated St. Kilda group of islands from the way it does on the British mainland. If two populations of a species remain separated for a long time and their song differences increase, and they then come into contact again, the differences in utterances may have become so great that they do not respond to each other's songs. In such instances they will not interbreed but will become increasingly distinct in behavior and appearance as well as in song. New species may thus evolve.

As everybody knows, some species of birds, and no other nonhuman creatures, are able to copy human words and phrases and, what is more, even utter these on appropriate occasions, as if they understood their meaning. Imitative learning is then most apparent.

SONG AND DISPLAY

In addition to vocal language, birds have a gesture language—visual signals that constitute their "display." These involve movements that often exhibit a bird's adornments, even those within its mouth, to best advantage. When displaying aggressively, many birds and mammals exaggerate their size by erecting feathers or fur to intimidate an adversary. In this situation, a bird may raise its crest or extend its wings as well as utter threat sounds. Normally both sexual and aggressive or defensive displays become "ritualized" and built into specific situations. In many species courtship pursuit occurs, and in some, as different as the European robin and various species of tern, "courtship feeding" is a feature of the ritual. Anyone who has observed a tern colony early in the breeding season is likely to have seen one of the birds carrying a small fish in his bill and pursuing a female to whom he will give it—so initiating or maintaining the pair bond between them.

The territorial and mating displays of many species involve flight, often accompanied by song or calls. A number fly up while singing or calling, thus adding to their conspicuousness and increasing the distance their utterance carries. The most notable performers of this aerial song and dance are birds which nest in open habitats, marshes, moorland, or tundra. The skylark flies up several hundred feet, singing continuously so that the bird-watcher is amazed at such a lavish expenditure of energy, and the prairie horned lark mounts higher and higher, uttering a twittering song. Bobolinks sing their bubbling melody from a tree and then

Facing page *A capercaillie, a large European grouse, crowing and displaying in a Norwegian wood.*
Below *Ruff in full display. The display of every male is unique, each having a different combination of feathers.*

Below *Vultures squabbling.*
Facing page (top) *Robins quarreling. During such an encounter, the birds put on a threat display, including aggressive calls and songs.*
Facing page (bottom) *Laysan albatrosses in courting display.*
Overleaf *The aquatic "dance" of the western grebes.*

fly circling and singing over the meadows. Their *chink* contact call is heard not only on the nesting grounds but as they pass high overhead on migration. Some waders engage in remarkable song flights. The spotted redshank flies back and forth over the marshes in Lapland uttering a distinctive call and exposing the pale underside of his wings as he swerves. The upland plover may mount to a height, uttering what one observer has described as "a prolonged mellow whistle, more like the wind than a bird's voice, which may be heard even at night, and is one of the most weird and never-to-be-forgotten sounds in nature."

Some aquatic species perform elaborate water dances. Pairs of western grebes act in consort, jerking their heads over their bodies; they then rise out of the water and scurry across its surface. As a climax they rear up and, paddling furiously, confront each other with very little of their bodies in the water. Great crested grebes swim back and forth and occasionally the male rises out of the water, holding a bunch of weeds in front of his mate. Black guillemots join in a group display, circling one another while they utter high-pitched wheezing notes, diving now and then and occasionally forming a long line, floating equidistant from one another. They open their beaks so that the vivid red coloration inside is exposed.

The displays of birds of paradise are noteworthy for the magnificence of the birds' plumes as well as their posturing. Some hang upside down or even perform a back somersault. A king bird of paradise sings a song resembling a skylark's, though softer, exposing his lovely fan-like side plumes and opening and closing them in time with his song, swaying his body with his two burnished green disks and long tail quills quivering over his head.

Americans need not go to New Guinea to see and hear a

Facing page (top) *A sharp-tailed grouse dancing during a courtship display.*
Facing page (right) *Two male grouse in a contest on the display ground.*
Below *Emperor of Germany's bird of paradise hanging upside down in inverted display, showing the ivory and golden plumes of its flank fans.*

very beautiful song-and-dance performance—the courtship of the rose-breasted grosbeak. H. R. Ivor described it thus:

> The cock crouched before the hen and the mating song poured forth from his open beak as he moved toward the female, weaving his head and body in an erratic dance in which he resembled some magnificent butterfly rather than a bird. The downward and forward sweep of his wings revealed in striking contrast the blacks and whites of the separated flight feathers, the vivid rose of the underwing coverts and the white of the rump. The song, quite different from the territorial song, was soft, low, and continuous, with a great variety of notes; some of the sweetest notes were so faint that I had to listen intently to hear them though the bird was only two feet away; for pure rapture I cannot recall any song which equals the courtship song of the rose-breasted (and black-headed) Grosbeak.

Many creatures from spiders and insects to apes perform crude dances, but birds surely surpass them, so far as our aesthetic judgments are concerned, for some combine gay coloration, song, and, in some instances, aerial or aquatic maneuvers in their displays.

In all of nature there are few more fascinating and beautiful sights to be seen than the displays of birds. The observer who takes the trouble to wait to see them will be well rewarded.

3
Birds in Prophecy and Magic

Above *Medieval stained glass pane showing a mythical bird called the caladrius. It was believed that a sick man whose illness was not terminal could return the steady gaze of the bird; having absorbed the disease, the bird was then said to fly up to the sun and disperse the sickness.*

Facing page *Condor being led by marchers in Cuzco, Peru. Considered a special bird in several Latin American countries, it plays a part in various rituals.*

Overleaf *Totem poles with thunderbirds carved on them in front of the house of the Chief of the Himpkish, Alert Bay, Victoria, British Columbia.*

Primitive man, far from thinking of himself as the lord of creation, is much impressed by the capabilities and adaptations of animals. This explains the development of animal cults, animal worship, and a general humility toward the animal world. Even though the native hunter may kill animals, he has respect for the wild creatures. He is observant of what goes on in the forest or wilderness and often has a knowledge of plants and animals which surprises and arouses the admiration of the civilized intruder.

Primitive folk notice that birds go about their business at the appropriate time and they may even interpret certain activities of animals as promptings or admonitions in regard to their own affairs. The biblical prophet Jeremiah declared:

> The stork in the sky knows the time to migrate,
> The dove and the swift and wryneck know the
>   season of return;
> but my people do not know the ordinances of the
>   Lord.

He was speaking to a peasant people who paid attention to "the signs of the times" as they worked in the fields and for whom seedtime and harvest had an importance that the modern city-dweller can hardly realize.

In European weather lore we find every type of prediction attributed to birds, from interpretations of bird activities prophesying the next day's weather to long-term auguries which, as we might expect, are founded on superficial associations and have been handed down for generations without study or thought. Short-term inferences from bird behavior may be reasonably accurate, such as that swallows fly low over water before rain and that fine weather is likely to follow when the robin sings from a high perch. The explanations are simple. In humid conditions insects fly low and so the swallows do likewise, and robins sing perched low in the bushes and trees until the spring of the year, warmer weather, and mounting sexual ardor impel them to choose more prominent song perches. In Suffolk in southeastern England the saying is:

> If the robin sings in the bush,
> Then the weather will be coarse;
> But if the robin sings on the barn,
> Then the weather will be warm.

But when the countryman seeks out prophecies indicating what kind of harvest or winter to expect, sometimes he does so by putting the cart before the horse, and finds answers in curious ways. Some people believe that plentiful berries in autumn, providing provender for the birds, foretell a severe winter—as if the shrubs could anticipate the needs of the birds. The French saying that when the magpie builds high, the summer will not be stormy implies foresight that even the most cunning

aue uł rore. Ceta nomina instructione discit. hinc est
illud. Psitatus a nobis aliorum nomina discam. hoc didici
p me disere. cesar aue. cui rostri tanta duricia; ut cum
e sublimi precipitat in saxum; nisu oris se recipiat. Qdam
qa fundamento utat ext ordinarie hi nuitant. Caput u
tantum ualens. ut signando ad discendum plagis sit admonen
dum. nam studet ut qd homines loquat. ferrea sit ferula
ubandus. Nam cu in pullo; atq adeo intra annum etatis sue
annu; q monstrata sunt; ea discit r retinet uenacius. pau
lo senior; obliuiosus est œ indocilis.

Caladrius sicut dicit phisiologus totus; albus nulla parte
habens nigram. cuius interior simus curat oculor caliginem.
hic in atriis regum inuenit. Dicaq; in egritudine ex hoc caladrio
cognoscit si uiuat an moriat. Si g; in infirmitas hominis ad mor
tem. mox ut uiderit infirmum auertit faciem suam ab eo; r qm

Mythical birds have been associated with sickness or death in many cultures.
Facing page *Drawing of a caladrius, the augur of health or death, in a thirteenth century bestiary.*
Left *Bird figure over Haida grave on Queen Charlotte Island, British Columbia.*
Below *Soul-bird hovering over a mummy on the back of a bull, as depicted on the lid of an Egyptian coffin.*

Below *A panel on a silver-plated cult vessel of the first century B.C. Found in Denmark but illustrating Celtic mythology, it may possibly represent a deity associated with the creation or fertility of birds.*

Facing page *Bird killing a snake-like dragon shown in an illuminated Spanish manuscript. The theme of a bird holding a serpent in its mouth is a widespread one in mythology and folklore, often symbolizing the conflict of cosmic forces.*

Overleaf (left) *Enamel eucharistic dove from France (c. 1250).* (top center) *Pre-Columbian gold eagle.* (far right) *Bronze bird from thirteenth century Italy, probably representing the gyrfalcon, the falcon of kings.*

sublimium adque lurcum

Right *Cover of a Crow Indian shield from Montana. The wing feathers of the prairie falcon are attached as prayers.*

Below *A fresco depicting The Miracle of the Raven, in which a jealous priest attempts to kill St. Benedict by offering poisoned bread to the monks. The wise Benedict orders a raven, shown at center and upper right of the fresco, to remove the bread.*

magpie does not possess. The Swiss call the waxwing *Pest-vogel* and *Sterbe-vogel,* "pestilence bird" and "death bird," because great flocks of these birds come south from their breeding quarters in Scandinavia and Russia when Europe is in the grip of snow and ice. In the Middle Ages such conditions often meant starvation, epidemics, and death; but the explanation is ex post facto and assumes cause and effect where there is only association.

The Norwegian belief that hard times are to be expected if the cuckoo utters his call after he has seen the first haystack may have some justification, in so far as late seasons are bad for the farmers' crops and possibly also for the cuckoo. In Borneo the Dayaks regulate their agricultural activities partly by observations of bird activities, and are prudent to do so. The first yellow wagtails appear in September and their coming is a reminder to get the rice fields ready for planting; and when they come in numbers about a month later, Dayaks know they must lose no time if the rice is to be harvested before the destructive weaver finches return in February. The farmers' observations enable them to adjust appropriately to the prevailing conditions.

We need not go so far off to find farmers who believe that the comings and goings of birds can help them. An ancient Greek writer, Theognis, refers to the crane's calling the plowman to his work. When the flocks of birds appear he should be in the fields. Another Greek, Hesiod, advised the farmer that "when the cuckoo sings among the oak trees it is time to plough," and "if it should happen to rain three days together when the cuckoo sings in the oak trees, then late sowing will be as good as early sowing." There was an English saying:

> When the cuckoo comes to the bare thorn,
> Sell your cow and buy your corn;
> But when she comes to the full bit,

> Sell your corn and buy your sheep.

It was only a small step from such ideas about the cuckoo's insight to supposing that the bird was not merely weather-wise but could divine what fate had in store for a man or woman. Over much of Europe rustics used to ask the bird how long they would live and then counted how many times he called. So Yorkshire children would sing:

> Cuckoo, cherry tree,
> Come down and tell me
> How many years afore I dee?

In Germany, girls would ask the bird to tell them how long it would be before they got married. Such ideas led to notions concerning good and bad luck. In Northumberland it was believed unlucky to hear the first cuckoo while walking on a road, and in England and Germany it was thought lucky to have money in one's pocket when one first heard that bird. If a person jingled the coins and made a wish, the wish would be gratified—if it was reasonable!

The mere appearance of a bird at some important juncture could be regarded as highly significant if it happened to be a species that had a good or bad reputation. When those who interpreted omens and auguries were mistaken, it was easy for them to discover subtleties which proved that they were right after all. Probably this was more often due to a recognition that the ways of God and nature are mysterious than to deliberate deception. If a "lucky" bird appeared but things turned out badly, it could be argued that in going away it had taken its good luck with it. So Cassius says in *Julius Caesar:*

> On our former ensign
> Two mighty eagles fell, and there they perch'd,
> Gorging and feeding from our soldiers' hands,
> Who to Philippi here consorted us.

Facing page *Coptic church painting of St. Anthony* (left) *and the Hermit Paul* (right) *with raven. When the Hermit Paul sought out St. Anthony in the desert they were fed by a raven.*
Below St. John the Evangelist writing his Gospel. Be- *cause it soared so high the eagle was associated with the exalted spirituality of the Apostle John, who was said by St. Jerome to have taken wings and ascended to the throne of God.*

This morning are they fled away and gone,
And in their steads do ravens, crows, and kites
Fly o'er our heads, and downward look on us
As we were sickly prey.

In any kind of augury the number of birds involved could be significant. The magpie may have gained prominence in folklore as a bird of ill omen because of its conspicuous black and white plumage and its associ- ation with ravens and other birds that gather around dead bodies. Also, because it may at times be seen in parties, various folk rhymes were concocted in England concerning the significance of each number in such parties. Two hundred years ago the country people in the west of England would say:

One for sorrow, two for mirth;
Three for a wedding, four for death.

But this was too dismal and didn't rhyme, so the version which became most widespread was:

One for sorrow, two for mirth;
Three for a wedding, four for a birth.

Other village rhymesters then added this:

Five a sickening, six a christening,
Seven a dance, eight a lady going to France.

Or, in Lancashire:

Five for rich, six for poor,
Seven for a witch, I can tell you no more.

There are other versions, showing that what was once taken rather seriously as augury had become playful. But there were developments in another direction. Cus- toms arose, not entirely playful, designed to avert the predicted evil—a significant evolution from belief to ritual. In England it was the custom in Derbyshire to cross oneself, but in Yorkshire a person seeing a mag- pie would cross his thumbs and say a kind of charm to annul the mischief:

I cross the magpie,
The magpie crosses me:
Bad luck to the magpie,
And good luck to me.

In other areas it was enough to bow, cross one's feet, look for a crow, the sight of which could ward off the evil portent, or spit over one's shoulder while saying:

Clean birds by sevens,
Unclean by twos;
The dove in the heavens,
Is the one I choose.

Thus these practices also illustrate the natural human impulse when disquieted by a sense of mysterious impending danger, to assert oneself, however il- logically, against it. Since the underlying belief, or fear, was that the devil must be up to mischief, some of the protective rituals had a Christian background.
In parts of southern India people paid attention to the

Facing page *Crossbill. According to legend, a caged crossbill could cure colds by transferring them to itself.*
Below *Great horned owl. Because of its nocturnal activity and strange calls, the owl has had a prominent place in mythology and folklore.*

number of times an owl screeched. One screech was supposed to indicate a death; two, the success of some project; three, a marriage; four, trouble; five, a journey; six, the arrival of visitors; seven, anxiety; eight, sudden death; nine, favorable happenings. The number nine is often significant in divination and folklore. The notion that the red-backed shrike impaled nine insects on thorns before it began its meal accounts for its name in German—"nine-killer."

BIRDS AS GUIDES

The statement quoted earlier from Jeremiah suggests another justification for the primitive person's feeling that birds seem not to be troubled by uncertainties. He might assume that a bird's ability to do clever things, such as weave a neat nest, is all its own, or that it is guided supernaturally to act in certain ways. The African forest-dweller knows that the honey guide not only is good at finding bees' nests but leads him to the nests by attracting his attention with its calls and flitting before him; whereas the Yakut on the Siberian tundra, seeing the skeins of geese and cranes disappearing in autumn and arriving in V-shaped squadrons in spring, regards them as under the guidance of the god Yassagai-Toyon. No matter how a primitive interprets the means by which birds find their way, he is impressed—as we are too—by their ability to do so. In the past it was assumed, and not only by people of lower culture, that birds could guide men. This belief was correct up to a point but, as with weather-forecasting, it was extended beyond the realm in which it was valid.

When Noah released the raven and the dove from the Ark, he was acting just as Babylonian mariners did when they used shore-seeking birds to tell them if land was near. When the birds set off purposefully, the mariners knew the direction in which to steer. In the *Dia-*

logues of the Buddha (fifth century B.C.) there is the following description of how shore-seeking birds were used:

> Long ago ocean-going merchants were wont to plunge forth upon the sea, on board a ship, taking with them a shore-sighting bird. When the ship was out of sight of land, they would set the bird free. And it would go to the East, the South, the West, and the North, and to the intermediate points, and rise aloft. If on the horizon it caught sight of land, thither would it go, but if not it would come back to the ship again.

A trivial experience impressed me with the value of sea birds in enabling seafarers to find their way without a compass. I was trying to reach a gannet nesting colony on an offshore rock stack when thick mist descended. Glimpses of birds converging in one direction assured me that the island was ahead.

Thus, men sailing from Taprobane (Ceylon or Sri Lanka) took with them birds which they liberated from time to time in order to ascertain the direction of land. The Vikings used ravens in the same way. According to the *Saga of Floki,* a legendary Icelandic explorer, Iceland was rediscovered with the aid of these birds. Floki took three of them with him and sailed westward for several days. He then released one which, after circling high in the air, flew back in the direction of Norway. Several days later when the second raven was set free it returned to the ship, but the third bird, released after several more days, flew westward and did not return. This was the clue Floki needed, so he continued westward and reached the southeast coast of Iceland.

Inevitably, stories were invented attributing to birds supernatural powers in guiding men. According to the tradition, when the population of Thera, an island in

Facing page *Raven. Practically everywhere that it occurs, this bird has been thought of as having supernatural powers and is the subject of strange tales.*
Below *Barn swallows. Because of its tendency to nest near human dwellings, this bird was the subject of many beliefs, such as that it was sacred to the household gods.*

the Aegean Sea, emigrated to Libya, ravens flew ahead to show the way. Similarly, Alexander the Great was said to have been guided across the desert to the oasis of Ammon by two ravens sent from heaven which encouraged stragglers with their croaking. Beyond all other European birds, ravens were believed to have occult knowledge. It was also said that birds led the Gauls during some of their invasions. And birds contributed to the discovery of the New World by Columbus: when his men wanted him to turn back, he pointed out that the birds which they were beginning to see indicated that land was not far away.

WEATHER LORE AND OMENS

These examples illustrate a principle which is helpful in interpreting folklore: once launched, a belief that something is uncanny or has hidden significance is likely to give rise to a crop of other beliefs; and these may attain an independent life of their own after the original source is forgotten. When a bird gets a reputation for being privy to information not available to men, its reputation may increase until it becomes a wizard, the messenger of a god, or the god himself.

For those engaged in any kind of agriculture the weather is more important than it is for food-gathering tribes that move to areas where particular animals or plants are most abundant. Farmers have usually been conservative folk, believing that it is hazardous to experiment with a new procedure, and they have always cherished ancient lore concerning the weather. Their weather lore ranges from the obvious to the fantastic. The belief, already mentioned, that swallows flying low presage rain is only one of a number of traditions which grew up around this bird that aroused interest and respect by its readiness to nest in or near human dwellings, its function as a herald of spring, and its reputation as a fire bird because of its red breast. In both East and West it has attracted attention as a neighborly bird. I have seen swallows nesting in open shops in the streets of Canton as well as in English barns. Aelian wrote of the swallow that it was sacred to the household gods, and naturally it became a bird of good omen. But such a bird can easily become a prophet of evil if it acts in an exceptional way. Shakespeare, echoing what he had obviously read in Plutarch's *Lives,* wrote in *Antony and Cleopatra:*

> Swallows have built
> In Cleopatra's sails their nests. The auguries
> Say they know not, they cannot tell, look grimly,
> And dare not speak their knowledge.

In 1602 another writer continued the tradition that the swallow was a bird of ill omen: "Swallowes followed King Cyrus going with his army from Persia to Scythia,

Facing page (top) Crane mask from the Awikinox tribe, Kwakiutl, Alaska.
Facing page (bottom) Watercolor of an Eagle Dance by a Kiowa painter of Oklahoma.
Below The owl on this coin, a tetradrachm, from Crete 267–200 B.C.) confutes various ancient authorities who thought that there were no owls on Crete. Among the Greeks the owl was variously considered a bird of evil omen or a portent of victory.
Overleaf New Guinea dancers wearing Princess Stephanie bird of paradise headdresses in a ceremonial dance.

as Ravens followed Alexander the Great at returning from India and going to Babilon; but as the Magi tolde the Persians that Cyrus should die in Scythia, so the Chaldean astrologers told the Macedonians that Alexander, their king, should die in Babilon, without any further warrant but by the above Swallowes and Ravens." The raven is not always a bird of ill omen. Despite its black plumage and sinister croaking and its feeding on corpses, it fed Elijah in the wilderness; and among the North American Indians it was a culture hero.

Augury from the behavior of birds was subject to tricky interpretations. An augur who was wrong could always argue that there was some aspect which had not been taken into consideration. Thus, in divining by means of birds, not only must their number be considered but also such details as the point of the compass at which the birds appear and depart. Where magic is concerned, the human mind finds what is complex and esoteric intriguing. A good example is the belief that a crossbill kept in a cage could cure colds and rheumatism, but only a bird whose mandibles bent to the right could be effective with men, and only one whose mandibles bent to the left could cure women.

Divination thus became a complex affair, too serious and subtle to be left to amateurs and interpretations by rule of thumb; thus only those who were considered experts were consulted—augurs, prophets and prophetesses, shamans, and priests.

Apart from these professional predictions, abnormal actions by birds were often interpreted as unpropitious. The Roman scholar Pliny tells us that "a woodpecker once came and settled on the head of Aelius Tubero, the city Praetor, when sitting on his tribunal dispensing justice in the forum. It showed such tameness that it allowed itself to be taken with the hand. Upon which the augur declared that if it were released the State would be menaced with disaster, but if killed, the praetor himself would suffer. In an instant he tore the bird to shreds." In spite of the Praetor's, patriotic action, the omen was fulfilled, for at the battle of Cannae in 216 B.C., Tubero and sixteen members of his family were killed.

The direction from which a bird came or called could be of oracular significance. The African people known as the Masai regard a woodpecker calling on the right as a good omen but on the left as a portent of evil. Ennius, the poet-historian, tells how it was decided whether Romulus or Remus would be the first king of Rome: each took his stand, one on the Palatine Hill, the other on the Aventine, waiting to discern the will of the gods. At dawn the sign was given: the most propitious of all birds (which kind this was is not mentioned) ap-

peared flying to the left of Romulus and twelve sacred birds surrounded him; there was no doubt whom the gods had chosen. In his *Asinaria,* Plautus, Roman comedy playwright of the third century B.C., has a rascal seeking to swindle his stepmother into purchasing a harlot say: "Tis settled: 'tis confirmed by auspices; on each side do the birds give good omens. The woodpecker and the crow on my right, the raven as well on my left. They are persuading me to it, and i' faith, I am resolved to follow your advice. (Starts and listens.) But what means this, that the woodpecker is tapping on the elm tree? (A bad omen.) That's for nothing. Troth and for certain, as far as I can gather omens from the augury, the rods are in pickle for my own back."

The Umbrians, before the Romans, were much given to divination based on the flight of birds (*auspicium*), and so probably were the Etruscans. Their outlook was a complete surrender to the divine will, so they were obsessed with discovering it by means ranging from the inspection of the liver of a sacrificed animal to interpreting the flight of birds. The Etruscans believed in demons, notably the horrid Tuchulcha which had the face of a vulture, the ears of a donkey, and serpents rising from its hair. Their wise men were reputed to understand the language of eagles.

The Romans, especially the lower classes, attached great significance to the *auspices*. The consul took his seat on a chair in an open-fronted tent, uttered a prayer, and awaited the appearance of the birds. He faced south, and as a result birds on his left were propitious, whereas those on his right, in the west, were unlucky, except for the raven.

The Romans also used fowl to make their decisions for them. Pellets of bread were fed to cocks; if they were so eager that some crumbs fell from their beaks as they fed, this was considered a good omen. The Greek prac-

tice was a little more subtle. Persons seeking guidance scattered grains of corn which were inscribed with letters of the alphabet. Predictions were made according to the order in which the grains were picked up. It seems hardly credible that any but the most superstitious folk could let important decisions be made in such a way.

More sophisticated people were not so gullible. When his men told Publius Claudius before the sea battle of Drepanum (249 B.C.) that they were troubled because the fowls would not eat, he replied, "Then let them drink," and threw them into the sea—but nearly all his ships were sunk. Cicero, who tells these stories, was a member of the College of Augurs. When Alexander the Great was about to set out on an expedition and this method of taking the omens was suggested, he killed the bird, remarking that if it could not foresee its own fate, how could it know the fate of an expedition? But the psychological effect of favorable omens on an army could be important. In the third century B.C. Agathocles of Syracuse was fighting the Carthaginians with an inferior force composed mainly of Greeks. Before the battle these men were greatly heartened by seeing owls, birds sacred to the goddess Athena, perching on their banners; they defeated the enemy. They did not know that their commander had arranged for the owls to be caught and released at the critical moment. Prognostications may act the other way and reduce morale. When the Spaniards arrived in Peru in the sixteenth century, it happened that auguries of impending disaster were current. If it had not been for these, which caused the Inca emperor to believe defeat inevitable, he would hardly have allowed a handful of invaders into his capital, thereby smoothing the way for his own death and the destruction of the empire.

Plutarch tells us that Alexander chose the site of the city

named after him and, as there was not sufficient chalk available, commanded that the outlines of the foundations be marked out with flour. But flocks of birds came from the banks of the Nile and consumed the flour. Alexander was perturbed, fearing that this portended a famine in the city, but the augurs reassured him, telling him that the significance of this bird invasion was that the city would prosper so much that it would be able to feed the whole world.

People liked to believe that some propitious event or sign from heaven was responsible for the foundation of their city. According to Aztec traditions, their forefathers wandered about in the Valley of Mexico until "they at length halted on the southwestern borders of the principal lake. They there beheld, perched on the stem of a prickly pear, which shot out from the crevice of a rock . . . a royal eagle of extraordinary size and beauty, with a serpent in his talons, and his wings open to the rising sun. They hailed the auspicious omen . . . as indicating the site of their future city, and laid its foundations by sinking piles into the shallows. . . . The place was called Tenochtitlán, in token of its miraculous origin." The Mexican emblem, the serpent-eating eagle on a cactus, commemorates this tradition. This story may be founded on fact, for certain eagles do prey on snakes. Stories and representations of eagles in conflict with snakes are ancient and widespread, and they are often symbolic of the conflict between good and evil. An eagle or vulture with wings outspread in the sun is a memorable sight: I still vividly recall a king vulture perched thus on top of a tree by a lake in the Panamanian forest.

The thoughts and activities of primitive people are naturally concerned with the basic appetites—having enough to eat and drink and propagating their kind. In the more arid regions of the world tribes folk live in fear that if the rains fail they may starve. When drought threatens, they know that they cannot take any practical measures to save their crops, stock, or themselves, so they resort to magic, often calling for the rainmaker or shaman to save them by means of charms, invocations, dances, or other activities.

BIRD DANCERS

Some primitive folk, having noted that certain birds perform dances or antics at the time of year when rain normally falls, assume that the birds are able to bring down rain, mistaking the coincidence of these events for cause and effect. Some of them also feel that if they imitate the birds, they too will be able to bring rain. Thus one of the two springtime dances of the Tarahumara Indians of Mexico is an imitation of the courting antics of the turkey. Since the gods grant the prayers

of the deer, as expressed in its courtship activities, and of the turkey, as expressed in its displays and gobbling, the men imitate the animals in order to please the gods and secure rain. The ceremonials of the Zuni of New Mexico at the summer solstice are almost entirely devoted to rainmaking. In their processions and dances they wear quantities of feathers. They also wear masks representing various creatures and are then considered to be the spirits they mimic.

In the Yukon, Eskimo dances were performed to please the ancestral spirits and so persuade them to send game and to increase the tribe. For the raven dance a man appeared wearing a raven mask. He partnered one woman, then another, their movements imitating the courtship displays of the raven. The shaman, wearing a spirit mask, danced in circles around the couple, working himself into a frenzy until he collapsed in a trance. When he came to his senses he proclaimed that the spirits had been pleased and game would be abundant. Another bird dance with, apparently, mixed motivation, is performed in the Torres Strait area between New Guinea and Australia. The young men's initiation ritual is followed by a "recognition" ceremony in which ten men hop about in a crouching posture, beating their chests and going back and forth. They imitate the Torres Strait pigeon and their forearms are painted black to represent its wing feathers. Since the pigeon is an important source of food in the area, the ritual is apparently performed both as an initiation ceremony and to secure a plentiful supply of the birds. The Chukchi of Siberia, another shamanistic tribe, mimic the display of the ruff—a bird named after its remarkable nuptial adornment. These birds gather at arenas, or "leks," where each takes a stance a foot or two away from other males. There they confront each other silently and make simulated attacks. In *The Voyage of the Beagle,* Darwin describes totemistic dances by two groups (phratries, as they are called) of Australian aborigines, the Cockatoos and King George's men, which he says were without meaning for him; this is understandable since he had no knowledge of totemism. The naked, painted men did an emu dance in which the performers each held up an arm bent to imitate the bird's head and neck.

Mimetic dancing, as it is called, frequently has more than one motive. In northwestern Brazil the Kobeua and Kaua Indians imitate a wide range of creatures in their masked dances in honor of the dead. Represented in these dances are the swallow, owl, and black vulture.

The underlying belief is that by imitating such creatures the dancer acquires some of their power and can bring the blessing of fertility to the village, its plantations, and nature in general.

It is a far cry from the Brazilian jungle to the Bavarian highlands, but the principal dance among the mountain folk is the *Schuhplattler*, in which the *Nachsteigen* represents "mountain cock mating." The man jumps along behind his partner, clicking his tongue and clapping. Finally he strikes the ground with one or both hands and bounds toward her with arms outspread or hanging down. The blackcock, like the ruff, is a bird which assembles in parties at selected arenas where the birds posture, dance, and engage in mock fights. Proof that the blackcock is indeed the bird imitated is provided by the tuft of its tail feathers that the dancers wear in their hats. The dance is now recreational, but its affinity with other such bird dances shows that it originated long ago in similar magical ideas and impulses.

WISHBONES AND OTHER CUSTOMS

Divination by means of the bones, liver, or other parts of an animal is very ancient. It survives in the playful breaking of the "wishbone" at the dinner table. This custom has venerable antecedents. Writing in the middle of the fifteenth century, a Dr. Hartlieb, physician to Duke Albrecht of Bavaria, mentioned that "when the goose has been eaten on St. Martin's Day or Night, the oldest and most sagacious keeps the breast-bone and allowing it to dry until the morning, examines it all round, in front, behind, and in the middle. Thereby they divine whether the winter will be severe or mild, dry or wet, and are so confident in their prediction that they will wager their goods and chattels on its accuracy." He describes a discussion with an officer who asked him on Saint Nicholas's Day what sort of winter to expect.

"This valiant man, this Christian Captain drew forth out of his doublet that heretical object of superstition, the goose-bone, and showed me that after Candlemas an exceeding severe frost should occur and could not fail. [He] told me that the Teutonic knights in Prussia waged all their wars by the goose-bone; and as the goose-bone predicted so did they order their two campaigns one in summer and one in winter."

Similarly, feathers have often been attributed with prophetic significance. Vultures were sacred to Mut, the goddess of maternity in ancient Egypt, and were reputed to ease childbirth. In Siberia tribesmen scattered kingfisher feathers on the water, believing that those which floated and were retrieved would cause any woman touched by one of them to fall in love with the man who preserved it. More than a century ago sailors setting out from the neighborhood of Hamilton in Scotland used to catch a wren and pluck some of its feathers, toss them in the air, and decide according to the way they fell whether the herring fishery would be profitable or not.

The purposive behavior of birds, their regular comings and goings, and their nest-building were regarded by primitive folk as indicating that neither the birds' activities nor those of men were random or unrewarded. They simply accepted the lesson that if there was such order in the doings of other creatures, there could and should be order in their own. This conviction was reasonable and heartening. Therefore we should not look down on primitive people because of their credulity where divination was concerned, such as their belief that whether a bird flew to the right or left could determine whether a people should go to war or not. For at the heart of the concept of divination is a belief in the order of nature, and a revolt against the idea that chance rules our fates.

4
Birds Fabulous and Mythical

Above *Nootka Indian drum from British Columbia painted to represent the thunderbird carrying off a whale.*
Facing page *Alabaster wall panel from the palace of Ashur-nasir-apal II, King of Assyria (885–860 B.C.), at modern Nimrud, Iraq, showing eagle-masked figures, probably priests.*

It is easy to understand why large birds of prey impressed people. An eagle circling upward with its wings gleaming in the sun is a magnificent sight, and early peoples assumed that such birds had an affinity with the sun god. But it is not clear why some less imposing birds achieved fame. Why, for example, did some of our primitive forefathers regard the woodpecker so seriously as to make it into a god? The largest European species, the black woodpecker, is a big bird but not to be compared in size or majesty with an eagle. Obviously conspicuousness and fierceness had nothing to do with the woodpecker's reputation as a magical bird. To understand its importance as a supernatural creature we must discard our twentieth-century sophistication and see it as men did centuries ago.

We must ask, Has the woodpecker any striking characteristic? It has. In springtime practically all species make a drumming noise which, to anyone unfamiliar with woodland sounds, may well seem mysterious and even ominous. Drumming on a branch is the way woodpeckers communicate with one another. African natives use drums for the same purpose, and some tribes believe that by imitating thunder with their drums they and their shamans, or medicine men, can bring rain when the ground is parched. Here we have a clue to the woodpecker's importance in folklore: it was regarded as a magician, a drumming rainmaker, who could thus save animals and crops from disaster. Moreover, it was assumed that birds and men could use drumming to communicate with higher powers. So strongly does the beating of the wings of the cock pheasant resemble distant thunder that I myself have sometimes momentarily mistaken it for the real thing. Another assumption was that birds are more weatherwise than men; hence the universal belief in particular birds as weather prophets. Obviously then, the woodpecker was a thunderbird, to be honored as a rain-bringer.

As long ago as the eleventh century, a Greek writer, Suidas, commented that the woodpecker foretells rain. In Europe it is known as the "rain bird" or "rain fowl" and in France it is called *Pic de la pluie* and *Le Procureur du Mennier* because, in times of drought, it was thought of as pleading for rain as urgently as the owner of a water mill. In England the green woodpecker's call is believed to forecast rain even though its utterance is like a very high-pitched laugh and not at all like thunder. The importance of the woodpecker as thunderbird and rainmaker is evident to anyone who analyzes even trivial folk anecdotes. Thus, according to a Norse folktale, Christ and Saint Peter once came to a cottage where a woman named Gertrude sat baking with a red cap on her head. In answer to their request for something to eat she rolled out a tiny scrap of dough. She

was so mean that she refused to give it to them even though it grew bigger and bigger until it covered the entire griddle. Because of her lack of generosity she was transformed into a woodpecker, condemned to seek her food in the crevices of trees and never to receive a drop to drink when it rains. She flew up the chimney to escape—which is why the woodpecker's body is sooty black—but she still wears a red cap on her head. "Gertrude's fowl," as the woodpecker is called in Norway, is said to be always thirsty and calling for rain.

In ancient Greece the woodpecker was considered an oracular bird and one seal shows a young warrior consulting it. The assumption was that a bird which could predict or bring changes in the weather could foresee other events. Plutarch tells us that it was specially honored among Latin-speaking peoples, and Dionysius of Halicarnassus knew that in some regions it was considered a god-sent bird and was set on a wooden pillar. In *The Birds,* Aristophanes gives us a clue to its history when he writes: "Zeus will not lightly restore the sceptre to the oak-tapping woodpecker." In other words, the bird was regarded as in some sense a deity who reigned before Zeus was acknowledged to be a high god by the Greeks.

The concept of a thunderbird is widespread. In ancient China the pheasant was such a bird and anyone who wanted rain danced a pheasant dance, imitating the movements of the bird and the flapping of its wings. "Thunder hides itself in the winter but is to be expected when spring appears. But first the pheasants must 'sing their song' and, as it were, beat a drum with their wings. Thus they create thunder. . . . Thunder is a pheasant"; thus wrote the distinguished French orientalist Marcel Granet.

In North America the thunderbird embodies traditions comparable to those concerning the eagle and other giant Asian birds. Such beliefs are, or were, held by tribes from Mexico to Hudson's Bay. One tribe, the Athapascans, pictured it as a titanic bird whose eyes flash lightning and whose flapping wings create the sound of thunder. In another tribe, the Tlingit on the northwest Pacific coast, the thunderbird was thought to be so immense that it could cause thunder by moving even one of its plumes, and lightning flashes when it winked. On its back it carried a lake and its movements spilled the drenching rain of a thunderstorm. The Eskimos also believe in the thunderbird, and in northern Siberia the forest Tungus imagine thunder to be something like a large swan. In Manchuria when the members of a certain tribe build a sacrificial platform, they erect near it a tall pole crowned by a large wooden swan. But in Mongolia and the Altai region, where the dragon, as elsewhere in the Far East, is a beneficent beast, bringer of rain and fertility, thunder is attributed to a flying dragon.

The thunderbird illustrates vividly how an idea, once conceived, can take on a life of its own. Thunder and lightning were mysterious phenomena to our forefathers. In India a friend of mine saw a tree that had been struck by lightning split open right down the trunk and immediately close up again. An unsophisticated person would no doubt attribute such a happening to some arbitrary power from on high. In early ages the response to a thunderstorm may have been primarily apprehension, but later, when primitive farming arose, the thunderbird became, on the whole, a benevolent creature that was supposed to bring much-needed rain for crops. Later, when man had begun to free himself from the bondage of everyday needs, imagination generated romance, and the giant bird was pictured as chariot of gods such as Vishnu, or of heroic figures, including Sinbad.

THE PHOENIX

In the Western world the phoenix is the best known of all mythical birds. Mention of it is virtually a cliché in connection with the revival of any enterprise that has almost disappeared. In Great Britain and the United States it has been adopted as the emblem of an insurance company, standing for reconstruction after fire and a new beginning after disaster.

The exact nature of this strange creature puzzled Greek and Roman writers but they accepted the tradition and added some elaborations of their own. The first known reference is attributed to Hesiod in the eighth century B.C., and we owe the first detailed if somewhat skeptical description to Herodotus. The accepted account was that a single phoenix came from Arabia every five hundred years. The fact that there was only one at a time presented no problem because a belief in spontaneous generation persisted until the Renaissance. On sensing the approach of its death, the bird built a nest of spices and died in it. From the remains a young phoenix was born and carried its parent's relics to the altar of the sun, where they were burned.

The myth arose in Egypt where the Nile rather than rain is the source of fertility. It probably gained currency through a misunderstanding: the Egyptian hieroglyph that is interpreted to mean "phoenix" is unmistakably a species of heron or egret. Such birds were very common in Egypt in ancient times and may still be seen in many African regions. The Egyptian word *bennu,* which was taken to mean phoenix, is ambiguous and could mean either a date palm or a bird. There was thus ample room for confusion. A second-century Christian writer, Tertullian, illustrated this confusion when he translated Psalm 92, line 12 as "The righteous shall flourish like the phoenix" instead of "like the palm tree." The Egyptian pictures of the creature showed a bird with golden and red plumage, resembling an eagle in size and shape.

An Arab writer, Kazwini, who confused the phoenix with the huge anka, or simurgh, asserted that it lives for seventeen hundred years and when a nestling is hatched the parent burns itself alive. He thus added a second quite different bird myth to the first.

Further details of the mythical bird's evolution come from the *Physiologus,* a Greek collection of beast tales which contains what we might dismiss as nonsense were it not for its immense influence. It was translated into many languages, and hardly a monastery was without a copy of this odd compilation. The *Physiologus* remained popular because it supplied imagery and analogies which could be used by preachers to explain Christian truths to simple people in pictorial terms. To the preacher or teacher the truth of the

Facing page *Kwakiutl two-headed thunderbird mask from Vancouver Island, British Columbia. Thunderbird myths associate thunder or lightning with a great bird. Among certain American Northwest Coast Indians the thunderbird is believed to be the creator of the world.*

Below *Fifth-century Byzantine mosaic showing a phoenix in a "field" of flowers.*

illustration was unimportant so long as it served to drive home some religious or moral message. The attitude to nature represented in it persisted to some extent until the Renaissance and even later.

It was the *Physiologus* that attributed to the phoenix the characteristics by which it became best known. It describes the bird as coming from India; when it arrives in Egypt it settles on an altar laden with spices and kindles a fire in which it is consumed. Next day, when the priest searches among the ashes he finds a small worm, but the day after that it acquires feathers and becomes a young bird. On the third day the bird salutes the priest and flies away. So the phoenix became a symbol of the Resurrection and eventually, as we think of it today, of a hopeful new beginning after a catastrophe.

Over the centuries the phoenix became ever more wonderful. The song with which it accompanies the rising sun was said to be very melodious. A medieval writer said of it: "The Phoenix is a bird more beautiful than the peacock, for the peacock indeed has golden and silver wings but the phoenix has wings of jacynth and emerald and is adorned with the colours of all precious stones. He dwells in India, lives five hundred years, and nourishes himself on the air by the cedars of Lebanon without food or drink. . . ." This splendid creature is depicted in many Christian buildings, notably the cathedrals of Tours and Le Mans, Magdeburg and Basel.

In an Old English poem the phoenix is depicted surrounded by all the birds and acclaimed by them as their king. English poets welcomed the phoenix as an adornment to their verse. Chaucer described the Duchesse thus:

> Trewly she was to mine ye
> The soleyn fenix of Arabye,
> For her lyveth never but oon [one]:
> Ne swich [such] as she ne knew I noon [none].

In *The Tempest* Shakespeare wrote:

> Now I will believe . . . that in Arabia
> There is one tree, the phoenix' throne, one phoenix
> At this time reigning there.

And in *Henry VI*, Part 3 he gives a twist to the tradition, making the bird stand for a longing for vengeance:

> My ashes, as the phoenix, may bring forth
> A bird that will revenge upon you all.

THE HALCYON AND PIOUS PELICAN

The halcyon has long been assumed to be the familiar kingfisher, but Greek and Latin authors, who were not interested in the behavior of kingfishers, endowed it with such fanciful characteristics that it must be con-

Facing page *Silk tapestry of the Ming dynasty (1368–1644) depicting two phoenixes.*
Below *The eagle renewing its youth. While the phoenix came to signify rebirth, the eagle was associated with rejuvenation. It was thought that in old age it flew aloft until the sun scorched off its old feathers; then it dived three times into a spring and became young again.*

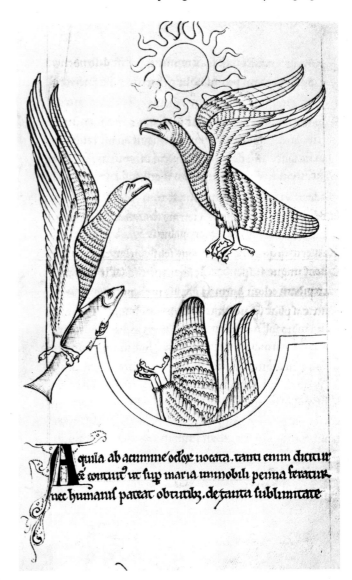

Nam id temporis fouendi ht
deputatum partubz quan
do maxime insurgit mare
litoribzq; uehemtior fluct
illudit q̃ magis repentine
placiditatis sollempnitate
auis huj eluceat gra. Haq;
ubi undosum fuerit mare
postus ouis subito mitescunt ꝯ õs cadunt uentox pcelle.
flatuq; aurarum mitescunt. ac placidu uentis stat mare.
donec oua foueat ablon sua. Septem aute dies fotus sunt.
q̃bz decursis educit pullos fetusq; absoluit. Is q̃ alios q̃ vij.
adiungit dies q̃bz enutat parte suo donec incipiant adoles
cere. Is interis tam exiguu nutritu tẽp cu absoluco fetuum
ta paucox dierũ sit. ht ut hos. xiiii. dies nautaci ꝓsuipte sere
nitatis obseruent. q̃s yalciomidas uocant. q̃bz null' mo
pcellose tempestatis horrescat.

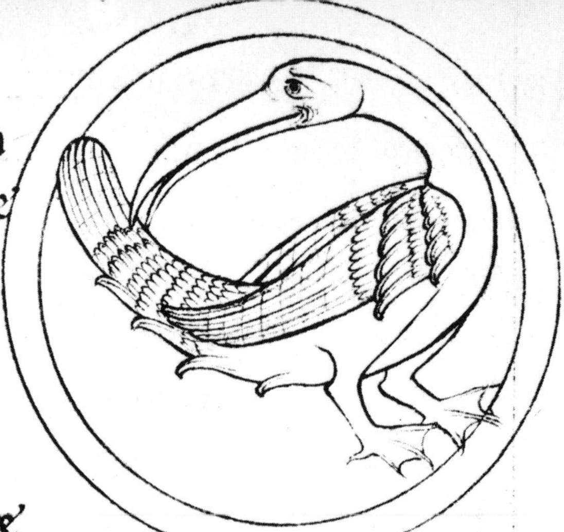

enix arabie auis dicta
q̃d colore feniceum ha
beat. ul' q̃d sit in toto orbe
singularis ꝫ unica. hec cũ
gentos ultra annos unuers.
dum se uiderit senuisse. col
lectis aromatũ uirgultis. rogũ

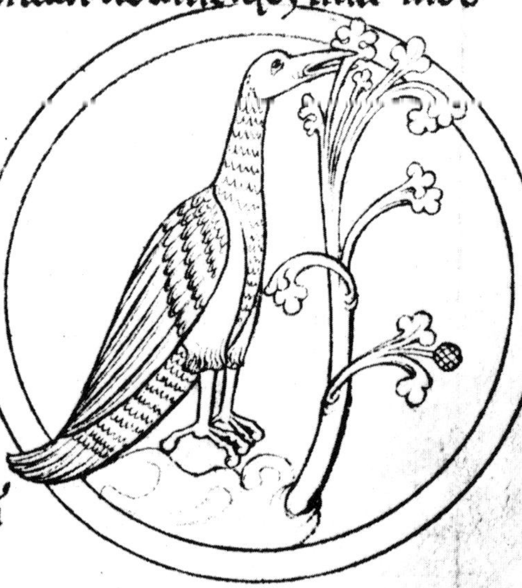

sidered a mythical creature. According to the ancient accounts, it sings, is loved by the sea nymphs, and the females carry the aged males on their backs. Unlike the actual kingfisher, the mythical halcyon breeds when four months old, lays five eggs in the winter, and launches her nest on the sea. Pliny, who was more of a bookworm than a naturalist, reported that the sea is calm for seven days before and after the winter solstice in order that the halcyon may rear its young. According to Greek myth, Aeolus, guardian of the winds, forbade the winds to vex the waters while the halcyon reared her young.

If the legend of the phoenix has survived to our own day because it symbolizes hope, references to the halcyon still appear because humanity has found in it a symbol of tranquillity and harmony. Shakespeare, who gave new life to classical avian symbolism, has Joan of Arc in *Henry IV*, Part 1, encourage the Dauphin by urging him to "expect St. Martin's summer, halcyon days." Southey referred to the original tradition when he wrote:

The Halcyon's brood around the foamless isles,
The treacherous ocean has forsworn its wiles.

Ideas about the halcyon having been transferred to the kingfisher, and this bird therefore being assumed to be weatherwise, it was also regarded as a weathercock. In his *Vulgar Errors* (1646) Sir Thomas Browne commented skeptically: "That a kingfisher, hanged by the bill, showeth us in what quarter the wind is, by an occult and secret propriety, converting the breast to that part of the horizon from whence they blow, is a received opinion, and very strange . . . conceit supported by present practice, yet not made out by reason or experience." Marlowe referred to this belief in *The Jew of Malta*:

But now, how stands the wind
Into what corner peers the halcyon's bill?

And Shakespeare in *Lear* makes Kent refer to those who

Renege, affirm, and turn their halcyon beaks
With every gale and vary of their masters.

The jumble of notions which accumulated around the halcyon-kingfisher over many centuries shows us how folklore evolves. A bird becomes associated with the weather; even when it dies this association persists, and Browne's statement suggests that among rustics the dead kingfisher may have been regarded not only as a weathercock but as a weather prophet. Another early belief may lurk in the background of this legend. In the twelfth century Giraldus Cambrensis wrote in his *Topography of Ireland* that a dried kingfisher placed among clothes preserves them from moths and "gives them a pleasant odour." Even more wonderful, he said,

Facing page *A page from a bestiary showing the halcyon* (upper right). *To indicate the bird's association with the sea, the artist has given it webbed feet, which no kingfisher has.*

is the belief that if the dead body is hung up by the beak, "they change their plumage every year . . . as though the vital spark still survived and vegetated through some mysterious remains of its energy." But surely the reason for the halcyon's longevity in literature is that just as the dove became a symbol of peace among men, so the halcyon stood for peace among the elements.

We have seen that fabulous birds range from recognizable species thought to have unusual attributes to creatures that are figments of the imagination, or products of misunderstanding, or the exaggerations of characteristics of known birds, or composite creatures invented to satisfy a craving for a supernatural symbol of ideas such as benevolence and power. We find examples of all types in the *Physiologus*. After a few words about a creature, sometimes introduced by a mistranslated text from the Bible, a moral was attached. A few examples will serve to show the extremes, ranging from a few true facts to the invention of fantastic characteristics for nonexistent birds. Thus it declares: "The woodpecker is a gay-colored bird. He gets up into the trees and pecks at them with his beak, and then listens with his ear. And when he finds the tree is hollowed and decayed, he builds his nest in it; but if the tree is sound to the heart, he flies away from it." The moral follows: the devil flies away from a virtuous person but stays with the weak and fainthearted. The modicum of ornithological truth in this is that woodpeckers are indeed brightly colored and some species may nest in unsound branches or tree trunks.

A popular medieval emblem, often depicted in church windows and sculptures, is "the pelican in her piety," a representation of a bird, only superficially resembling a pelican, bending over chicks huddled beneath her breast. The legend in the *Physiologus* is: "They love their young very much. When the young are born, and as soon as they are a little grown, they strike back and kill them. But presently the parents begin to have compassion on the young and, after they have mourned three whole days over the children they killed, the mother . . . opens her side and drops her blood on the dead bodies of the young and arouses the life in them." This crude and inconsistent legend bears evidence of having been clumsily put together to illustrate the rejection of Christ, his resurrection, and man's redemption. According to another version, which seems to have been worked over to make its Christian message clearer, the snake blows venom on the bird's young and kills them. When their mother sees that they are dead, "she looks up to a cloud and flies there; and striking her side with her wings till blood streams, she lets the drops fall . . . on the young ones and they come to life again."

In medieval bestiaries, which continue and elaborate the *Physiologus* tradition, and also in church representations, the bird is shown pecking her breast to rain down reviving blood on the chicks. The moral is that the pelican is Christ, and the snake the devil, but Christ raises up those who die in sin. Originally the bird in a comparable story was the vulture, which, since it feeds its young with bloody meat, might be imagined by a casual observer to be feeding the chicks with its own blood. An Egyptian writer, Horapollo, remarked that a vulture signifies a compassionate person because if food is unobtainable during the first 120 days of the nestling period, "it opens its own thigh and permits the young to partake of the blood, so that they may not perish from want."

Once the pelican was established as a symbol of self-sacrifice, Christian writers and artists seized upon it. It appeared prominently in literature, especially in the works of Shakespeare. In *Hamlet,* Laertes speaks of "the kind life-rend'ring pelican," King Lear refers to his "pelican daughters," and in *Richard II* Gaunt says:

> That blood already, like the pelican,
> Hast thou tapp'd out and drunkenly carous'd.

GERAHAV AND BARNACLE GOOSE

Another bird in the *Physiologus* which was almost completely imaginary is the gerahav. It was alleged to inhabit the sea and to lay, with great effort and pain, huge eggs. It deposits these in the depths of the ocean and watches continually over them for fear of its enemies. "Then, rising to the surface of the water and with eyes fastened on the depths, it broods over the eggs until the young creep out of the shell. Then the bird dives down into the depths, and leads the young ones to the shore and feeds them." This, of course, is fantasy, but it includes the idea mentioned in other fabulous stories that

a bird could brood its eggs by fixing its eyes on them. The moral is that God looks down from heaven and broods over His children and draws them out of the ocean of their misery. The gerahav was too far-fetched to become a popular symbol. Perhaps some monk, seeking an apt illustration for a sermon, created the bird to serve his purpose.

It seems incredible that the belief that barnacles can turn into geese survived almost to the present day. A generation ago it was recorded that goose was considered legitimate Lenten fare all along the Kerry coast of Ireland. The most eminent student of Irish folklore, Professor J. H. Delargy, once wrote to me: "I met a teacher in Kerry who told me he had often shot barnacle geese and had them for Friday's dinner, this type of fish being popular locally on that day. He was quite serious."

The legend can be traced back to about the tenth century. A diplomat from Moslem Spain to the court of the Emperor Otto said of the country of "Shashin" (most probably Ireland):

> There is something marvellous there, such as is nowhere else in the world. On the seashore grow trees, and from time to time the bank gives way and a tree falls into the sea. The waves toss it up and down so much that a white jelly is formed on it. This goes on until the jelly increases in size and assumes the shape of an egg. Then the egg is moulded in the form of a bird with nothing but both feet and the bill attached to the wood. When Allah wills, the wind that blows on it produces feathers and it detaches the feet and bill from the wood. So it becomes a bird which scuttles . . . about the surface of the water. It is never found alive, but when the sea rises it is thrown on the shore, where it is found dead. It is a black bird similar to the bird which is called The Diver.

There is no suggestion here that the bird is a goose, but the mention of black birds found dead on the shore suggests that the legend may have arisen from the observation that at times after a storm some parts of the British coast are littered with the bodies of little auks. In 1186, after a visit to Ireland, Giraldus Cambrensis read a paper in Oxford in which he claimed to have seen the birds being generated from shells attached to floating timber. He called them *Bernacae* and declared that religious men regarded them as legitimate fare during periods of fasting "because they are not flesh nor born of flesh." At the end of the sixteenth century Gerard, in his *Herball* published an illustration of the geese hatching from barnacles. So the legend became fixed and widely accepted.

Three factors were responsible for its origin, acceptance, and persistence. First, no educated man at that time had ever seen the nest of a barnacle goose because they breed far north of the British Isles; and second, the concept of spontaneous generation was unquestioned. Moreover, such people as the poverty-stricken Irish countryfolk were glad to have an excuse for eating roast goose during Lent, and their ecclesiastical superiors had the good sense not to be too fussy about zoological categories. They knew that a man who had secured a goose out on the wind-swept mud flats or on one of the islets in the stormy seas off the western coast of Ireland had earned his supper.

THE CHINESE CRESTED LOVE PHEASANT

Although it is often miscalled the Chinese "phoenix," the fêng huang, or love pheasant, is quite a different creature from the phoenix of Western tradition. A Chinese writer writes of it: "It resembles a wild swan before and a unicorn behind, has the throat of a swallow, the bill of a cock, the neck of a snake, the tail of a fish, the forehead of a crane, the crown of a mandarin drake, the stripes of a dragon, and the vaulted back of a tortoise. The feathers have colors named after the five cardinal virtues, and it is five cubits in height; the tail is graduated like the pipes of a gourdorgan, and its song resembles the music of that instrument, having five modulations."

The story goes that once upon a time three strange and exquisite birds came to a terrace near Nanking. Their songs were so melodious that all the birds for miles around were attracted. When it was seen that all the other birds were paying homage to them, they were recognized to be fêng huang, birds with every grace and beauty, harbingers of good fortune, joy, friendship, and love, and emblems of an empress. The name signifies "male-female," so they also symbolized marital accord. Li T'ai-po, one of the most eminent of all Chinese

Facing page *The pelican legend illustrated in a bestiary, showing the adults killing the young.*
Below *Chinese silk painting (c. 1470) showing the mythical queen of paradise with a phoenix.*

poets, who lived in the golden age of Chinese literature during the Tang dynasty (A.D. 618–907), wrote of a lonely wife's "keeping ready half the quilt" as she awaits her absent husband:

> Beneath the quilt of the Fire-bird on the bed of the
>   Silver-Crested Love-Pheasant,
> Nightly, nightly, I drowse alone.
> The red candles in the silver candlesticks melt and
>   the wax runs from them,
> As the tears of your so Unworthy One escape and
>   continue constantly to flow.

The fêng huang is often embroidered on fabrics and furnishings, and I have seen it as a decoration on a temple in south China.

Another poem, entitled "Ascending the Terrace of the Silver-Crested Love-Pheasants at the City of the Golden Mound," begins:

> The silver-crested love-pheasant strutted upon the
>   Pheasant Terrace.
> Now the pheasants are gone, the terrace is empty,
>   and the river flows on its old, original way.
> Gone are the blossoms of the Palace of Wu and
>   overgrown the road to it.
> Passed the generations of the Chin, with their robes
>   and head-dresses;
> They lie beneath the ancient mounds.

The fêng huang is represented in various ways, depending upon the artist. Usually it is depicted in brilliant colors with extravagantly long and ornate tail feathers, against a multicolored background representing the sky, clouds, and sun. The origin of the image is uncertain, but it probably stems from one of the ornate south Chinese species of pheasant.

The love pheasant is one of the four most important Chinese supernatural creatures, the others being the unicorn, the tortoise, and the dragon. In very early annals it is mentioned as appearing at the court of virtuous monarchs as a sign of heaven's favor. This concept is deeply rooted in Chinese thought. A ruler or regime believed to have lost such favor was regarded as doomed. In the faraway time of the mythical Emperor Huang Ti the fêng huang appeared and told the emperor to teach his subjects the use of wooden, earthen, and metal utensils, the construction of wheeled vehicles and boats, and the function of currency. His wife showed the people how to rear silkworms and make silk. The appearance of this bird was believed to have heralded the ordered government, harmony, and prosperity of the Golden Age.

The concept of the soul as a bird goes back to ancient Egypt, where the soul was represented as a human-headed bird. Among the Chinese, tradition recorded that in the time of the aforementioned mythical em-

peror a kind of leopard attacked and killed a woman. After her burial a bird flew out of her tomb, crying out that the woman had been killed by mistake and that it was her "wounded soul." Later, when a person was deemed to have died before fate decreed, such soul birds gathered in the fields and forests. When a usurper of the throne, Wang Mang (33 B.C.–A.D. 23), killed many innocent people, flocks of these birds appeared, screeching piteously.

Among a number of other mythical Chinese birds was one which crowed like a "male phoenix," fed on jade, had magical virtues, and drove away dangerous beasts. It was numerous for some years and then disappeared. To induce it to return, people carved images of it and hung them beside their door, but in vain. This is said to be the reason that pictures of red cocks are displayed at the Chinese New Year—an instance of an explanation manufactured for an ancient custom, the true origin of which has been forgotten. Another mythical Chinese bird is the three-legged cock, which is said to live in the sun and is embroidered on the sacrificial robes of Chinese monarchs. Still another is the pi fang, which is like a crane with one leg and one wing, and has red and blue plumage and a white beak. It carries fire in its mouth and presages the burning down of any house where it appears.

LEGENDS OF GIANT BIRDS

Wherever eagles have occurred they have always been viewed with respect and often with awe. The imagination seems to have been stimulated to magnify the significance and power of such huge birds and to endow them with mystery, magic, and sanctity.

Historically, the eagle comes into prominence with the rise of city civilizations in the Middle East. The falcon and the vulture (which has often been confused with the eagle), rather than the eagle itself, achieved prominence in Egypt because eagles were not as conspicuous there as in the mountainous lands farther north. Another early civilization that adopted the emblem of the eagle was the Sumerian city of Lagash; it used a frontal view with wings and legs outstretched and the head in profile. When Babylonia subjugated Sumeria and then was itself conquered by the Assyrians, the eagle symbol was adopted by both conquerors in turn. The emblem of the Babylonian god Ashur was an eagle, and his ministers are shown on a frieze from the palace of Ashur-nasir-apal at Nimrud (now in the British Museum) wearing eagle masks and wings during their rituals. The early Anglo-Saxons hung an eagle over the gate of a conquered city. In modern times the symbol was adopted in Turkey, Austria, Germany, and Russia, among others. After the subjection and partition of

Facing page *Chinese silk painting of a mythical bird, probably a phoenix, but perhaps a pi fang, since it stands on one leg like a crane.*
Below *Neolithic painting from Turkey of a giant bird, probably representing a vulture, attacking two headless men.*

The eagle has been used symbolically more often than any other bird.
Facing page *Fourteenth century Byzantine banner depicting an eagle with two crowned heads. The emblem was brought to Europe from the Middle East and was adopted by the Russian and Austro-Hungarian empires.*
Left *The eagle on an Egyptian coin of the third century B.C.*
Below *A representation, dating from about 1840, of the national emblem of the United States of America.*

Poland in 1795 its eagle was shown with its wings closed, but after 1919 it had them outspread. It is evident that the eagle has been associated with the more predatory relationships among peoples.

In ancient Egypt the Pharaoh was regarded as a living incarnation of Ra, the sun god, creator of the world. Later, when the sun god was represented as a falcon-headed man, the king of Egypt was clothed with the garb of the god together with birdlike gear. It is difficult for us to comprehend how a human being can, by putting on certain clothes or a mask, become in the eyes of his fellows a supernatural being; but ancient peoples thought that since the eagle and falcon show themselves to be "sun birds" by flying up to the sun, anyone who can identify himself with the bird becomes endowed with sun-god attributes.

Large flesh-eating birds were treated with respect or reverence not only in Egypt and Asia but also in North America and Australia. Hopi Indians, for example, went through a rite of purification before hunting an eagle, and the Blackfeet observed taboos in connection with it. In Australia, the eagle hawk was deified.

All this may seem to belong to an imaginative world of far away and long ago, but the prestige of the eagle lives on in modern ritual and heraldry. It is depicted on the robes of British royalty and the arms of Mexico, and is the national bird of the United States.

Another ancient tradition is the use of the eagle on the scepters of kings and other high dignitaries. At Olympia an eagle crowned the scepter of Zeus, and Roman scepters carried a model of the bird. The eagle was also important in Roman augury; and the figure of an eagle attached to the Temple at Jerusalem by King Herod was greatly resented by the Jews.

According to the *Rig-Veda,* a collection of sacred Hindu verse, the eagle brought the sacred intoxicating liquid,

soma, to mankind. In northern Asia one tribe regards the eagle as a shaman sent by the good spirits to counter-act the evil powers. To another group of the same region a tree containing an eagle's aerie is holy, and still another considers it a crime to kill an eagle. North American Indian tribes held analogous views. The Zuñi and Dakota kept eagles in order to adorn themselves with their feathers, and the Hopi and Ojibwa con-sidered the eagle a good omen.

The eagle as well as outsized mythological birds are often believed to have associations with the sun, the clouds, thunder, and the wind. Northern peoples more readily pictured the wind as a bird than did dwellers in the tropics, although in Malaysia, when clouds obscured the sun, people used to say that Gerda (a colossal bird) was spreading his wings to dry. The Indian giant bird Garuda is also identified with the wind. Similarly, when David sang a jubilant song after his defeat of Saul's army, he referred to the Lord as being "seen upon the wings of the wind." According to the Norse *Edda,* Hraesvelgr is a giant who sits at the edge of heaven in the shape of an eagle. When he flaps his wings the winds rise from beneath them. A giant of the Norse sagas, Thiaxi, could sometimes appear as an eagle, and Odin could change from a serpent form into an eagle. Such shape-changing in the sagas reveals how the un-stable identity of these creatures in ancient legends left traces in later literature.

THE ROC

Among mythological birds which have had special sig-nificance in religion, magic, and storytelling are those which are exaggerations of the size or ferocity of the larger flying predators. Perhaps the most familiar of these monstrous birds is the roc, or rukh, which figures in the fifteenth-century treasury of Near Eastern stories popularly known as *The Arabian Nights.* In the best known of these tales, Sinbad the Sailor on his second voyage reaches a mysterious island, apparently in the Indian Ocean, where he finds a dome without a door-way which turns out to be a huge egg. He concludes that it must have been laid by a colossal bird which was said to feed its young on nothing less than elephants. In order to escape from the island he creeps beneath the egg and when the roc arrives, fastens himself to one of its legs. When the roc flies away he is carried to a ravine strewn with diamonds and swarming with snakes. The natives of the country throw down carcasses and the birds bear them off with diamonds sticking to them. The natives then obtain the diamonds by collecting them from the aeries of the monstrous birds.

We might suppose that these tales were invented by an imaginative Arab, but an almost identical story was told

Facing page *Worship being offered to the falcon-headed god Harakhete, as depicted on an Egyptian stele of about 1400 B.C.*
Below *Detail of coffin lid from Saqqara, Egypt, show-ing the winged goddess Isis. Isis was a goddess of na-ture and agriculture and also of love and maternity; the cult of Isis began about 1700 B.C. and persisted into the Christian era.*

in China about the beginning of the sixth century A.D. We can trace the essentials of this tale even further back, first to a book by a bishop in Cyprus during the fourth century, and then to Lucian, a Greek satirist born in Syria in the second century. The latter wrote a book parodying "tall" stories; in it he related how seafarers came on a nest seven miles in circumference and containing five hundred huge eggs. When they hacked open one egg the chick inside was bigger than twenty vultures.

GRIFFINS, GARUDA, AND OTHERS

The history of such stories makes it clear that widely known folktales often grow by accretion and elaboration. Once they have set forth on their wanderings, no one can tell in what strange places and forms they may end up. The storytellers were plainly interested only in telling a good yarn—let those who will believe it. We are able to intercept one of these giant-bird tales midway on its meanderings when it crops up in the narrative of the travels of Rabbi Benjamin of Tudela. Rabbi Benjamin set out from Saragossa, in Spain, in 1160 on travels which lasted thirteen years and took him to Constantinople, Jerusalem, Persia, and the frontier of China. When he reached the banks of the Tigris he was informed that on the sea voyage to China many vessels had been lost but that the crews had learned how to save their lives: each man armed himself with a knife and, having sewn himself into a cow's hide, plunged into the sea. Soon "a large eagle called a griffin, spying what it took to be cattle, would swoop down and carry the man to land." As soon as it set the sailor down he killed the bird with his knife and "tried to get back to an inhabited country."

Once a strange monster has been designated, proof of its existence may be produced by those who think they can gain profit, prestige, or fun by doing so. So with the roc. According to Marco Polo, its wings were sixteen paces across and its feathers were ninety "spans" long. One of these "feathers" was obtained and presented to the Great Khan; actually, it was the dried remains of a frond of the *Raphia* palm. It is an odd coincidence that Madagascar, where this palm grows, was the home of the giant flightless *Aepyornis* discussed in our chapter on prehistoric birds.

During the Middle Ages travelers into remote countries expected to find the unexpected, especially barbaric customs and weird animals. Thus, another medieval European traveler, Friar Odoric, who started out in 1318 and eventually reached China, reported that while he was passing through Ceylon he saw birds with two heads. In all probability he caught a glimpse of rhinoceros hornbills, which have a large excrescence at the base of the

Facing page *An imaginative Persian representation of the mythological roc carrying off a man.*
Below *A sixteenth century Italian plaque showing an eagle devouring the heart of a human corpse. This strange legend occurs in both Aztec and classical mythology.*

ولایک پرواز کرد و بال کشاد مرغ که را برجای برو چون‌داد

۲۴

Facing page *A Balinese girl in a dance representing the movements of a mythological bird named Garuda. King of birds and storm-bringer, it serves as the mount of the Hindu god Vishnu. Garuda is prominent in the mythology of the Indochinese region.*
Below *Javanese brass oil lamp in the form of Garuda. Such lamps have served since the eleventh century to illuminate the performance of Balinese* wayang, *a type of theater in which traditional Javanese and Hindu legends are enacted.*

bill that a casual, credulous observer might take to be another bill on a second head.

Yet another monstrous bird is the Persian simurgh, a magnified eagle or vulture. It acts as an aerial steed and carries the hero Rustam to the China Sea in a single night. There Rustam finds a tamarisk tree and from one of its branches fashions the arrow he uses to slay his enemy Isfranchiyar. The simurgh becomes the protector of Rustam's family and heals the hero's wounds.

Such giant-bird stories probably served to reassure people that the monsters they feared might be outwitted or even enlisted to help them.

Further east, in India and Indochina, dwells Garuda, the sacred "eagle" of the sun god Vishnu. Garuda is a huge winged monster who feeds on snakes which lurk deep in lakes. He may be seen in all his gigantic, menacing splendor in Cambodia where, a century ago, a path was hacked through the jungle to reveal at Angkor Wat the most extraordinary complex of temples in the world.

At a corner by the door of one of these temples I came on Garuda, jutting forth from the stonework, his immense beaked countenance dwarfing a human figure standing beneath him. He holds aloft the tails of cobras and their menacing heads curl at his feet. King of birds and storm-bringer, Garuda acts as a steed for Vishnu, one of the Hindu divine Trinity. If we compare this Hindu mythology with the Sinbad stories of *The Arabian Nights,* we see how a concept, originally religious, having traveled far and been modified by peoples with different cultural backgrounds, became just an entertaining yarn.

The association in Arabia, as in India, of gigantic, helpful birds, snakes, and treasures, suggests that we are dealing with branches of a tradition rooted far back in history and, probably, prehistory. In a Persian (Pahlavi)

translation of an Indian story the simurgh is substituted
for the anka, which has some of the characteristics of
the phoenix. It lives seventeen hundred years and when
a youngster is born, the parent of the opposite sex burns
itself alive. Here two traditions have met, for although
avian giants may be "birds of a feather," the phoenix belongs to a different tradition.

The griffin was of a rather different lineage from the
roc but had affinities with Garuda. As described in the
Physiologus, it is the largest of all birds and two of
them rise at dawn and fly to the sunset. They are said
to stand for the Holy Trinity, the Archangel Michael,
and the Virgin Mary; this confused identification of
the griffin shows that the creature had not yet found a
definite place in Christian imagery.

In the West a transmogrified griffin appeared and was
called a hippogriff in the *Legends of Charlemagne.*
The hero, Rogero, spurs the flying monster toward the
orc, a man-devouring marine beast, drives his lance into
the orc, frees the naked Princess Angelica who had
been abandoned on a rock as prey for the beast, and
carries her to safety on the back of the hippogriff.

The ancient stem from which most of these tales
branched may be found in the *Jatakas* of India, the
oldest and most complete collection of folklore in the
world. The *Jatakas* were gathered in the third century
B.C. and include stories reproduced much later in the
West in the fables of Aesop. In one of them we are told
of a huge bird which lived in a tree on an island far out
in the ocean. It took human form and so was able to
kidnap the queen of Benares, in India. The distressed
king commissioned a musician to try to discover where
she was concealed. The musician succeeded in finding
the haunt of the creature and by hiding himself under
its wing managed to rescue her.

A titanic storm bird, the phang, appears in Chinese
records. It is a transformed fish and when it flies its
wings are like clouds all across the sky. It goes to the
southern ocean, the pool of heaven, flapping over the
water for a thousand miles. Its back is like a mountain
and on it rests the blue sky. Similarly, the Japanese tell
of a pheng, a bird that lives in the southwest ocean, is
able to swallow a camel, and, in flight, eclipses
the sun.

All these stories are obviously related to one another
and the origin of the ideas basic to them can be traced,
ultimately, not to flights of fancy but to religious beliefs.
The multitude of symbols and meanings that every civilization has found in birds is testimony to the way
man's imagination has been stimulated by the intriguing ways, awesome beauty, and seemingly magical
powers of these remarkable creatures.

5
Birds in Sport and Recreation

Above *Duck hunting in a lagoon near Venice as shown in a painting by the Venetian painter Pietro Longhi (1702–1762).*
Facing page *A nineteenth century impression of hunting ruffed grouse.*

Occasionally sportsmen today eat the game birds they kill, but by and large we are safe in defining sport as the killing of birds without any intention of using them for food. In the distant past birds were trapped or were shot with bow and arrow for food, but long before the invention of firearms most peoples had progressed beyond the stage where they depended on hunting for subsistence.

There is, however, much of the hunter in civilized man and he still likes to exercise his skill in pursuit of birds and beasts. As a result, most countries have had to introduce laws defining how, when, and where animals may be killed. In addition, there are often unwritten laws as to what is "sporting" in hunting. Governments exercise control by regulating the hunting seasons as well as the use of firearms, by setting up preserves, and so forth. An example of an unwritten rule is the widely accepted convention that a "sitting bird" should not be shot. Apart from humanitarian considerations, the principle underlying these rules is that any sport involving the death of an animal should be regulated lest the sport itself peter out through lack of quarry. Some field sports have become almost ritualistic. Thus, in Scotland, numbers of tweed-suited sportsmen descend on the moors on "the glorious twelfth," the date in August when the grouse-shooting season starts; similarly, when the "open season" on deer comes in the fall in the United States, hunters head for the woods in droves. The attitude toward so-called "blood sports" varies according to upbringing, interest in animals, sentiment, and the extent to which a person enjoys physical exercise and skills. In some the love of animals may be dominant, and in others the love of sport, and such is human nature that sometimes there is a love of both. The situation is seldom clear-cut. For example, in England even the animal enthusiast who loves watching fox cubs play near their den must admit that the fox, being prone to attack poultry and newborn lambs, might be wiped out in parts of the countryside were they not allowed to live for the benefit of fox-hunters. There are others who deplore hunting in general but regard fox-hunting as an acceptable traditional sport because it has hazards for the participants as well as the fox. Then again, some persons see deer-stalking as a sport calling for endurance and field craft, and others see it as a useful operation to prevent the animals from increasing to such an extent as to destroy their own habitat. Scientific investigation has shown that shooting wood pigeons does little to affect their numbers because other factors would reduce the population if man did not. It is thus increasingly realized that sportsmen and conservationists basically need not be at odds since ultimately their interests are the same—the preservation of the animal. In many

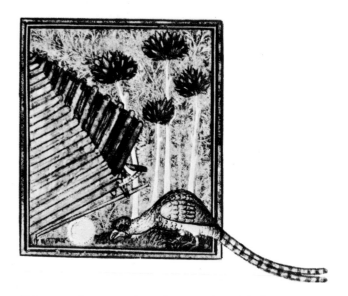

American communities hunting-license fees are in fact incentives to protect the animals from excessive hunting or cruel practices. Unfortunately there are still countries in Europe and South America that have not come around to this view and where populations of birds have consequently been sharply reduced. There are situations in which conservationists complain that their efforts merely provide more birds to be killed.

CATCHING AND TRAPPING BIRDS

A great variety of devices have been used throughout the ages for capturing or killing birds—traps, nets, missiles, or simply clubs. One very old practice is the liming of twigs with a sticky "lime" made by macerating holly bark so that the bird gets stuck when it alights on the branch. This method is constantly referred to by the Elizabethan poets. Shakespeare alluded to liming as well as other devices in *Macbeth:* "Thou'ldst never fear the net nor lime/The pitfall nor the gin." Some ancient devices are still used in the countryside, or were until recently. As a boy I watched birdcatchers in Ireland stretch a long net over a shallow stream, set a linnet (a finch) in a cage beneath it as a decoy, and, when birds arrived, pull a string attached to the props that held up the net. My father showed me how to make a "klaven" to catch birds. It was a pyramidal wooden framework propped up a few inches above the ground with a net stretched over it. When a bird entered under the framework and perched on a curved twig, it knocked out the prop and trapped itself.

Bas-reliefs from the ancient civilizations of the Middle East depict mainly the hunting of larger beasts, especially the lion, yet, as Egyptian paintings show, wildfowling was carried on in marshes and along the banks of great rivers. Birds provided a much-appreciated addition to what must have been rather dull fare. Ancient representations remind us of the immense differences in the attitudes of people toward killing animals. The motives of an Assyrian king hunting lions and a peasant capturing birds for his supper were very different.

THE "EVIL OSTRICH"

In early civilizations when artists depicted conflicts between bird and beast they were symbolizing the beliefs, hopes, and fears of the communities in which they lived. Those beliefs or feelings were externalized by religious or magical motifs down the ages. The ostriches on Babylonian seals represented evil, probably because the birds lived in the desert, a hostile and dangerous area which was regarded as the dwelling place of mysterious, uncanny, or malicious beings. In the Bible (Lamentations) we come upon such expressions as "cruel as the ostrich in the wilderness." By association, the ostrich could be regarded as in league with or embodying alien and antagonistic powers. The eagle, which circles up to the life-giving sun, represented good. It was thought of as opposed to a composite monster that had a lion's body and a bird's wings and tail. About the eighth century B.C., the Babylonian god Marduk in the form of an eagle was depicted as in conflict with an ostrich, which stood for Tiamat, the power of evil. This design, a bird attacking another bird, mammal, reptile, or fish, recurs in many later cultures. Whether some lingering tradition of such a conflict survived into Roman times is doubtful, but combats between man and ostrich were occasionally staged in Rome's Circus. The ostrich stood little chance against a man with a sword; it was soon decapitated. For the mob the amusement lay not in so unequal a combat, but in watching the beheaded bird running about. The treatment of ostriches in Rome was not always so bar-

Left *Trapping a pheasant with a mirror as portrayed in a fourteenth century French manuscript. Peasants were not allowed to hunt or hawk so they used ingenious devices such as this to trap birds.*
Below *An ancient Babylonian seal illustrating a man driving ostriches.*

baric. The Emperor Ptolemais Philadelphus had eight of them trained to draw a chariot; and a statue of his queen riding one of these birds was erected on Helicon.

COCKSHYING AND OTHER GAMES

On Shrove Tuesday in England and France, villagers participated in another cruel "sport": a live cock was hung up and sticks were thrown, or shied, at it. He who killed it could take it home and eat it. In the fifteenth century, Erasmus commented that "the English eat a certain cake on Shrove Tuesday on which they immediately run mad and kill the poor cocks." The cockshy was a sport at the court of Henry VII, and in the seventeenth century there was a satirical song:

> Cocke a doodle doe, 'tis the greatest game,
> Takes a cocke from his dame,
> And binds him to a stake,
> How he struts, how he throwes,
> How he swaggers, how he crowes,
> As if the day newly brake.

Participants paid two pence for three "shys" from twenty-five yards away, and had to catch the cock before it rose to its feet after being knocked over. If the bird had been well trained it could elude the sticks for a considerable time and so the owner of the cock was well remunerated.

Hogarth, who held a mirror to his age, made throwing at cocks the subject of prints which he called *The Four Stages of Cruelty*. Another British commentator wrote: "We have several groupes of boys at their different barbarous diversions; one is throwing at a cock, the universal Shrove-tide amusement, beating the harmless feathered animal to jelly." In spite of occasional protests, cock-throwing continued here and there in England until at least the end of the eighteenth century.

Another hardly less objectionable practice consisted of tying a hen to the back of a boy with bells attached to him and then having a gang of blindfolded boys armed with branches chase and try to beat him and the hen. Naturally the boys frequently hit each other. The girls did the blindfolding but often contrived to make a peephole for a boyfriend.

COCKFIGHTING

Cockfighting is the sport of getting gamecocks, male domestic fowl, to fight each other. They are bred and trained for this purpose. Man learned many centuries ago that some male birds are very aggressive when at close quarters with other male birds. In order to provide entertainment they exploited the fighting which often takes place in such circumstances. An amulet seal from 1500 B.C. found at the ancient Indian city of Mohenjo-

Facing page Disguised as an ostrich, a stalker approaches his quarry.
Below A Flemish or Dutch scene showing the operation of a net trap in winter.

Right *Cocks fighting.*
Below *A cockpit as portrayed by the eighteenth century artist William Hogarth.*

daro shows two jungle fowl in a fighting attitude. Partridges may also have been trained to fight, as partridge-fighting is still popular in this area. Pottery model cages with birds at their entrances found here are probably partridge cages. This sport satisfied the same aggressive emotions as the bullfights that still attract large crowds in Spain and Latin America, or the bear-baiting popular in Britain until it was prohibited in 1835. In June, 1670, the English diarist John Evelyn wrote: "I went with some friends to the bear-garden, where was cock-fighting, dog-fighting, bear and bull baiting, it being a famous day for all these butcherly sports, or rather barbarous cruelties. . . ."

Cockfighting was introduced from the East where it was popular in Persia, India, and China. Themistocles was said to have brought the sport to Greece in the fifth century B.C. It was reported that, seeing two cocks fighting as he led his troops against the Persians, he called on his men to copy the valor of the birds. The sport spread throughout the Greek world and was adopted by the Romans. It became popular in spite of disapproval by the early Christian church. Columella, in the first century, inveighed against spectators who lost all their money betting on contests, and Lactantius condemned cockfights as inhuman spectacles to be avoided by Christians.

The Romans are said to have brought the sport into Britain but it may have been adopted earlier. During the reign of Henry II schoolboys arranged fights, especially on Shrove Tuesday. They were abetted by their masters, who then appropriated the dead birds. Henry VIII added a royal cockpit to his palace in Whitehall and the sport, over which the king presided, was called "the royal diversion." Shakespeare repeatedly refers to cock fighting.

Cockpits were circular and had a matted stage about twenty feet across surrounded by a barrier against which the crowd pressed. A "battle royal" was a conflict between a number of birds which continued until all but one had been killed or disabled. This champion was reckoned "cock of the walk"; hence our use of the term "cocky" to describe a very self-confident person. The term referring to the tail feathers seen when a timid bird flies away—"showing the white feather"—has also been applied to man. Perhaps because cock-fighting was enjoyed by all classes, it has added more expressions to the English language than has falconry, which in Europe was never a sport of the common man.

The fighting spirit of cocks was fostered by their training. Normally most male birds in the wild maintain a "territory," an area which they defend against intruders of their own species and sex. This permits breeding to take place without serious disturbances from rivals. Also, social species, such as jackdaws, form a hierarchy or "pecking order," with one boss and so on down the scale to the lowest individual in the flock. In a hen run, where birds are abnormally close together, dominance and subservience are more obvious and accentuated than in the wild.

Birds in training for cockfights were fed with stimulating food such as bread, sugar candy, and a mixture of eggs and oatmeal saturated with beer. Birds would be set to spar against each other with their spurs so wrapped up that they could not inflict serious injury. After Shakespeare's time the birds were equipped with iron spurs, and this may also have been an ancient Greek practice. Before a fight, cocks were made to fast for a few days, their spurs were sharpened, and their wings were cut short to expose the quills so that they could do maximum damage to an adversary.

There were cockpits throughout England until they

were declared illegal in 1849. Cockfights were also popular in the United States but they were discouraged in New England and the sport was made illegal in Massachusetts in 1836. Probably the growing popularity of horse-racing, with its appeal to a wider audience, had as much influence as did humanitarian sentiments in bringing about legislation against this barbarous pastime. However, it is said to be still practiced surreptitiously in various parts of the United States, especially in communities where Latin Americans live, and in the north of England. It is common in the Caribbean and Central American area, and in a number of Eastern countries.

QUAILFIGHTING

Very similar to cockfighting was quailfighting. It too was introduced to Europe from the Orient, where it is still enjoyed by the Chinese and Malays.

It was practiced in England but was never popular there. Shakespeare mentions quailfighting as well as cockfighting in *Antony and Cleopatra*. The Soothsayer has just left and Mark Antony, referring to Caesar's luck, soliloquizes:

> He hath spoken true. The very dice obey him,
> And in our sports my better cunning faints
> Under his chance. If we draw lots, he speeds;
> His cocks do win the battle still of mine,
> When it is all to nought; and his quails ever
> Beat mine, inhoop'd, at odds.

Shakespeare owed this allusion to Plutarch, who had written of Antony and Caesar: "It is said that as often as they drew lots of pastime, who should have anything, or whether they played at dice, Antonius always lost. Oftentimes they were disposed to see cockfights, or quails that were taught to fight one with another. Caesar's cocks or quails did ever overcome." Shakespeare was not alluding to quail as good eating but to Agamemnon's fighting prowess when he wrote: "Here's Agamemnon, an honest fellow enough and one that loves quails" (*Troilus and Cressida*). In the allusion already quoted, "inhoop'd" refers to the enclosure or "hoop" in which the birds were placed. This sport came to Europe, like cockfighting and so much else, from Asia, where it is still popular in China, Sumatra, Malaysia, and other Far Eastern lands.

Probably the custom of keeping quail as pets also originated in Asia. What might be called "quail-fancying," on the analogy of "pigeon-fancying," is still popular in Japan, where birds are bred for excellence in song, color, and form. Pet quails were highly esteemed in ancient Greece and were given by a lover to his beloved. At Athens quails were placed in a circular arena and whichever bird chased the other out of the ring was

Facing page *A quailfight in South China watched by sailors from sampans.*
Below *A cockfight in Japan.*

the winner. In North Africa I have seen a quail in a cage made of wooden lattice hung up at the entrance to a house where the occupants could enjoy its mellow notes. Together with fighting cocks, quails were among the birds given as presents to Roman boys as object lessons in courage, and one later writer, Glaucus, deplored the degeneracy of young men who had become too sophisticated to appreciate such gifts. For a time quail-fighting was in vogue in Italy, where it was customary to feed two birds lavishly, place them at opposite ends of a long table, and throw millet seeds between them to provoke a quarrel.

FALCONRY

Man's closest relationship to animals has been with those with which he can establish some kind of rapport. The most familiar such relationship is with the dog, which he has taught to serve him in many ways, from guarding property and retrieving game to leading the blind, and with which he can also establish an understanding almost like that between human beings. In general, training an animal, whether elephant or bird, to do one's will establishes a bond which can be emotionally satisfying. This explains how differently we have regarded the horse in comparison with the cow.

It is easier to establish such a tie with some mammals than with birds. And yet someone who has taught a budgerigar to speak may be greatly upset when it dies. But perhaps the most unusual kind of relationship is that between a falcon and its trainer. The attraction here lies in the satisfaction of training a bird to hunt at its master's behest—all the more gratifying because the bird is notably fierce and powerful—so well described in T. H. White's remarkable book *The Goshawk*. To subdue such a creature seems to minister to man's pride.

Falconry has a good claim to being the oldest sport. Even if we question the belief that it was practiced in China as long ago as 2000 B.C., there is a Khorsabas bas-relief in Iran dating from about 1700 B.C. which appears to depict a falconer with a hawk perched on his wrist. There is little doubt that the sport was known in China in the seventh century B.C. and not much later in Japan, India, Persia, and Arabia. In all these regions falconry is still practiced. Some years ago in Peking I was surprised and fascinated to see a man with an eagle on his wrist being drawn through one of the main streets in a rickshaw. Later, on returning to England I was also pleased to meet on the street in Cambridge an undergraduate carrying a falcon on his wrist. Nowadays demonstrations are sometimes given at farmers' gatherings in England's East Anglian countryside.

Below *Falcons flying at a heron, in a miniature from* The Book of King Modus, *a fourteenth century French work.*
Facing page *A boy with his hooded falcon in a painting by the seventeenth century Dutch artist Albert Cuyp.*
Overleaf *A hawking party depicted on a sixteenth century Flemish tapestry.*

One of the treats at an ornithological conference in Russia a few years ago was a demonstration of hunting with eagles. Since falconry is most successful in open country, the East Anglian marshes, which in medieval times extended over an area of about two thousand square miles, were more suitable than forested area. Bones of the pelican and crane as well as the remains of common wading birds dug up in the peaty soil testify to the rich variety of quarry available. A picture in a tenth-century manuscript shows falcons being released where ducks are swimming on a lake and a crane is feeding on the bank. The *Lex Alaman* of the seventh century lists "a hawk that flies at cranes" as worth six shillings while an untamed hawk was worth only half that.

One of the earliest of all sporting books is *The Art of Falconry* by Emperor Frederick II, king of Sicily, which appeared in 1248. In England during the eleventh century hawking by the clergy was frowned upon, but later they approved of it and certain priests even had the right to bring the birds into church. When one fourteenth-century bishop of Ely left his hawks in the cloister of a church, they were stolen and he promptly excommunicated the thieves.

Men and women became very fond of their hawks. A fifteenth-century Central Asian grandee was said to have been heard moaning, after one of his hawks had died, that he had rather it had been one of his sons. Marco Polo tells us that the Great Khan had trained gyrfalcons, and hawking has long been a popular sport in India and other parts of Asia. Even ladies took part: among the gifts sent to Queen Mary of England in 1556 was "a large and fair white jerfawcon, for the wild swan, crane, goose, and other great fowls." Olaus Magnus, who lived from 1490 to 1558, in his *History of the Gauls* called the gyrfalcon "the most noble bird of all" and wrote, "She is so strong that she will carry an eagle, and so full of animosity that if she be let fly in the ayr after four or five cranes, she will never forsake the prey till she strike them all down to the ground one after another. . . ." He was aware that the female is larger and more powerful than the male. Dame Juliana Berners's treatise, *The Boke of St. Albans,* classified hawks according to an owner's rank in society: the eagle was the emperor's bird, the gyrfalcon belonged to a king, the peregrine to a prince, the sparrow hawk to a priest, the merlin to a lady, and the kestrel to a peasant. Falconers today rate the kestrel very low because it feeds on small mammals and insects.

Late medieval and Renaissance poets liked to show their knowledge of falconry. Spenser does so in *The Faerie Queene,* and Shakespeare in *Romeo and Juliet*

Facing page *A present-day American falconer with his martial eagle.*
Below *An Arab falconer and his bird in Morocco.*

parades his acquaintance with the craft when Juliet, using the term "tassel-gentle," referring to a male peregrine falcon, says:

Hist, Romeo, hist! O, for a falc'ner's voice,
To lure this tassel-gentle back again!

Books on falconry recommended that a falconer should be not only a good horseman and swimmer in order to follow his bird, but capable of calling it in a loud voice. Such a shout was uttered when the "lure," a tuft of feathers with meat attached to it, was swung on a string to "take down" a bird when it strayed. Shakespeare is using such a call when he has Hamlet cry: "Hillo, ho, ho, boy! come bird, come," Referring in the term "haggard" to a wild-caught bird, and to the fact that when a falconer wanted to get rid of a disappointing hawk he flew her "down wind," Othello, suspicious of Desdemona's behavior, says to the villain Iago:

If I do prove her haggard,
Though that her jesses were my dear heart-strings,
I'd whistle her off, and let her down the wind.

Fastened to each leg a hawk had jesses, narrow strips of leather attached to a swivel from which hung the "leash." When the hawk was flown, the jesses and leash were removed and bells of silver or brass—referred to in Act II of Shakespeare's *Richard II*—remained, enabling the falconer to trace his bird. Elsewhere in *Richard II* there is the line, "Imp out our drooping country's broken wing," an allusion to imping, a way of repairing a broken feather by inserting a needle in the broken quill and attaching a fresh feather to it.

A "hood" is put over the hawk's head and eyes when it is carried out of doors to prevent its becoming excited by the activity around it. A dog is used to locate game birds, such as partridges or grouse, when the hawk is unhooded and released, ready to "stoop" (that is, dive). The familiar phrase "at one fell swoop" (*Macbeth*) refers to the swift descent on the quarry.

Some birds that one might suppose to be "easy game" are not as helpless as they seem. Tramping over the tundra in Lapland, I flushed a whimbrel. A gyrfalcon suddenly appeared and plummeted down on her at great speed but, to my astonishment, missed, because at the critical moment the whimbrel adroitly swerved and side-slipped. Both birds rose higher, the falcon making strenuous efforts to rise above the whimbrel. He swooped again and missed. For nearly ten minutes the aerial maneuvers continued, the whimbrel eluding the falcon every time until they were both specks in the sky. Then the falcon acknowledged defeat and flew away.

Each species of hawk has its own hunting technique: the merlin flies swiftly over moorland and seizes small

Facing page Lady with a Hawk, *an Indian miniature* (*c. 1760*).
Overleaf *A German military falconer and his charges* (*c. 1767*). Far right (top) *Falcons on their perches, a detail of a page from the famous early work* The Art of Falconry (1248), *by Frederick II, King of Germany.* Far right (bottom) *Falcons with their masters, a scene from* The Art of Falconry *by Frederick II.*

Es anciens phi
losophes a qui
dieu auoit en
lumine lenten
dement et donne cuer denat
ur choses prouffitables qui
consideroient que toutes cho
ses qui sont soubz le ciel sot
crées de dieu pour prouffit
humain. Si pensèrent par
soubtil enging comme bestes
cuer de terre et deaue qui po
le peche du premier pere es

toient inobedient a homme
si sapient pasez. Et ace trou
uerent plusieurs cauteles
dont les hommes ont vse z
tousiours depuis en soy soub
tillant ont trouue plusieurs
autres engins et y adioustet
que pou de gens sceuent. Si
me suis pourpense den escri
re plusieurs selon ce que iay
peu sauoir. Et preme
rement comment len pret
les oiseaulx. Secondement

birds such as meadow pipits as they are collecting food for their chicks; the sparrow hawk swerves around trees and bushes and seizes the unwary thrush or warbler. The nobler falcons, hunting larger game, put on a grand display, and we can understand a falconer's satisfaction when he sees his bird outfly and seize its quarry, however much we may regret the death of its victim.

In Europe and the United States the use of DDT has seriously reduced the numbers of hawks, rendering the eggshells so thin that the brooding birds are liable to break them. The sport of falconry, involving the collaboration between man and bird, still fascinates men today, but the depletion of the hawks in Europe and America means that the small but enthusiastic bands of men that still practice the art must rely on birds imported from elsewhere. Attempts are being made to breed birds of prey in captivity, but this has its own problems.

THE CORMORANT AND MAN

In many places along a rocky coast frequented by cormorants these birds may be seen standing upright, often with wings outspread to dry. Apparently their likeness to black-garbed church dignitaries was noticed independently in south and north Britain, for in Hampshire they are called "Isle of Wight parsons" and in Scotland, "Mochrum elders." In *Paradise Lost,* referring to the bird as a symbol of greed, Milton was less complimentary. He wrote of Satan that he,

> On the tree of life,
> The middle tree, the highest there that grew,
> Sat like a cormorant.

Similarly, Shakespeare in *Richard II* speaks of the "insatiate cormorant."

But in other times and places people have been more interested in making use of the bird than in its symbolism. Possibly it was a falconer in Japan who had the bright idea that if hawks could be trained to catch birds, it should be possible to use cormorants to catch fish. Although the relationship between trained cormorants and their master is comparable with that between falcon and falconer, it is less close. At all events, the first Far Eastern reference, in Chinese annals of about 600 B.C., relates to trained cormorants in Japan. In tenth-century Japan, falconry and cormorant-fishing seem to have been regarded as allied sports. Cormorants appear in a fishing scene depicted in the tomb of Mera dating from the sixth Egyptian dynasty (about 2200 B.C.), but there is no evidence that these were trained.

Since cormorant-fishing is not mentioned in China until the Sui dynasty (A.D. 589–618), it may have been

Facing page Shooting birds, an illustration from an illuminated French manuscript.
Below Flightless cormorant from the Galapagos Islands. Other relatives of this rare cormorant are used for fishing in India, China, and Japan.

Below *Using cormorants for fishing in Japan.*
Facing page *Trapping birds, an Egyptian wall painting from the Tomb of Khnum-hotep (about 1900 B.C.). In the trap are various species of geese, ducks, and grebes, while in the flowering acacias are a hoopoe, a redstart, a dove, and shrikes.*

one of the few arts which the Chinese acquired from the Japanese. But if it began as a local rustic practice, it may not have been considered worth mentioning until it attracted the attention of the educated nobility in the tenth century.

In China, fishing with cormorants is mainly confined to the lower Yangtze area. The birds are bought by fishermen from the breeders. When they have been trained, they are taken out on boats and perched on the gunwale where they can see into the water. They are usually on a leash, but sometimes they are allowed to swim freely with a ring or strap fastened around the neck so that they are unable to swallow the fish they seize. This requires very exact adjustment lest the birds choke. They are usually rewarded from time to time with some of their catch. At a signal from the fisherman they plunge into the water, and since they are very agile in the water they are often successful. Sometimes fishermen in several boats collaborate and use their birds to drive the fish into nets.

For references to cormorant-fishing in Japan a thousand years ago we may turn to that delightful book *The Tale of Genji,* written by the highborn Lady Murasaki in the eleventh century. She describes how some gentlemen rode out to join her party in the country. "We should have been here sooner," they said, "had we not become involved in a hawking party that one of the chamberlains has got up. . . . It was no easy matter on the spur of the moment to provide entertainment for so large a number of persons. However, the cormorant-fishers who ply their trade on the Katura river were hastily sent for, and promised to secure food enough for the whole party. . . . The falconers, who had decided to camp in the open country, sent a present of small snipe, each bird tied to a bunch of sedge-leaves."

Another passage describes a visit by the emperor. The bridges and pathways were carpeted with brocade and a wall was pulled down to enable him to see the brilliant autumn coloration of the maples. The party set out in boats on the lake and the head cormorant-fisher from the palace gave an exhibition in which his birds caught a number of small fish. The fish were presented to the emperor for his approval and then Genji's falconers appeared with their birds and these were submitted to the emperor by another colonel of the guard. Thus cormorant-fishing was regarded as more than a way to obtain a meal. Like so much in Japanese life, past and present, it became part of a ritualized way of life.

On the basis of these few allusions it would be going too far to call fishing with cormorants "the sport of emperors," but for a time it became the sport of the kings of England. A diplomat sent to China during the reign of James I published an account of his experiences, which included cormorant-fishing. Probably through his recommendation or that of other visitors to the Far East, cormorant-fishing was introduced in England. King James kept trained cormorants for many years and sometimes took them together with his falcons when he traveled in the countryside. The cormorants were kept by the river at Westminster and their keeper, John Wood, was given the title of Master of the Royal Cormorants.

A manuscript diary in the British Museum written in old French by an aide who came to England with the Duke of Würtemberg on a diplomatic mission contains an account of how the party was entertained at Thetford in Norfolk in May, 1610: "His excellency supped again with His Majesty. After the meal they went by carriage to the river where they saw the cormorants, birds which on a sign from their Master dive into the water and catch eels and other fish. Moreover, at another sign they disgorge their prey alive—a very extraordinary sight."

One "John Harris, gentleman" took Wood's place after the Restoration and there are records of his receiving sums of money for "repairing yearly unto the north parts of England to take haggard [untamed] cormorants for His Majesty's disport in fishing." The birds may have been brought from the Farne Islands off the northern British coast, where the cormorants still breed. Probably these were young birds.

In England fishing with cormorants never became more than a dilettante sport for king and courtiers, and it ceased entirely with Charles II. Men who lived by fishing had more efficient methods. But rather more than a century ago the sport was for a time revived by some English country gentlemen who were also interested in falconry. If it was revived again the birds might be studied scientifically and even exhibited to the public. They would be no more difficult to manage than the gray seals which have been successfully tamed and trained in England, or the seals and whales in the great aquarium theaters in Florida and California.

THE CONDOR-BULL FIESTA

To us the sight of a condor with a wingspan of almost ten feet soaring over the mountains in the wild regions it frequents would be an unforgettable experience, but to the people in remote Andean villages of Peru the bird is simply one of a number of scavengers. Since it is also, at least in some South American regions, symbolic of racial or national identity, and its likeness has appeared on the coins of Bolivia, Chile, Colombia, and Ecuador, we may hope that in Peru too it may eventually be respected and protected.

The Andean condor is a native of such harsh wildernesses that it is not yet menaced with extermination like its relative the California condor; but when we learn that one man has shot as many as forty-six in one summer and realize that condors do not breed until they are eight years old and then lay only one egg at a time—sometimes every other year—no one can feel confident that this bird will not rapidly become one of

the vanishing species. At present there are localities such as California's Condor National Park where visitors can still see condors in flight almost any day. Others should be established in areas of the Andes to preserve the birds for future generations.

In northern Peru, villagers have a custom called *arranque del condor* or *condor-rachi* wherein a condor is suspended from a kind of gallows and horsemen ride at it and strike it with their fists until it expires— sometimes after an hour of such treatment. Then it is lowered to the waiting horsemen and subjected to the final brutality of having its tongue bitten out by one of the riders, who may not even wait until life is extinguished. No condor ever survives. At some fiestas two birds are thus tortured and slaughtered. Happily, there are some indications that the gratuitous cruelty of the *arranque* is being recognized and the custom has even been prohibited in some areas. The motivation behind these ceremonies resembles that which prompted Incas and Aztecs to sacrifice animals and human beings to their gods. The procedure itself resembles a European practice in which horsemen rode at high speed at a suspended chicken and tried to wrench off its head as they passed.

A more sophisticated ritual is staged by villagers in the mountains of southern Peru on national and religious holidays, such as July 28, September 8, and December 8. A condor, representing the indigenous Indians, is tied to a bull, representing the invading Spaniards, by means of a rope passing through holes pierced in the bull's hide. The condor-bull is released in a bullring while the crowd, wild with excitement, shouts and cheers as the bird tears at the frantic bull's ears. The show goes on for about ten minutes and then the bull is lassoed and the condor untied and removed. It is looked after for a day or two and then set free—if it has recovered sufficiently. In spite of the belief that the bird's death foreshadows misfortune for the villagers, it is frequently mortally injured as the maddened bull charges against a fence or, in the mountains, falls into a chasm. About a third of the condors die; at one fiesta where twelve condors were involved, half of them

perished. Humanitarians are trying to modify the practice, advocating that only one bird a year be treated in this way, that supervision be imposed, and violation of the rules punished. Realizing that complete prohibition would be difficult to enforce, they are trying to introduce changes gradually.

As the preceding pages indicate, so-called sports in which birds are involved have unfortunately often been barbarous. This does not mean that all killing of birds should be prohibited. But, as in any other sport, rules should be drawn up by enlightened sportsmen who have given thought to the preservation of the stock of their quarry and avoiding needless cruelty. It is deplorable that there are still countries where a man with a gun can use it as he chooses on wildlife.

Once a person's interest in birds has been aroused, he usually feels that it is more enjoyable to watch birds than to kill them. Bird lovers can infect others with their enthusiasm. Outings by bird clubs are one way of doing this. Witnessing a single interesting incident in bird life can transform a person's attitude toward birds.

"Shooting" birds with a camera is another ideal substitute for shooting them with a gun. A long-focus lens makes it possible to obtain interesting group photos where birds gather in numbers: prairie chickens at their display ground, pelicans at their nests or flocks of flamingoes feeding. There is a special pleasure in hiding in a blind and seeing birds going about their business at the nest, unaware that they are being watched. Even more of an achievement is getting an unusual photograph, such as a shot of a loon sliding on to its nest or a bird of prey alighting on its aerie. The photographer may become so interested in what he sees that he forgets to release the shutter!

Recording bird calls and songs with a tape recorder is the newest sport with birds. The whole repertoire of any species has seldom been recorded, so a challenge awaits anyone who sets out to do this. It was not until I had been studying the wren for some years that I discovered that when the female came into the nest to feed the nestlings, she stimulated them by singing a chittering song so quietly that I was able to hear it only by putting my ear to an opening in the side of the nest-box. By playing a bird's own song to it you can attract it closer in order to photograph it.

Bird-watchers may become bird-banders. Mist nets are commonly used and strict rules must be observed so that the captured birds come to no harm. This hobby is also valuable scientifically because it identifies individual birds and their migration routes and winter quarters. An intensive study of any species may involve color-banding a small local population.

Facing page *Bird-watching in the marshes.*
Below *A photographer here "freezes" the flight of an egret.*

6
Birds Friendly, Decorative, and Useful

Above *British titmice have become so domesticated that they have learned to peck holes in caps on milk bottles.* Facing page *Ornamental Chinese geese in Battersea Park, London. A patch of ice having been broken for them in the frozen lake, they congregate for hand feeding.*

Where birds are unfamiliar with man they may be quite "tame" in the sense that they do not recognize him as dangerous. When sailors landed on Rodriguez Island in the Indian Ocean in the seventeenth century they were able to kill the flightless solitaire with sticks, and so it soon became extinct. On the Galapagos Islands a tyrant flycatcher surprised a friend of mine by alighting on his head to collect hair to line its nest; a mockingbird pecked at his boots and the buzzards were very tame—Darwin was able to poke one with the muzzle of his gun. The Galapagos birds have become more wary as a result of unpleasant experiences. Another of my friends, roaming the Australian bush, had to protect his head from birds seeking nest material.

By gradually accustoming a ringed plover to my presence, I have been able to put my hand under its breast while it was brooding. A number of species can in this way be induced to feed from the hand. A cock wren which undertook responsibility for the nestlings when his mate deserted was so preoccupied with the task that he readily perched on my hand when entering his nest. The house bunting is so named because it seeks food in houses. Thus some species have no innate fear of man and others can be tamed by kindness.

Such learning is gradual, but in young birds it may take place much more rapidly. Newly hatched goslings have an inborn tendency to follow. This instinct is vital to their survival but is vague to the extent that they will follow any large moving object, including a human being or, as experiments have shown, even a box dragged along by a length of string. What is more, goslings may become fixated or "imprinted" on a person or object to such an extent that at maturity they may regard him or it as an appropriate mate. When a budgerigar is caged without bird companions it may react in this way and learn to "talk." Such imitation of human speech is due to the deflection of thwarted impulses toward a substitute.

Probably this reaction explains why geese were among the first birds to be domesticated. We can imagine a brood of goslings following a primitive man to his cave or shelter and being allowed to forage around until they were big enough for the pot. So geese may have domesticated themselves. At all events, Old Stone Age men were sufficiently interested in geese to engrave pictures of them on stones. A statuette found at Ur of the Chaldees shows a goddess, Gula the Healer, seated on four flying geese, and an Egyptian wall painting of Nefer-Maat in the tomb of Medum (dating from before the Great Pyramid) shows three species, the white-fronted, red-breasted, and bean or greylag, depicted so exactly that we feel sure the artist was working from tame models. These birds were sacrificed in the autumn

to the gods Isis and Osiris. According to Homer, Penelope kept geese, and in Rome geese on the Capitoline Hill gave warning of the approach of the Gauls. At present geese are kept around a whisky distillery near Glasgow to give the alarm if trespassers intrude. The Germanic tribes sacrificed geese to their god Woden, and Caesar recorded that the Celtic people of Britain kept geese "for entertainment" and not for consumption—an indication that the birds had ritual significance. The *hansa* or sacred goose had a place in ancient Indian ritual, and in the Far East the Chinese goose was domesticated very early. The ritual use of a bird or beast does not preclude its being an article of diet.

DOVE AND PIGEON

There are 289 species of dove and pigeon, some no bigger than a skylark, others as large as a hen turkey. Since all members of this family of birds are good eating, we may be sure our remote ancestors were interested in them; but very early in historic times some species acquired religious significance. The ancient Semitic peoples regarded one or another species of dove with reverence. The dove was sacred among the Phoenicians and Philistines. The Syrians would not eat it, and if a person or his clothes touched one he was considered "unclean" for a day, but the Egyptians had domesticated it by 2600 B.C. and used it as food. Among the Hebrews it was reckoned a ritually "clean" bird, but it is never mentioned in the Old Testament as being eaten though it figured in ancient ceremonies. Pigeons and turtledoves were sacrificed and their blood applied ritually for cleansing a sufferer or a house afflicted with leprosy. In Old and New Testament times turtledoves were offered in the temple by women after childbirth. Stalls for the sale of doves were situated in the temple precincts at Jerusalem and were not beyond the means of the poor.

Images of the dove dating from 3100 B.C. have been found in the Middle East. This bird was associated in successive cultures with goddesses of fertility and love —Atargatis, Astarte, Aphrodite, and Venus—evidence of the influence of Eastern religion in Europe. At Mecca doves are still regarded as sacred, and the tolerance, or affection, extended to pigeons in Venice throughout centuries seems to be due to Eastern influence.

Why should the dove have become so closely linked with religion? The rock dove or pigeon, the ancestor of our domesticated pigeon, was, like the swallow, regarded with reverence in the Middle East and in the West. It perches and nests on ledges of buildings, and no doubt in antiquity enlivened temples with its courtship displays and cooing. Because of its conspicuous amatory activities it became associated with love and

Facing page A carving of geese on a tomb at Saqqara, Egypt. Geese were among the earliest birds to be domesticated.
Below Girl holding doves as seen in a Greek grave relief (c. 450 B.C.).

fecundity and was regarded as sacred to the goddesses who bestowed these blessings.

Since ancient times doves have also provided tasty morsels for human palates and have been reared for this purpose, sometimes on a large scale. H. B. Tristam wrote in his *Natural History of the Bible* (1867):

> At this day in Syria, the pigeon is the invariable companion of man wherever he has a settled habitation: the village sheikh marks his wealth by the possession of a large separate dovecote, built of mud or brick and roofed over, filled with earthen pots with a wide mouth, each of which is the home of a pair of pigeons. The poorer people rear them in their houses, and in the villages about Carmel there is a row of small, square pigeon-holes formed in the wall just under the roof opposite the door, each of which has a pair of tenants, who fly in and out over the heads of the family through the common door.

Thus our term *pigeonhole* has an ancient ancestry! The custom of establishing dovecotes spread to Europe. In medieval times they were attached to monasteries and manor houses. In those which survive, the pigeon-holes may be seen in rows ranked one above the other. The dovecote in a monastery at Willington in Bedfordshire accommodated fourteen hundred birds. These dovecotes were the medieval equivalent of our large-scale chicken "factories."

HOMING AND RACING PIGEONS

Even in antiquity the homing capacity of pigeons was recognized. The dove sent out from the Ark returned, indicating that the floods were still widespread, but when sent out later it brought back an olive leaf, proclaiming that they were subsiding. The tree and the bird are still associated with peace. According to the *Odyssey,* doves carried messages for Zeus. At the original Olympic games homing pigeons were kept in readiness to be released with messages notifying cities of the winners. Pliny tells us that pigeons carried messages into camp during the siege of Mutina.

Before the days of telephones an interesting sight could be seen near the old Mongol market. As soon as the exchange rate was announced about 4:30 A.M., a flock of carrier pigeons were released, each bearing a strip of paper giving the exchange rate. After circling around to get their bearings, the pigeons made off individually to the various banks.

Homing pigeons have been used in Europe to establish a "pigeon post" mail service especially when other means of communication failed or were obstructed. But homing pigeons achieved their greatest fame when Paris was beleaguered during the Franco-German War. Dispatches and private letters were micrographed on

Facing page   The Dispatch of the Messenger *by the French painter Francois Boucher (1703–1770). The portrayal of so large and clumsy a missive is a romantic exaggeration by the artist.*
Below *Soldiers attaching a message to a pigeon.*

Facing page (left) *This remarkable parrot has learned to feed itself with a spoon.*
Facing page (right) *Tame hoopoe. Instead of its usual insect diet, this bird has become accustomed to a boiled egg for breakfast.*
Below *An Amazonian Indian boy with his pet parrots.*

pellicles so light that 50,000 separate messages could be carried by one bird. The pellicle was stuffed into a quill fixed to the pigeon's tail so as not to interfere with its flight. A million private as well as 150,000 official messages were sent. Over 360 pigeons were employed, of which 57 returned safely. Homing pigeons were also used during World War II, dropped by parachute to Resistance groups in the occupied countries. Of nearly 17,000 birds, some 2,000 came back with information. Pigeons helped save the lives of many airmen. When an aircraft crew was in difficulties after "ditching" their plane in the sea, a bird would be released with a message that helped to locate the plane.

PIGEON RACING AND FANCYING

Although hobbyists have enjoyed breeding and flying pigeons for centuries, racing the birds competitively is a comparatively modern sport. It has many more devotees, especially in urban areas, than is commonly realized. A few years ago it was estimated that there were about two million birds in British fanciers' lofts. Training begins when a bird is four months old. It is then flown for progressively longer distances, with a few days' respite between flights.

The sport became popular in the Low Countries, especially Belgium, at the beginning of last century. The first race of more than a hundred miles was organized there in 1818, and five years later birds were raced from London to Belgium. By 1878 regular races were being flown in the United States. Birds a year old will fly distances of three hundred miles, and a few of the older, more experienced birds cover distances of almost a thousand miles in the United States.

Pigeon-fancying is an ancient hobby. In Greek and Roman times white birds were admired. One chronicler (Babur) recorded that devotion to pigeons cost the life of a fifteenth-century king of Fergana, in central Asia. He was a great sportsman, flying falcons and keeping tumbler pigeons (so named because they check and fall back in flight) on the brink of a ravine at his mountain fortress. In 1494 the king himself tumbled, together with his pigeons and their loft, into the ravine. His obituary recorded: "He fell with his pigeons and their house and became a falcon."

Breeding has long occupied the attention of enthusiasts; indeed, no other bird has been as assiduously bred, not only to look different from the original ancestor but to behave differently. The roller performs on the wing (as its name implies), the pouter has a large inflatable gullet, the Jacobin has neck feathers forming a hood, and the fairy swallow has thickly feathered legs and feet. One or two of these breeds are shaped so abnormally that they are unable to feed their squabs, which have to be tended by other pigeons.

The sounds "uttered" by pigeons may be changed in strange ways. When I was in China in the 1930s it was pleasant to hear from time to time a weird, sustained, ethereal chord in the heavens. The sound came from a flock of pigeons, each of which carried a tiny open, hollow gourd that caught the current of air and acted as a resonator. Now that so much of traditional Chinese life has been discarded, I cling to the hope that this evocative, otherworldly chime still floats down to the crowded streets.

BIRDS AS PETS

Pets may be kept for both sentimental and utilitarian reasons. A hunter's dog may be a good companion as well as useful for fetching game birds. When Columbus arrived in the West Indies he found that the aborigines reared macaws for food much as Europeans reared poultry; but they probably also regarded them as pets.

Facing page *Bird cages in a fourteenth century manuscript.*
Below *Ducks and ducklings in a Roman mosaic (c. 100 A.D.). Ducks easily become accustomed to man and feeding them by hand has been a popular pastime since ancient times.*

Macaws are the largest of the parrot family, the red and blue reaching a length of two feet eight inches, the green, two feet four inches.

G. M. Bechstein, whose authoritative book on cage birds appeared in 1794, wrote of the latter: "It is exceedingly docile and talkative. The specimen which I have seen imitated everything that was said, called all the family by name, and was exceedingly obedient, faithful, and good-tempered." This may be somewhat exaggerated but it indicates how readily natives might to some extent regard a macaw as "one of themselves." The nineteenth-century explorer Alexander von Humboldt saw an aged parrot that had been reared among the Atures and had learned some phrases; since the tribe had become extinct, that parrot was the last to use their language.

The ability of birds to learn words has intrigued mankind for many centuries. Ctesias, an ancient Greek writer, commented on a blossom-headed parakeet which uttered sentences in an Indian language, and Pliny remarked that certain parrots saluted emperors, but became lascivious when they had drunk too much wine. A minor Greek poet, Crinagoras, wrote of a parrot which had learned to say "Hail" to the emperor; it escaped, so it was said, and taught all the woodland birds this greeting.

Konrad Lorenz, famous student of bird behavior, tells of a hooded crow which was stolen and returned after some weeks with a broken toe. It came out with, "Got 'im in t' bloomin' trap"—obviously the exclamation of the person who had trapped the bird. Bechstein mentions a gray parrot that was purchased by a cardinal because it could say the Apostles' Creed without a slip. It also dreamed aloud. Many other species are vocally imitative and quite a number can mimic human speech. The Indian myna is probably the most expert but its relative, the starling, can also be trained to "talk." Some of the stories told of talking birds are surely exaggerated. A bird often learns to associate phrases with particular people and situations without in any way understanding what it is saying.

CAGE BIRDS

Cage birds are not as popular as they were fifty or more years ago, but many people still keep such pets. There are, too, people who specialize in breeding unusual species. Private zoos have aviaries for land birds and ponds for water birds, and at the larger zoos techniques for feeding cage birds and for heating and lighting their quarters have greatly improved. Bechstein's *Cage Birds* is still of interest not only for its practical advice but as representing an age when trapping birds was an accepted practice. Thus he tells us that snow

te sanctus pro lege dei siu
pectauit usqs ad mortem et
a uerbis impior non timuit.
fundatus enim erat supra fir
mam petram. v. Corona au
rea super caput eius. expressa
signo sanctitatis glorie horis.
Oremus: Cornelij Aia an.

buntings could be caught with "horse dung covered with lime twigs," and nightingales with "a few limed twigs or a falling net adjusted on two cross sticks."
The linnet was once very popular as a cage bird, partly because a nestling, reared separately, will acquire the songs of other species and any melodies that are whistled to it. Bird-fanciers appreciated such a bird since, if they taught it the nightingale's song, they could enjoy that song even during the months when no nightingales sing. Of course this meant that one had to have a caged nightingale to "teach" the linnet. As a result the nightingale-catchers in eighteenth-century Germany pursued the birds so mercilessly in some regions that the authorities began to fine them.

Certain birds have been particularly popular as pets at different periods. The canary, imported during the sixteenth century from the islands after which it was named, is easy to breed and consequently there are many varieties. Some were named after their color, such as gay spangles, jonquils, and lizards. Other strains are notable for their songs. Oliver Goldsmith commented that a century before his time canaries had fetched high prices but had since become plentiful and cheap. One of the most interesting uses of canaries was in coal mines. Since a canary is affected by foul air or deadly fumes more rapidly than human beings, a canary in a cage was taken down into a mine to provide a warning. But this practice was abandoned years ago.

During the eighteenth and nineteenth centuries there was such a craze in Germany for keeping chaffinches that after a while in Thuringia a good singer was seldom heard because if such a bird appeared in the woods it was soon trapped; so the remaining wild birds had no opportunity to learn from a good singer. Recent research has shown that there is a critical time in a young chaffinch's second year when it improves its innate song by learning from its neighbors.

Although budgerigars were brought from Australia by John Gould in 1840, they became very popular only during this century. They are brightly colored, have confiding ways, and if reared in isolation from other birds, learn to say phrases in a queer, high-pitched, crackly tone. Their quick movements and tiny, mustachioed faces add to their charm. They may be allowed to fly around a room, they breed easily, and are relatively inexpensive. Another bird which can be taught to "talk" is the myna. It is able to enunciate words most distinctly, but its voice is so loud as compared with a budgerigar's that after a time some owners tire of having familiar, irrelevant exclamations ring out at odd times and get rid of such birds.

Among other popular species now kept as pets are the Java sparrow and certain types of finches.

Facing page *A pet sheepdog has learned to put up with the antics of a flock of doves tamed by his owner.*
Below *A budgerigar and a dachshund make friends.*

PEACOCKS AND OTHER ORNAMENTAL BIRDS

The outstanding ornamental bird is the peacock. Of the two species, the blue and the green, the former has been domesticated for more than two thousand years. The Assyrian King Tiglath-pileser IV (745–727 B.C.) received peacocks as tribute and the Greek historian Diodorus Siculus says that some were kept in Babylon. Since peacocks are native to the forests of Indian and Sri Lanka, the stock must have come from these regions. Therefore the familiar passage in the Bible telling us that King Solomon's fleet came home every three years bringing ivory, apes, and peacocks cannot be trusted. The translation of all three words is doubtful, and "peacocks" is certainly erroneous.

The peacock has always attracted attention if for no other reason than that it is so magnificently endowed and so ready to strut and display. Apparently the English eighteenth-century naturalist Gilbert White was the first to record that the train, erected during the display, springs from the lower part of the bird's back; the unimpressive tail is hidden underneath. Most Europeans regard the bird's scream as harsh and unpleasant, and in India there was a saying that the peacock had angel's feathers, a devil's voice, and a thief's walk, but other associations accounted for its being considered a beneficent bird. Because its mating period coincided with the rains, it was regarded as a prophet of fecundity, heralding a fertilizing downpour by screaming and dancing. These fertility associations were transferred to women. Thus ancient marriage manuals declared that the voice of a desirable woman was "like that of a peacock." The association with rain traveled with the bird to Europe. The *Hortus Sanitatis,* first published in 1490, asserted that "the peacock when he ascends on high betokens rain," and during my boyhood in Ireland it was an accepted belief that the bird's screaming precedes rain.

The peacock is not indigenous to China, but chronicles record that during the Tang dynasty (A.D. 618–907) many districts paid their tribute in peacocks because the feathers were used as decorations during imperial processions and were also bestowed upon officials as a reward for faithful service. Peacocks were kept in the precincts of Indian temples and appear in Hindu and Christian art. The bird became a symbol of the Resurrection and a representation of salvation through Christ, perhaps because during the molt it lost its splendor but in the course of time regained it.

The Greeks admired the peacock and at one time people would travel to places where the birds were on show, but later references indicate that it became fairly common. It was the symbol of Hera (Juno), the queen

Facing page *An Indian princess with her pets as seen in an Indian miniature of the Malwa School (c. 1680).* Below *Male peacock displaying.*

of heaven, because its starry feathers and brilliant train seemed as representative of an empress as an eagle did of an emperor. Because of the "eyes" on its feathers it was also associated with the "hundred-eyed Argus" who, urged by Juno, spied on Io.

The peacock's beauty inspired efforts to conserve and propagate it. Alexander imposed a heavy penalty on those who killed the birds in India, and the Greeks reared them on islands where they were not exposed to mainland predators. A number of writers describe the peacock's flesh as unpalatable, but having partaken of a peahen at a banquet in the United States I can testify that it is excellent eating.

Among the birds commonly kept in parks or large gardens because they are "ornamental" we should include the turkey cock—a fine sight when in full display—and pheasants, especially the golden. The silver pheasant is also very beautiful and easy to breed. In grounds with a lake or ponds various waterfowl such as the mute swan and the Canada and the Chinese goose add interest. The Muscovy duck is sometimes kept in farmyards, but the most beautiful species likely to be seen in parks are the mandarin and the wood duck.

BIRDS AND EGGS AS A RESOURCE

The domestic fowl is descended from a species of jungle fowl native to Southeast Asia. It may have been domesticated in the fourth millennium B.C., but one of the earliest representations we have is on a coin from Ephesus of about 700 B.C. Not only did fowls and their eggs become important as food, but the birds were associated with religion and magic to such an extent that a large volume would be needed to relate the beliefs and rituals in which they figured. As is well known, chicken-farming and egg production have become important industries. Geese and ducks are farmed on a lesser scale, though in central Europe and China they have long been an important source of food. Guinea fowl were eaten by the Romans, but the turkey was not imported into Europe until the sixteenth century though it had been domesticated earlier in Mexico. The many uses of feathers are treated in the following chapter.

Apart from their use as food, eggs have figured in rituals in many parts of the world. The "Easter egg" has pre-Christian antecedents and its religious importance is derived from its Resurrection symbolism: out of it comes life. The custom of painting Easter eggs is ancient. Eggs were not eaten during Lent and were colored red for Easter Day to signify rejoicing (in the Far East red signifies joy). The Easter egg rolling on the White House lawn has become a tradition in Washington. But it is, of course, as a food that eggs are of major importance all over the world.

Facing page Peacocks, a crane, a squirrel, and a monkey in the foreground, and a displaying turkey and flying swallow in the background as seen in a painting by the Dutch artist Melchior D'Hondecoeter (1636–1695). Below Hen and egg mosaic. A detail of the pavement in the synagogue of Ma'on, in Nirim, Israel (sixth century A.D.).

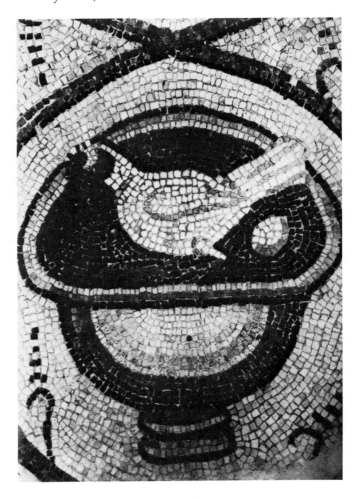

Below *Bronze sculpture from Nigeria, Court of Benin (eighteenth century). Roosters apparently had special significance among the Bini people of Benin, since images of them were placed on the altars of the mothers of chiefs.*
Facing page *A barnyard rooster. The proud bearing and aggressive behavior of these birds have made them the subject of innumerable legends.*
Overleaf *Belgian Mille Fleurs bantams, one of several species fancied by some breeders for their remarkable appearance.*

GUANO

The dung of fish-eating birds is a valuable fertilizer, but it occurs in exploitable quantities only where fish are very abundant and the climate is so dry that the droppings accumulate. These conditions characterize the Peruvian coast and the offshore islands where colonies of the Peruvian booby, cormorant, and brown pelican nest. Early in this century the exploitation of the guano had reached such an extent that it was evident the nesting areas were being destroyed. Measures were taken to "farm" the islands in a controlled way and to create protected nesting areas on the mainland. Overfishing of the anchovies on which the birds feed is forbidden, although this has involved restricting the fish-meal industry. The management of guano collection and fish-meal production is an important example of how the interests of man and bird can be reconciled to the advantage of both.

THE DOMESTIC FOWL

No bird, apart from the goose and dove, has had a closer association with man throughout history than the domestic fowl. Its flesh and eggs have been valued as food and it has had a prominent role in magic, religion, and sport. Domesticated breeds of fowl have been able to accommodate themselves to the most diverse conditions, from African villages to mechanized chicken farms.

Domestication of the red jungle fowl, from which all modern breeds are derived, occurred long ago in Asia, where it is found from northern India to Sumatra. Tame fowl seem to have been kept in the Indus valley about 2500 B.C. and an ancient Indian law prohibited their use as food, possibly because they were thought to have magical powers. There is evidence of fowl in Crete and Phoenicia a thousand years later. In Egypt a white and yellow hen was sacred to Anubis, and a chick, either of domestic fowl or quail, appears in hieroglyphic inscriptions, where it was used for the letter *u*. The Chinese believed that fowl were introduced into China from the region of India or Burma about 1400 B.C. In Europe the first known representation of the bird is from Crete. Its appearance in Greek art after the sixth century B.C. may have followed the Persian invasions, as Aristophanes in *The Birds* refers to it as "the Persian bird." He commented facetiously:

Of this therefore we have many proofs that not the gods, but the birds, were rulers of and kings over men in ancient times. For example, I will first point out the cock to you, how he was sovereign and ruler over the Persians before all . . . so that he is still called the Persian bird, from that his domain. On this account, then, even now, he only of the birds struts

about with the turban erect on his head like a great king. And so powerful was he . . . that still even now . . . when he merely crows at dawn all jump up to their work: braziers, potters, tanners, shoemakers, bath men, corn factors, lyre turners, and shieldmakers; and they trudge off, having put on their shoes in the dark.

Only a few of the countless beliefs concerning the cock may be mentioned here. The above quotation from Aristophanes indicates three characteristics that gave rise to much of the ritual and folklore. First, the bird has a prominent crest; second, it is dominating and aggressive; and third, it utters a clarion crow at dawn. The first and last of these characteristics inspired the conviction that the cock is a solar bird. It is crowned with the color of fire and daily announces the sun. In ancient times the color red on a bird suggested a connection with the gods or heavenly powers. Thus the Greeks sacrificed it to Asclepius, a solar deity, patron of medicine and healing. In north China it was the custom, when a man died outside the Great Wall, to have his coffin transported to the ancestral burial place with a cock in a basket on top of it. The belief was that by its crowing it guided the soul so that it could follow the body. Another ancient Chinese custom was to sacrifice a red cock to the sun.

Heliodorus suggested the cock crowed because it rejoiced in the sunlight, so its crowing became synonymous with the dawn. Probably as an extension of belief in it as a solar bird and because of its loud calls it came to be thought of as a weather prophet, and by extending still further the belief that it could predict the future it was used in augury. Christian ideas about it were primarily based on its behavior in warning Saint Peter of his shame in denying any knowledge of Christ. Despite the adoption of the cock as a Christian symbol, some European customs that had their origin in older beliefs survived until recently. In Wales, boys used to fix a representation of a cock to a stick and carry it around on May Day, and at Schiermonnikoog in Holland a basket holding a live cock was suspended from a green bough fastened to the top of a Maypole.

Poultry-keepers have produced some remarkable breeds of fowl. Some have bred birds that can lay almost an egg a day throughout the year, and others have sought to make the fowl an aesthetic wonder. Marco Polo saw "a curiosity" in the "large and splendid city" of Kienning-fu—"hens that have no feathers but have hair like cats and are pure black." This breed, known as the silky hen, is still preserved. In Japan specimens of the Yokohama or long-tailed cock may still be seen, with some showing feathers fifteen feet long. Probably it is merely a legend that the breed arose because of a rivalry

among courtiers to see who could wear the longest feathers. The birds are kept on high perches, and when they walk around an attendant has to raise the feathers to prevent them from being soiled and abraded. In Europe there is little interest in maintaining "fancy" breeds since poultry-keepers are commercially minded, keeping hens on deep litter or in a coop with a sloping wire floor so that the eggs roll into a receptacle in front. In Britain, about three hundred people still keep rare varieties, such as the buff medway, which has a face so feathered that it looks bearded. The Sicilian flower birds and the gold-laced variety have died out; only three Scots dumpie hens, squat and short-legged birds, survive (but with no purebred cock); but La Flèche hornets, black with red "horns," have been saved from near extinction. Many people regard fancy breeds as monstrosities, and indeed such fowl are more interesting than beautiful. But like fancy pigeons they reveal the capacity of a species to adapt its appearance and behavior.

TURKEY AND GUINEA FOWL

The turkey was domesticated by Mexican Indians who were sufficiently interested in birds to keep them in aviaries. Turkeys were first brought to Spain in 1519 and they proved so acceptable for the table that these large and tasty birds soon superseded the peacock as a delicacy. The wild species still survives in a few wooded areas in North America, and one may come upon families in some of the national parks there.

Our farmyard guinea fowl is one of the African species. Marco Polo wrote of an Abyssinian species: "They have cocks and hens the most beautiful that exist." In Greece, sacred guinea fowl were kept on the island of Leros and were sacrificed at the temple of Isis in Tithorea. They were also kept on the Acropolis in Athens, and in southeastern Greece (Boeotia) they were trained as fighting cocks. A British writer in 1760 stated that these birds were rarities in his youth but "are now become a common Fowl in England." Many farmers keep a few of these birds, but commercially the birds and their eggs, which have thick shells, have little value.

Facing page *Long-tailed Yokohama cocks in Japan.*
Below *A turkey depicted in a wall painting from India (c. 1612). The turkey was originally a native of South and Central America. The Spanish explorers took it back to the Old World.*

7
Feathers and Finery

Above *A ten-pfennig coin issued in New Guinea (1894) showing the beautiful feathers of the greater bird of paradise.*
Facing page *Blackfoot chief in headdress.*

Who among us, if asked to design a superlatively beautiful bird, could improve on those which already exist? Throughout the centuries Chinese artists have tried their hands at this, picturing the mythical love pheasant or fêng huang, but they could do no better than exaggerate the plumage, adornments and coloration of birds they already knew, giving them very long tails, extravagant plumes, and prominent crests. They leave us unconvinced that if their birds were to come to life they would surpass in grace and loveliness those we know. In the Middle Ages in Europe the most talented and fanciful of the artists who illuminated manuscripts never conceived a bird so beautiful as the greater bird of paradise, then unknown to the civilized world. Nature can and does surpass art. The world became a much more beautiful place when birds evolved from reptiles.

From very early times bird plumage aroused man's interest and was used for his own personal decoration. In a Spanish cave, the Cueva de la Vieja, there is an Old Stone Age painting depicting a remarkable scene in which human figures are shown among antlered beasts. The men are naked, with sexual organs connected to some of the animals by double lines. In their hands the men hold what appear to be light spears, and their heads are adorned with bunches of feathers. They are engaged in hunting-magic apparently designed to render the animals vulnerable but also, possibly, to increase their own fecundity and abundance. They evidently considered it more important to decorate themselves with birds' plumage than to wear clothing, which they could easily have made from the hides of the animals they hunted. But we should not assume that the feathers were merely decorative. Since the scene depicted is inspired by magical ideas, as the double lines indicating outgoing power suggest, we may infer that its function was to enable the hunters to enlist the help of supernatural forces. Certainly the design is more than merely pictorial. Magical virtues were attributed to wings and their feathers, for with their aid birds could come and go mysteriously and mount skyward toward the sun and heavenly bodies. Thus they could keep in touch with unseen higher powers. Such are the conceptions of the tribal folk of northern Asia, who appear to have retained some of the patterns of thought characteristic of Old Stone Age communities.

A painting such as this raises the question, Why was clothing invented? The answer that would spring to the minds of most of us—to keep people warm—has a grain of truth in it but is certainly not the whole explanation. Even in a very inclement climate primitive folk may go without clothing, as Darwin noticed when he visited Tierra del Fuego.

Facing page *Detail of featherwork in a garment from Brazil.*
Left *Feather decorations representing a bird on a Tlingit Indian mask from Alaska.*

Similarly, the notion that clothing owes its origin to shame, modesty, or sexual prurience is probably mistaken. Such feelings are not innate. Humboldt, referring to a tribe which went naked, wrote: "The excessive heat of the air, the profuse perspiration in which the body is bathed at every hour of the day and a great part of the night, render the use of clothes insupportable. Their objects of ornament, and particularly their plumes of feathers, are reserved for dances and solemn festivals. The plumes worn by the Guipinares are the most celebrated; being composed of the fine feathers of manakins and parrots." (Manakins are smallish birds with brilliant feathers on crown and throat, which the cocks display in a lively way at a set gathering place among forest bushes.)

Actually, people have been moved to wear clothing for many, and often mingled, reasons: to protect the skin, to conserve warmth, to abide by conventional standards of modesty, to augment sexual attraction or conceal lack of it, to indicate one's wealth, to impress enemies, for aesthetic reasons, to prevent the entry of evil spirits into the orifices of the body, or to identify oneself with some animal, perhaps a totem, which the group feels it must propitiate. Garments and decorations, apart from other considerations, have nearly always had, and still have, a special function as uniforms or insignia, revealing a person's status at a glance.

FEATHERS AS ORNAMENT

There is more scope for the decorative use of plumage in the neotropical region than elsewhere because it is the richest in bird life. Moreover, a large number of the tropical birds are brilliantly colored, since the canopy or dense undergrowth enables them to conceal themselves from birds of prey. Anyone from a temperate region who visits the tropical bird aviary at a zoo is amazed at the rich contrasts in plumage exhibited by the birds.

Alfred Russel Wallace, who visited South America from 1848 to 1852, arrived at a Brazilian village where he was delighted to find himself "in the presence of the true denizens of the forest." The women went completely naked. When he attended a dance the men wore coronets of red and yellow toucan feathers set in circlets of plaited straw. In each man's hair was a comb adorned with feathers, and from it a bunch of egrets' plumes hung gracefully down the back. Tufts of white downy feathers were set in their ears. From their arms hung bunches of seeds ornamented with bright-colored feathers, mainly those of the great red macaw. First, the natives would pluck out the feathers from a living bird and inoculate the wound with a milky juice from the skin of a small frog or toad. When the feathers grow out again they are brilliant orange or yellow, without any blue or green as is their natural color. This involves keeping the birds as pets, a custom common among South American tribes.

Wallace was also interested in ornamental feather headgear he saw when he went to New Guinea. He found that at Humboldt Bay the men went naked but used the plumes of birds of paradise to decorate themselves. Tom Harrison, a British scientist who has lived in New Guinea, has written of headdresses: "Lemon, pink, scarlet, violet, black, orange, and white may all merge in a superb mélange, imaginative and wildly dynamic. Some of the finest effects come by the arrangement of shimmering blue breast feathers and from the glorious tail-spread of the greater bird of paradise."

Among the many South American tribes which ornament themselves with feathers may be mentioned the Carajá of Bananal Island, in Brazil, who wear beautiful headdresses of long black, blue, and white-tipped

spikes, and achieve a radiating effect by fixing the feathers in long tubes. The Jivaro, another South American group, adorn their heads with a black and white circlet in which are set erect blue and yellow feathers. Complementary or vividly contrasting colors please these people just as they do us.

In Brazil, as in Borneo, headhunting tribes wear feather headdresses made of eagle feathers. The wearing of gaudy headdresses in some regions is possibly related to the belief that the head is what makes a man a man—is, in short, the dwelling place of his male spirit. The sexual organs are not regarded as the real seat of virility; in this view manliness is proclaimed by the headgear.

FEATHERS AS STATUS SYMBOLS

The widespread importance of feathers as symbols of rank among primitive folk is made plain in the accounts of early travelers. When Columbus on his second voyage arrived at Jamaica, his chronicler, Bernáldez, recorded that the local chieftain, or cacique, came out in a massive canoe "together with his wife and two daughters, one of whom was very beautiful. . . . They were, of course, completely naked. . . . He had a herald in his canoe, who stood in the prow wearing a cloak of red feathers. . . . Some of the men had their faces painted in the same colours, each wearing a large feather headdress." The cacique naïvely asked for his whole party to be taken to Spain, but Columbus, noticing how his crew eyed the girls, declined. Among primitive peoples there are few exceptions to the rule that men, and not women, wear feather decoration, reversing the customs of modern westernized society, but corresponding to nature's own rule that among birds and many mammals the male is the more decorative. The reason for this is that, with some excep-

tions, the male initiates the courtship, and needs to be easily identifiable and able to attract and stimulate the female. Loud calls, bright colors, and enlarged plumes are effective in this way. He may, however, make up for the lack of the latter by stimulating displays. Thus both sexes of the wren of Europe and Asia (the winter wren of North America) have inconspicuous brown plumage, but the cock courts the hen with his lovely warbling song and stimulates her by fluttering his half-opened wings.

Throughout most of the world the wearing of special feather adornments is often the privilege of men of high status. The elaborate American Indian feather headdress, extending down the back, was the prerogative of the chief and indicative of his authority. (When a party of such Indians visited the pope in 1974 they presented a feather headdress to him.) A North American Indian brave, moreover, wore a feather for each man he had killed. Such an attitude accounts for our use of the expression, "a feather in his cap." But feathers can have the opposite significance; thus, to show a white feather signifies cowardice. This interpretation may be based on the way retreating birds show their tail feathers; the water hen, for example, exposes the white feathers in its tail as it walks or swims away. A feather may indeed have whatever significance society may choose to give it. Thus, among the Kikuyu of Africa a girl had to wear a feather of Hartlaub's touraco one day in the year as a sign that she would respond to the blandishments of the first youth whom she met.

Eagle and hawk feathers are used decoratively in North America, Borneo, and elsewhere. The Pueblo Indians reared eaglets and kept them caged in order to have a supply available for their dances and other rites. Similarly, the Rio Negro Indians of Brazil kept

Facing page *Ostrich feather fan from about 1900.*
Left *Fashionable young woman wearing ostrich plume
hat in the late nineteenth century.*
Below *Photograph (c. 1890) showing ostrich feathers
being sorted into bundles according to color.*

wore a small bonnet with feathers bordering the brim. Gentlemen kept a plume in place with a jeweled brooch. The sixth wife of Henry VIII, Catherine Parr, wore a velvet hat decorated with feather aigrettes tipped with pearls. In the next generation, when Queen Elizabeth I visited Cambridge, her hat was spangled with gold and decorated with a bunch of feathers. In a report to his government in 1618 the Venetian ambassador to England noted that Englishwomen wore a plume on the head, "sometimes upright, sometimes at the back, and sometimes even transverse." The typical seventeenth-century English cavalier hat was low-crowned with a wide flexible brim decorated with a feather, and women's hats were similarly adorned. After about 1625, when ladies went riding they wore broad hats from which trailed ostrich plumes. As part of the elegance of the Restoration court, Charles II introduced the "French hat" with its wide brim, shallow crown, and several plumes.

The "conquest of the air" by Lunardi in a balloon in 1783 inspired a type of woman's hat called the Lunardi or balloon hat. It bulged out high above a woman's head and sometimes carried three or four large ostrich feathers at one side. At the end of the century it became fashionable for women to wear two or three ostrich plumes in their hair and this remained a custom among debutantes presented at the royal court.

Abrupt changes in the dress of men and women occurred after the French Revolution. Conspicuous was an emphasis on simplicity; tight lacing was abandoned and few underclothes were worn. But after about 1820 there was a return to large hats, bonnets, and bulky garments. In 1820 the English *Lady's Magazine* reported that at the king's birthday celebrations several paradise plumes appeared: "Bandeaux were much worn and a profusion of feathers, diamonds, topazes, and antiques were general." The plumes of birds of paradise were imported into Europe by devious routes even before Papua was explored.

From about 1860 the craze for birds' feathers reached extremes. Whole birds nestled on milady's hats and there was a lucrative plumage traffic from South America and the West Indies. Hummingbirds were imported by the thousands. When public protests were made, the periodical *Milliner and Dressmaker* retorted that a ban would create unemployment among the girls who worked in the trade.

Today, when artificial personal adornments involve a variety of products, it is difficult to realize how highly women esteemed ostrich feathers at the beginning of this century. In 1912 about 160 tons of such feathers were sold in France. They were used as trimming and were made into fans and into the long, fluffy scarfs

Facing page *Cartoon of about 1820 showing birds swooping on a lady whose head is lavishly adorned with feathers in a style of the time. Her skirt, also decorated with feathers, is being attacked by larger birds.*
Below *Lithograph of Therese, Queen of Bavaria, wearing aigrettes.*

Facing page *Snowy egret. The passion for the egret's plumes nearly resulted in the extinction of this beautiful bird.*
Below *Stage entertainer in feathered dress and costume.*

known as boas. Ostrich-farming became a profitable industry in South Africa and is still carried on to a limited extent. The tail feathers of the birds are cut about three times every two years but it does them no harm. But due to wartime austerities the market for ostrich feathers collapsed after 1918.

Ladies also adorned their headgear with egret plumes, which were most easily obtained when the birds were nesting. Vast numbers were killed and their young died. A warden appointed to guard a "rookery" was murdered. My friend the late Dr. Frank Chapman, famous ornithologist of the American Museum of Natural History, wrote in 1908: "As long as egret plumes are worth their weight in gold there will be someone to supply them." But they ceased to be so valuable when it became widely known how great was the carnage, how beautiful the bird, how ruthless the hunters.

Up to 1914 bird feathers were still fashionable and it was considered chic to wear two in a hat at opposite angles, but humanitarian agitation and the revelations of the barbarities suffered by large colonies of beautiful birds made women realize that hat feathers were tokens of brutality. It is a credit to conservationists that they succeeded in discouraging Victorian ladies and hussars alike from wearing feathers in their hats. In-terest in birds was increasing and a realization of the extent to which ignorance and apathy had contributed to the loss of the great auk and passenger pigeon stimu-lated the foundation of societies and the passing of legislation to protect birds. In 1913 the United States prohibited the traffic in plumes and Great Britain followed suit rather tardily in 1921.

To some extent magnificent plumed headdresses have retained their popularity in such places of entertain-ment as the English music hall. The glamour girl Jessie Matthews appeared in a feathered headdress so im-mense that she had to be photographed standing against a wall to support it. Even before our permissive age, the shapely girls of the Folies Bergères of Paris strutted in elaborate feather headgear and nothing else. It should be added that the very large headdresses sometimes worn on the modern stage are made of artificial plumes.

Today in the Western world, feathers, usually those of the domestic fowl, are still occasionally used to decorate women's hats, but apart from this they are no longer important. Fashion and the conservation move-ments have combined to save the plumed birds of the world from the barbarities of mankind.

8
Endangered Birds and the Struggle to Save Them

There is special interest and excitement in watching a bird which you have never seen before. Such excitement is greatest when you know that the species is so rare that it may soon become extinct and future generations may never have the opportunity to enjoy the sight of it. A few years ago I had such an experience. As I stood on one of the grassy ridges in the wetlands of the Everglades I turned my head, and there, twenty yards away, was an Everglades kite, wavering in its flight as it peered down, searching for the large snails (*Pomacea* or *Ampullaria*) which are its prey. It was immediately recognizable by its fine, curved beak, very different from the robust, short bill with which raptorial birds tear the flesh of birds and mammals. At that time it was reckoned that the world population of this bird did not exceed ten or twelve. Over an immense period of time the species had adapted to a diet consisting exclusively of these snails which themselves had become adapted to this damp environment, clinging to plants and the stems of shrubs above the water level and thereby available for this snail-eating kite. It grasps the snail in its talons until it pokes out of the shell, then stabs its nerve center with the point of the curved bill, thus paralyzing it. Any bird so specialized as to depend mainly on a very few species for its food is in great danger of extinction. The population of some birds of prey decreased when rabbits in Great Britain were almost exterminated by myxomatosis. The decrease in numbers of the Everglades kite is not due to direct persecution by man but to the reduction of its habitat by all that is involved in "development"—drainage, cultivation, road construction, house-building, and so forth. This has been the fate of many species. Watching this remarkable bird, my fears for it were somewhat assuaged as I recalled that wise and strenuous efforts were being made to save it.

THE DODO

The extinction of the dodo has become a classic in the chronicle of vanishing wildlife. Its name proclaims what mariners who first saw it on the island of Mauritius thought of it. The Portuguese called it *doudo,* a simpleton, because it had no fear of the men who encountered it, and Linnaeus, the great Swedish classifier of animals and plants, took this cue in naming it *Didus ineptus.* The Dutch sailors who landed on the island in 1598 described the birds as being the size of swans, with large heads and curly tail feathers. They named them *Walghvogels,* "nauseous birds," even though they found the birds' breasts quite palatable. When specimens were brought to Europe, several artists painted portraits of them. In 1628 an English observer, writing home, said: "You shall receive . . . a strange

Above *A restoration of the extinct dodo.*
Facing page *The bald eagle, emblem of the United States. Native only to North America, it has become more and more rare except in Alaska and in a few colonies in the western United States.*

fowle which I had at the Iland Mauritius called by ye portingalls Do Do which for the rareness thereof I hope will be welcome to you." Little more is known of it. About ten years later a man strolling along a London street noticed a crude painting of a peculiar bird displayed outside a house and, presumably after paying an entrance fee, saw a large bird "somewhat bigger than the largest turkey cock and so legged and footed, but shorter and thicker." The custodian demonstrated how it would swallow "large pebble stones . . . as big as nutmegs." One François Cauche who landed on Mauritius in 1638 recorded that the dodo laid a single large white egg on a heap of grass in the forest and had a call like a gosling.

Seafarers had a custom of letting pigs loose on remote islands to provide victuals for other ships. Whatever dodos the men didn't kill, the pigs did. The last reference to a living dodo occurred in 1681. One of the few complete mounted specimens is in the Cambridge Museum; it may be described as a giant pigeon grown corpulent from a life without competitors or predators.

The dodo is only one of a number of interesting birds that evolved on Madagascar, Mauritius, and other nearby Indian Ocean islands and were destroyed by man. On Mauritius four other species besides the dodo have been exterminated and three others are in danger. Reunion Island was not settled by Europeans until 1662, but within about seven years a pink pigeon and a parakeet species were gone, as well as a relative of the dodo, the solitaire. Rodriguez Island has lost eight bird species including the solitaire.

The solitaires were bulky, superficially gooselike birds. For their behavior we have to rely on a narrative by François Leguat that was published in London in 1708. Its accuracy was questioned, but the discovery of skeletons confirmed his statements that the base of the bill had a ridge like "a widow's peak," that it had a long neck (which Leguat says it carried with "stateliness and good grace"), that the hind parts were "rounded like the crupper of a horse," and that there was a "little round mass" of bone on the wing "as big as a musket ball." The males, which were larger than the females, weighed forty to fifty pounds and stood approximately three feet high. Most interesting is his description of altercations between the males. They whirled round and round many times, making a loud noise with their wings. There seems no doubt that the knobs on their wings were used in territorial fights, for a number of bones dug up on the island had grown together after being cracked. Indeed, Leguat's description of the behavior of solitaires has a strong claim to being the first detailed description of the defense of territory. The nest was a heap of palm leaves on which a single white egg was laid. Incubation was shared by both birds. The Reunion solitaire was extinct about 1746, the Rodriguez species about 1791.

So far as evolution is concerned the extinction of these species is a most impressive illustration of how drastic may be the effect of the extension of the range of such an organism as man. In our own lifetime England has had a mild reminder of this phenomenon: colonization by the collared dove has driven the wood pigeon, a robust and successful species, from areas which it had probably occupied since before man arrived.

Some reference has already been made to the extinction of species in general, but there are lessons to be learned from the fate of three birds in particular, one exterminated about the middle of the last century, the other at the beginning of this century, and the third even more recently.

The great auk, or garefowl, once bred in island colonies

on both sides of the North Atlantic. Mounted specimens may be seen in the British Museum and in Cambridge, where Alfred Newton, professor of zoology for forty years, wrote its history. In 1887 he met an Icelander who claimed to have killed one of the last survivors about 1840 on Stac an Armin, an impressive rock pinnacle off the main island of the St. Kilda group northwest of Scotland. In appearance and behavior the great auk had much in common with penguins, being flightless, nesting in colonies, and so unaccustomed to man as to be at his mercy—if that is the right expression concerning a bird which was persecuted mercilessly. Seamen boiled them in large cauldrons to extract the oil from their bodies. Extermination may be said to have begun in the sixteenth century when Jacques Cartier landed on the Bird Rocks off the coast of Newfoundland. Like all seamen on long voyages at that time he was anxious to provision his ship with fresh food. According to Hakluyt's *Voyages* he recorded the following in his journal for June 25, 1534:

Wee went southeast, about 15 leagues, and came to three Ilands, two of which are as steepe and upright as any wall, so that it was not possible to climbe them: and between them there is a little rocke. These Ilands were as full of birds, as any field or medow is of grasse, which there do make their nestes: and in the greatest of them, there was a great and infinite number of those that wee call Margaulx [gannets], that are white and bigger than geese, which were severed in one part. In the other were onely Godetz [guillemots], but toward the shoare there were of those Godetz, and great Apponatz [great auks] like to those of that Iland that we above have mentioned: we went downe to the lowest part of the least Iland, where we killed above a thousand of those Godetz and Apponatz. We put into our

boates so many of them as we pleased, for in lesse than one houre we might have filled thirtie such boates of them: we named them The Ilands of Margaulx.

This was the beginning of the extirpation of the great auk, but other mariners soon took further toll of the nesting birds. Thus, according to Hakluyt, when

Mr. Hore and diuvers other gentlemen visited Newfoundland and Cape Breton in 1536 and came to the Island of Penguines . . . they went and found it full of great foules, white and grey, and big as gese, and they saw infinite numbers of their egges. They drave a great number of the foules into their boates upon their sayles, and took many of their egges, the foules they flead [flayed], and their skinnes were very like honey combes, full of holes; being flead off, they dressed and eat them, and found them to be very nourishing meate.

One Joseph Bartlett said that "he had often heard his father, who died in 1871 at the age of seventy, speak of the Pinwing [penguin], and that crews occasionally got on the Funks, built enclosures, lit fires, and burnt the birds to death for sheer mischief." The great auk was the original penguin, and some islands are still called after it. On Funk Island, off the coast of Newfoundland, and probably the last resort of the birds, the enclosures used for massacres still stand.

The birds were very trusting. The specimen in the British Museum was obtained by a fisherman holding out fish to the bird and then killing it with an oar. Another, in Waterford harbor, Ireland, was enticed by throwing small fish to it and capturing it in a landing net. It was kept alive for four months and learned to prefer freshwater trout to marine fish! The last two great auks were killed in 1844 on the island of Eldey, off the coast of Iceland. The great auk's disappearance

was the result of persecution, but nature took a hand in 1830 when a rocky island off Iceland frequented by these birds was swallowed by the sea during a volcanic eruption.

Little need be said of the extermination of the passenger pigeon since the story of its extermination is familiar and fully documented. The disappearance of an exceptionally abundant bird within about twenty-five years revealed to thinking people that the survival of a species could not be taken for granted. In 1885, "millions" were reported assembled twenty-five miles northwest of Bedford, Pennsylvania. In a book published in America in 1866, W. R. King wrote:

Hurrying out and ascending the grassy ramparts, I was perfectly amazed to behold the air filled and the sun obscured by millions of pigeons, not hovering about but darting onwards in a straight line with arrowy flight, in a vast mass a mile or so in breadth, and stretching before and behind as far as the eye could reach. Swiftly and steadily the column passed over with a rushing sound, and for hours continued in undiminished myriads advancing over the American forests in the eastern horizon, as the myriads that had passed were lost in the western sky.

A Wisconsin nesting site in 1871 was a hundred miles long and from three to ten miles in width. For years carcasses of the birds were loaded into railway trucks to provide cheap food for the cities. The last forlorn bird died in the Cincinnati Zoo in 1914.

Many theories have been advanced to account for the passenger pigeon's rapid extinction—disease, the disruption of its highly social behavior, the destruction of trees—but undoubtedly it was man who was primarily responsible.

In spite of strenuous efforts to save the heath hen in its last stronghold, Martha's Vineyard, off the coast of

Massachusetts, to which it had been restricted since 1830, it died out. The decline of this and other species of the prairie chicken is mainly due to the cultivation of the grasslands, but it may be that birds which display socially at certain traditional leks, year after year as these birds do, may be most likely to suffer if their pattern of display behavior is disrupted. Perhaps this was one of the reasons why the ruff ceased for a time to breed in England.

The extinction of species throughout the world proceeded at an accelerating pace from the seventeenth century to the twentieth as shown by the data below, quoted by Prince Philip and J. Fisher in *Wildlife Crisis* (1970):

Period	Species exterminated	Period	Species exterminated
1600–49	3	1870–79	5
1650–99	9	1880–89	5
1700–49	9	1890–99	11
1750–99	11	1900–09	10
1800–29	4	1910–19	5
1830–39	7	1920–29	2
1840–49	2	1930–39	3
1850–59	2	1940–49	4
1860–69	3	1950–59	0
		Total	95

Human activity was directly or indirectly responsible for the loss of all of these, though forces of nature not under man's control sometimes contributed.

In recent times North America has lost more species than Europe. In addition to the great auk, passenger pigeon, and heath hen, the following have gone forever: Cooper's sandpiper, the Townsend's bunting (1833), the Labrador duck (1875), and the Carolina parakeet (1914). The probable reason for this is that the agricultural and industrial development was much more rapid there than in the Old World.

The list of American endangered species is so long as to arouse serious concern. Among these are some magnificent species—the bald eagle, the national emblem of the United States; the ivory-billed woodpecker; and the whooping crane. The Audubon Society organized a research program into the status of the ivory-billed woodpecker, culminating in an ominous report published in 1942. Since then the news has not been reassuring. During the 1950s no fully authenticated sighting was reported, but a few were seen in 1960 and 1961. At Big Thicket, Texas, between five and ten were observed in 1963, so there is some hope that it may still survive. Only about a dozen of the once-abundant Cuban race remain.

Facing page *Farmers shooting passenger pigeons in Iowa. This nineteenth century engraving suggests the vast flocks that once filled the skies in America.*
Below *"Martha," a passenger pigeon, the last of her species, who died on September 1, 1914 in the Cincinnati Zoo.*
Overleaf *John James Audubon's watercolors of the nearly extinct ivory-billed woodpecker and* (far right) *the Carolina parakeet, extinct since 1914.*

The situation of another splendid bird, the California condor, is also disquieting. It occupies an ecological niche similar to that once occupied by the incredible teratorn, though the condor's wingspan, huge as it is, measures not much more than half that of the teratorn. Long ago its range extended from British Columbia to Florida, but by about the beginning of this century its breeding was restricted to California. Realizing the bird's plight, the National Audubon Society organized a survey between 1939 and 1947 which showed that only about sixty survived. Another survey in 1963–64 revealed a decrease of 30 percent. Although carrion-feeding birds need a wide area in which to search for dead animals—an African lammergeier has been known to range over two hundred square miles— lack of food does not seem to be a primary cause of its decrease. Between 1947 and 1965 at least nine were shot in spite of legal protection. Development of part of the area, including the building of roads and a dam, has been prejudicial to its survival. It may justly be said of this magnificent creature that if it becomes extinct, the blame and shame are ours.

Because the whooping crane, which breeds in Canada's Wood Buffalo Park, now winters only at the Aransas Refuge of Texas and other islands close by, its world population can be accurately checked. There were fourteen in 1937 and 1938, then the number increased to more than thirty but fell back to twenty-odd in the 1950s. In 1967 thirty-nine mature birds and nine young wintered at Aransas. A few birds have been bred in zoos, so the outlook is hopeful, especially since there is much public concern for the birds, with the press carrying reports on the cranes during their migration periods. The campaign on their behalf may be reckoned one of conservation's triumphs.

In Britain, too, the record has its brighter side, such as the new species that have been added to the list of breeding birds. There was, for example, no record of the nesting of the snowy owl until a few years ago when a pair reared young in the Shetland Islands. They have continued to do so, watched over by the warden of the bird sanctuary there. The osprey has come back to nest in Scotland. The little ringed plover has also returned in some numbers after its first recorded nesting in 1938. The avocet, black-tailed godwit, and ruff are again breeding in the English wetlands. The firecrest has joined its close relative in the conifer plantations with which the Forestry Commission has too generously clothed the English hillsides. The collared dove has become established after a progressive extension of its range from southern Europe. Since the 1920s small numbers of the black redstart have nested.

As long ago as 1898 the League of American Sportsmen

Facing page (top) *Snowy owl with prey. A bird of the high latitudes, it is rarely seen south of Arctic or Subarctic regions.*

Facing page (bottom) *California condor. With a wingspread of more than ten feet, this orange-headed bird is the largest flying creature in North America. Less than fifty still survive, but efforts are now being made to protect them.*

Below *Whooping cranes in flight. Less than fifty of these birds are left in North America, but a few have been bred in captivity.*

Overleaf *Flock of greater sandhill cranes, another endangered species, at their winter feeding grounds. They winter in California, Texas, and parts of Mexico.*

Facing page *Catching a ruby-throated hummingbird in a mist net in order to band it.*
Below *Banding a female wood duck.*

was strong in its condemnation of "game hogs." It was during the period when plume-hunting was rife that ornithological societies were founded, the British Ornithologists' Union in 1859, the American Ornithologists' Union in 1883. At the second annual meeting of the latter a committee was appointed to consider what could be done to protect American birds. The National Association of Audubon Societies, named after the famous artist and ornithologist, was incorporated in New York State in 1905. It is now the National Audubon Society and like its sister society in Great Britain, the Royal Society for the Protection of Birds, has an educational function and maintains wildlife sanctuaries where colonies of birds or rare species breed or winter. These and other comparable societies and institutions publish journals, some mainly scientific, others with the aim of arousing sympathy for birds and spreading knowledge about them. In the United States, the Fish and Wildlife Service and the Bureau of Sport Fisheries and Wildlife work together in a field in which it is increasingly apparent that scientific understanding of wildlife is in the interests of both sportsman and quarry. Action needs to be on a world-wide scale when a bird's breeding and wintering quarters may be three thousand miles apart. Two international societies are of particular importance because among their activities is the collection of data concerning endangered species and the coordination of efforts to preserve them. The International Union for the Conservation of Nature and Natural Resources, with headquarters in Switzerland, together with the Survival Service Commission, compiles a *Red Data Book* providing particulars of the status of threatened species. The International Council for Bird Preservation issues reports dealing with birds.

Thus there is widespread interest in the preservation of bird fauna. We are becoming well informed about en-dangered species except in areas not easily accessible, but we are far from having solved all the problems involved in achieving a happy relationship between men and birds. The approach to conservation may differ from one country to another for historical reasons. In the United States, game belongs not to the landowner but to the state, while in most European countries, including England, the landowner owns and controls the wildlife. Thus in America the management of wildlife is a public responsibility exercised through various agencies. In practice, wise legislation, efficient management, and public spirit can make either system effective. But some governments are dilatory in passing the necessary legislation because of vested interests, traditional customs, ignorance, or apathy.

In Italy there is annually an extensive slaughter of small passerine birds. In justification it is argued that many of these birds do damage, but in some instances the opposite is true. Thus the farmers in the Salentina—the "heel" projecting into the sea between the Adriatic and Ionian seas—were permitted to kill starlings and thrushes and, in practice, many other birds, because of their apparent ravages in the olive groves. Then a forester found that each of the five or six olives eaten per day by these birds contained one or more larvae of the olive fly. At the third generation the progeny of one female fly are capable of destroying thirty thousand olives. Yet it is estimated that in one region 1.3 million starlings and thrushes were recently slaughtered in a month!

The greater bird of paradise is an example of how a social custom may lead to the persecution of a bird. The bird's scientific name, *Paradisaea apoda,* is a facetious reference to the practice of exporting skins without legs. According to an old tradition, the natives of New Guinea and the Molucca Islands adorned their head-

Facing page *Salvadori's red bird of paradise, which occurs only on two isolated islands near New Guinea.* Below *Pheasant-tailed jacana. A marsh bird found mainly in India and southeast Asia, its survival depends on the preservation of fragile wetlands.*

dresses with the feathers of this magnificent bird, but before World War I the bird was protected and was not in danger. However, in 1957, when the Moluccas became an Indonesian troop center, high-ranking army officers were honored with a gift of a bird of paradise. A skin, worth nearly seven hundred dollars, was all the more prized as the trade in them was illegal.

The web of life is so intricately woven, and in some places so frail, that introducing any bird or other organism into a new environment may sometimes have disastrous consequences. When, for example, mink-farming was introduced into Iceland no one thought of the possibility that some of the animals would escape. They have done so and have become a menace to the birds.

Ecologists are sometimes confronted with a very difficult problem when a species extends its range naturally. Should they interfere or not? The collared dove has recently advanced across Europe and is now established throughout most of England. It is a "hanger-on" of man, and was first noticed around farm buildings. As we have noted, in certain areas it has driven away the wood pigeon, which has a more soothing call. If the collared dove becomes a pest, eliminating it would now be impossible, so firmly established has it become.

Lest it should be assumed that the balance of the argument is against deliberate "interference" with nature, it must be emphasized that it is just because man has already interfered so much and will do so increasingly that it is necessary that he should step in to adjust the balance when he can do so with reasonable hope of success. This may entail keeping the remnants of some populations in captivity so that eventually their progeny can be released to augment the original stock. Thus some oryx—an Arabian antelope—have been brought to Arizona to form a breeding group because in its native haunts the species was being exterminated by "sportsmen" who hunted it in jeeps. Similarly, eagle owls have been bred in England and sent back to Scandinavia to augment the stock there. But this procedure has its pitfalls, too. Hawaiian geese have been reared in England at Slimbridge and released in Hawaii, but it is now known that this inbred stock has genetic deficiencies which could hurt the native population. Good will must be allied with knowledge. Even extremely common species can become extinct. Twenty years before the last passenger pigeon died no one believed that the species was doomed.

Homesick English immigrants to Australia and New Zealand brought or sent for birds from the British homeland so that seven species are now naturalized in Australia—skylark, song thrush, blackbird, greenfinch, goldfinch, house sparrow, and starling—and thirteen

Facing page *Many birds have survived or even flourished because they have adapted well to man. Here storks are shown nesting on a housetop in Alsace, where a special society has been established to preserve the birds.*
Below *Purple martins nest in houses of gourds made by farmers eager to have their help in insect control.*

in New Zealand, to the detriment of native species. This occurred because Australian and New Zealand birds evolved in greater isolation than European species, and never had a chance to adapt to man, his pets, or the changes he makes in the environment.

Island birds are more vulnerable to alien species than are continental birds. The Maoris found a wonderful bird life when they landed in New Zealand about A.D. 950. Forty-three species have gone. The rate of extinction accelerated with the arrival of European colonists and birds as well as mammalian predators. In Hawaii the Polynesians who settled the islands are not known to have exterminated any species, although they used brilliant feathers to adorn their ceremonial robes. They did not alter the environment drastically. In contrast, European settlement has involved the extinction of fourteen species, and the fate of many others hangs in the balance. In many areas the birds have so adapted to each other and to indigenous predators, such as the cat, mink, and mongoose that numbers of both are maintained in approximate equilibrium, but some bird species cannot adapt quickly enough to marauders. The success of many European species introduced elsewhere has often been due to immigrants who have unintentionally prepared the way for them by altering the landscape, cutting down forests and tilling the land. In Britain only the tops of the mountains, some islands, and wetlands are virgin nature. Perhaps the house sparrow and starling arrived after man for they depend on him to a great extent for nesting sites and, directly or indirectly, for food. They are commensals, even parasites, and would not have prospered in an uncultivated countryside. During journeys through the forests in Lapland and the far north of Scandinavia I noted house sparrows only at railway stations, where they could nest in crevices and pick up scraps. The house sparrow has extended its range to North America, much of South America, Australia, and South Africa, and New Zealand, Hawaii, and many other islands.

In Britain, for example, a naturalist becomes aware that our common birds are common because we have made them so by providing habitats for them. Swifts, swallows, and house martins find nesting sites on our buildings, and sand martins in our gravel pits; the blackbird and song thrush feed on our lawns, the rook forages in our fields, and warblers nest and feed in our hedges. Kestrels sometimes nest where buildings provide artificial cliffs. In North America, duck hawks occasionally nest on tall buildings, and the chimney swift and house wren choose nesting places provided by man. Thus in some areas people and birds have reached a *modus vivendi*.

But the losses are great. The problem in highly devel-

oped countries is to provide enough suitable habitats for birds. Some, notably the large birds of prey such as eagles, marsh hawks, buzzards, and kites, need large hunting grounds. Others, such as shore-nesting species like ringed plovers, oystercatchers, and little terns, are disturbed by vacationers. Agricultural machinery destroys the nests of ground-nesting species, drainage reduces the marshland birds, and disturbance by aircraft disrupts the nesting of other birds. The reclamation of the Waddenzee in Holland has reduced the feeding grounds of myriads of migratory and marine species despite strenuous efforts by bird-protection societies to reserve suitable areas for them.

THE MENACE OF POLLUTION

One day in the summer of 1969 a fisherman of the Scottish Isle of Cumbrae was puzzled by the strange behavior of some sea birds: they did not fly away when his boat drew near. At first he paid little attention, but he encountered lethargic birds again and again. On the other side of the Irish Sea, in Strangford and Belfast loughs, numbers of birds were reported dying or dead. By November it had been ascertained that between 100,000 and 500,000 guillemots and razorbills had died in what became known as the 1969 Sea-Bird Wreck. They were found to have been poisoned by PCB (polychlorinated biphenyl) chemicals, which are used in paints, plastics, and as insulators. These chemicals reach the sea in many ways, build up in plant tissues, then in organisms which feed on the plants, then in the fish which eat the organisms, and finally in the birds which devour the fish. This is but one example out of many that might be quoted of how toxic chemicals can kill animals at the end of a food chain—and man, of course, is at the end of many of the chains.

Rachel Carson in *Silent Spring* cited many other instances of bird disasters in the United States attributable to chemicals. She may have overstated the case but did an invaluable service by bringing this situation to public attention. The side effects of pesticides may be insidious and become evident only when much damage has already been done. It was only after considerable research that it was discovered that the decrease in peregrine falcons was due to the effect of DDT, which made the eggshells so thin that the weight of the brooding bird broke them. The oceans are being contaminated by the dumping of sludge containing toxic lead, chromium, and cadmium. Thor Heyerdahl's Ra expedition found huge areas of the surface of the Atlantic Ocean contaminated.

Many vacationers—including my own family—have been annoyed to find their clothes stained with sticky clots of black oil after sitting on a beach and have thus

Facing page *Razorbill.*
Below *Guillemot in flight. Perhaps as many as half a million razorbills and guillemots died of chemical poisoning in the 1969 "Sea-Bird Wreck" in the Irish Sea.*

193

Facing page *Wild turkey. The fearless, inquisitive nature of these birds and their abundance led to their wanton slaughter by early settlers in North America. Conservation efforts have increased their numbers somewhat, and today they are even reappearing in such states as New York and Pennsylvania where they had been absent for generations. Domesticated turkeys are bred for food on turkey farms.*

Below *Monkey-eating eagle. This immensely powerful and spectacular bird of the Philippine Islands is seriously menaced. It apparently subsists almost entirely on the Philippine macaque (a short-tailed monkey), which accounts for its name.*

realized the plight of birds which, unlike us, cannot change their clothes or rid their plumage of this lethal slime. No matter what precautions are taken, accidental oil spills will occur.

As society is now organized, the higher the standard of living, the greater the pollution of the environment. This is especially so if, as at present, pollution control is lax. To meet demands for more food, many poisons are being used to spray crops, but the farmers' insect foes are becoming immune to them. The chemists are hard put to keep a step ahead of the pests, and their products often kill the natural enemies of the pests. Biological control—the introduction or encouragement of the natural enemies of a plant or animal—is sometimes more effective. But one of the difficulties involved in introducing a bird or mammal outside of its normal range is that higher animals are often able to switch their interest to another kind of prey.

Another basic problem, indeed some would say the most fundamental, is the rapid and accelerating increase in human population. At present the population increase amounts to about 192,000 daily. It is certain that for a long time to come the increase in the numbers of *Homo sapiens* will reduce the living space for other creatures. Where there are too many people, there are too few birds.

PRESERVING RARE ANIMALS IN CAPTIVITY

In the past the prestige of potentates was increased if they had rare animals for display in gardens, aviaries, or parks. Today English landowners continue the practice by devoting portions of their grounds to miniature zoos and charging admission fees to pay for the upkeep and cope with high taxation. The ancient Egyptians kept various animals in captivity, but the first "zoological garden" appears to have been the "Intelligence Park" founded by the first emperor of the Chou dynasty about 1100 B.C. The Romans kept captive animals, including ostriches, not for exhibition but to be slaughtered at gladiatorial shows. The Aztecs maintained royal parks where game was protected. In England Henry I (1100–1135) established a menagerie which was later transferred to the Tower of London and continued until the nineteenth century, and Louis XIV of France maintained a *menagerie du parc* at Versailles. Aviaries were included in these zoos.

The concept of a national park is very different from that of a zoo, for a zoo or aviary implies that the animals or birds are enclosed. The former is an area, usually large and scenic, preserving interesting fauna and flora undisturbed except for the admission of visitors

and for supervision. Appropriately, a poet, Wordsworth, was perhaps the first to advocate establishing a national park in England. In his *Guide Through the District of the Lakes* (1835) he wrote that the Lake District "should be regarded as a sort of national property, in which every man has a right and interest who has an eye to perceive and a heart to enjoy." In our own time "the Lakes" have officially been recognized as a national park.

National parks belong to the people and in this they differ from earlier hunting grounds and estates. It was the prerogative of English monarchs until Magna Carta to convert any area they chose into a forest where they could enjoy the pleasures of the chase. The definition of such a hunting ground was:

> A certain territory of woody and fruitful pastures privileged for wild beasts and fowls of the forest, chase and warren to rest, and abide there in the safe protection of the king, for his delight and pleasure; which territory of ground so privileged and bounded with unmovable marks . . . and also replenished with wild beasts of venery or chase, and with great coverts of vert, for the succour of the said beasts there to abide; for the preservation and continuance of which said place . . . there are particular officers, laws, and privileges belonging to the same . . . and proper only to a forest and to no other place.

Thus, although these reserves were hunting grounds, emphasis was placed on the conservation and even the well-being of the animals. Only privileged persons were allowed to hunt, so there was no danger of overkill, and conditions were such that hunting grounds provided refuge and protection for the whole fauna and flora apart from beasts of the chase. The wolf was hunted as well as the deer, so the balance between predator and prey was not seriously upset.

To some extent later estates maintained this tradition and were bird sanctuaries except that the welfare of such favored game as pheasant or grouse was given such priority that the birds and beasts which preyed on them or their eggs were regarded as "vermin." Hawks, crows, and magpies were slaughtered along with rats and weasels by the keeper so that he might earn the commendation of "the guns" when the shooting season came round; but this meant that small songbirds nesting on or near the ground, such as the nightingale, skylark, willow, and wood warblers, could breed more successfully, undisturbed by predators.

As for establishing national parks in the modern sense, here the United States led the way. Picture a party of rugged, sunburnt men chatting by their evening campfire one evening in 1870 amid awesome scenery. They are thrilled by the wonders of what they had found during the exploration of what became known as the Yellowstone National Park. What would become of this magnificent area? What mineral treasures might lie underground? How valuable the timber! What sport awaits the hunter! How could all this be exploited? Then up spoke one of the party, Judge Cornelius Hedges: "Are dollars all that matter? Here we have found marvellous scenery where grizzly bear, wapiti, bison, and deer roam and bald eagles, white pelicans, and many other big, beautiful birds nest. We have been among the few to have set eyes on one of the wonders of the world. Could not this place be set apart forever so that all who come after us can enjoy it?" Such was the gist of their conversation, and then and there they dedicated themselves to realizing this dream.

They were so successful that in May, 1872, Yellowstone Park was established, the first of many such parks. Other countries all over the world have copied this example. Thus on the huge expanse of the Serengeti

plains you may watch at close quarters an oxpecker in search of ticks climbing a giraffe's neck as if it were a tree, or see a ring of hungry vultures waiting around until a lion has moved from his kill. There are tiny reserves where a rare orchid or butterfly is guarded. The success of national parks brings problems in its wake as increasing numbers of people, cramped in cities, seek less artificial surroundings. In one recent year the United States Parks and Reserves were visited by 163,990,000 people. A writer describes the crush of cars in famous Yosemite Park on an average weekend; the concreted acreage of parking spaces, the hotels, cabins, paved roads, and souvenir shops, and how in the evening the valley lay beneath a pall of exhaust fumes and campfire smoke, and pots and pans clattered to the accompaniment of transistor radios.

This is a somewhat biased report because in the great American parks, it is good to know, steps are being taken to limit car travel and it is possible to escape the crowd by relying on one's own two feet. Some years ago in the Grand Canyon I walked down to the river without meeting another person, but on a Sunday high in the Usambara mountains of East Africa, where I expected to find tranquillity, I instead found boys carrying around transistor radios turned up full blast.

It is a very worthwhile experience to motor through or be guided around a national park whether in the United States or Africa. Large animals and birds become so accustomed to human beings that they are easily approached—lions and ostriches in Tanzania, bears in the Smokies, alligators and turkeys in the Everglades. The aim of the American National Wilderness Society System, established by Congress in 1964, is to ensure that nine million acres still "unspoiled" will be preserved in their pristine beauty, excluding automobiles and human exploitation or settlement. The United States and Canada are fortunate in still having large tracts of country in this condition.

In Europe the national park movement has made progress since Sweden set apart several areas in 1909 and Iceland established nature reserves in 1905 and its first national park at Thingvellir in 1928. The latter is a bleak area clothed with moorland vegetation where the snow bunting sings and the great northern diver's half-human wailing emphasizes the loneliness. Holland has four national parks and many national nature reserves. Large numbers of marine and wading birds nest on Texel Island, and the Naardemeer, close to Amsterdam, is a bird paradise with nesting spoonbills, purple herons, bitterns, black terns, marsh hawks, and great reed warblers. France has two thousand reserves large and small, including the Camargue, a vast area of wetland. It is hoped that the flamingoes which nested there until a few years ago will return; their desertion is attributed to aircraft flying overhead. Now the famous Coto Doñana in southwestern Spain, a curious mixture of swamp and desert, is the only place in Europe where they and the imperial eagle nest. At the other extreme from this flat area is the Swiss National Park in the Engadine where golden eagles soar over high peaks and ibex and chamois graze on cliffs and slopes. The ibex came from the neighboring Gran Paradiso Park in Italy. The Gran Paradiso had been a hunting park since 1836 and has been under royal patronage since the late 1850s.

There is now scarcely a European country without national parks and nature reserves, and on the other continents, too, governments have created parks, refuges, and reserves. The East African parks are so popular with tourists that the governments of several countries there rely on them for a goodly proportion of their revenue. It is a marvelous experience to cruise across

Facing page Lesser flamingos. A vast number congregate on their ancestral breeding ground at Lake Natron, Tanzania.
Below Pigeons in St. Mark's Square, Venice. Pigeons exemplify birds that have adjusted so well to man that they have sometimes become a nuisance.

the Serengeti and watch leopards, rhinoceroses, and elephants at close quarters, to see a procession of migrating wildebeest stretching to the horizon, to gaze at huge Lake Nakuru pink with thousands of flamingoes, to listen to the nicely timed duets of boubou shrikes, and be diverted by the comings and goings of brilliant flocks of starlings. The visitor may readily observe the tiny honeycreepers hovering daintily at tree blossoms, acting the role of the New World hummingbirds, and admire ostriches feeding.

In Asia much is being done to safeguard wildlife. Since 1958 seven national parks have been created in Turkey and more are planned, Israel is acting in a very enlightened way, and Jordan has established the huge Azraq Desert National Park, following suggestions from British naturalists. India has many rich preserves and Japan has twenty-three national parks. Mention should also be made of the scientific centers established on two groups of islands, the Galapagos, that volcanic cluster off the coast of Ecuador, and the Aldabra Islands in the Indian Ocean.

Much is being done to protect birds and their habitats, but the overriding problem remains—that as increasing mouths need food, housing, clothing, not to speak of other paraphernalia of civilization, the world's fauna and flora have to give way to that most wasteful organism, man. The utmost vigilance is necessary to avoid unnecessary spoliation. In February, 1975, the European Parliament, meeting at Brussels, was told that of 408 species of wild bird living within the states of the European Economic Community, the numbers of 221 species are diminishing. This is a tragic situation which should be regarded as a warning to the entire world.

9
Birds in Art

Long before writing was invented, man expressed himself graphically and on so grand a scale that a decorated cavern, such as that of Lascaux in southern France, can justifiably be called a picture gallery. The visitor finds himself surrounded on every side by life-size, or larger, colored renditions of animals, realistically depicted, except for one large figure of an imaginary beast with long, straight horns projecting from its forehead. There are many other such "galleries" in southern France and northern Spain, and although there are differences of opinion as to the significance of this Old Stone Age art, it can be assumed that these paintings were not executed for purely aesthetic reasons nor to while away the time. They had magical significance and were probably designed to establish and maintain what was considered to be an appropriate relationship with the animals. Paleolithic man wanted these animals to be numerous —hence he sometimes painted them pregnant—and vulnerable, but he held them in great respect, amounting even to awe.

Probably, like some primitive hunting peoples today, he did not feel superior to the animals but rather experienced an affinity with them. Thus the Tlingit hunter in Alaska apologized to an animal he had killed.

Designs on cavern walls illustrating birds are rather rare, as, indeed, are portraits of man himself, but there are interesting pictures of birds in flight or displaying in some Spanish caves and rock shelters. There are also a number of designs of birds on stone and bone. Some of the most interesting bird pictures are hidden away in remote corners of the caverns. One group, showing a pair of snowy owls with their chick, is engraved on a wall in the last passage of the Trois Frères cave, and another engraving, of two birds, one auklike, is on a rock at the end of a winding fissure in the cave of El Pendo. The secretive location of these designs suggests that they had some esoteric or magical significance.

When I visited Lascaux some years ago, before it was closed to the public, I persuaded the guide to allow me to descend by ladder into a rockbound pit not normally shown to visitors. Standing at the bottom I found myself close to a painting about six feet across, very small in comparison with those in the gallery above. Unlike them it depicts a violent scene of bloodshed, with a man as the center of interest between a retreating rhinoceros and a furious, charging bison disemboweled by his javelin. The man is represented with a bird's head painted in a simple, vigorous style, and close by in the same style is a bird perched on a post. This scene is in the most secluded nook of the cave. There is obviously a magical relationship between the bird and the bird-faced or bird-masked man.

Among other Paleolithic works of art which throw

Above *A Paleolithic cave painting known as* The Birdman of Lascaux. *The bird-headed man is depicted between a charging bison and a rhinoceros (not shown in this detail).*
Facing page *The "Vulci" vase (c. 550 B.C.) showing Hercules using a sling to drive away the swan-like birds which, according to Greek mythology, had infested Lake Stymphalis.*

Facing page (top) *Prehistoric petroglyphs of various water birds found in Kazakhstan, Russia.*
Facing page (bottom) *Representations of bird-headed men occur in the art of many cultures, such as this rock carving of two birdmen found at a ceremonial site on Easter Island.*
Below *A wooden mask surmounted by the figure of a bird. From the Guro tribe, Ivory Coast, West Africa.*

light on "the Birdman of Lascaux" are the designs in the depths of the Trois Frères cave representing a bear with its body bristling with arrows, and a clay bear at Montespan scarred with the marks of arrows indicating that magical attacks had been made on it, probably in order to bring success to the hunter. Acting out what you wish to happen has always been a feature of magical ceremonies.

To this day the hunting tribes of Manchuria, the Tungus, erect posts surmounted by a wooden model of a bird and set beside sacrificial platforms. Their culture preserves characteristics which may have lingered since the Old Stone Age; for instance, their shamans perform a ritual in which they wear feathers and leap around waving their arms as if flying. So they claim to establish contact with the heavenly powers.

Clearly bird art has long had a magical or magico-religious significance. The bird-headed man is one of the oldest artistic motifs and has occurred in many cultures —Paleolithic, Egyptian, Assyrian, Babylonian, medieval European—and in the paintings of the Dutch master Hieronymus Bosch and in modern artists such as the American painter Leonard Baskin. It appears in the art of Melanesia and Polynesia and is prominent in rock carvings and the script of remote Easter Island. Anthropologists have pointed out possible affinities between the bird-man in New Zealand art and ancient Asian designs. Such extraordinary diffusion in time and space of this motif testifies to the profound feeling that man has always had for birds.

EARLY CIVILIZATIONS

The discovery in Neolithic times that certain plants, particularly those bearing grain, could be cultivated and regular crops obtained by saving and sowing seed meant that permanent settlements could be established and animals domesticated. As such settlements were extended and the size of communities increased, civilization grew up in the area now known as the Fertile Crescent—the Nile valley, Israel, northwestern Jordan, western Syria, Lebanon, southeastern Turkey, the Tigris and Euphrates valleys. A settlement at Ur was established by the Sumerians at an early date. They came from elsewhere—perhaps from somewhere toward the Indus valley—bringing with them, so far as we can tell, their traditions, including a knowledge of agriculture, metalwork, and writing. At this royal city, the capital, evidence of the importance of domestic animals and wild birds was found in the temple remains. To the rear of the temple platform was a lintel above which was a copper relief of an eagle and stags. Along the top of the platform was a frieze of resting cattle and above it a frieze of birds, probably doves. At

Mecca these have long been regarded as sacred. Thus both wild and domesticated animals had religious significance. Elsewhere was another frieze showing a bull with a lion-headed eagle on his back tearing at his rump. We do not know precisely what myth is illustrated here, but it must surely represent the conflict which man sees in the universe and which he experiences in his relationships with others. In various forms this symbol is one of the most long-lived. It appears as a design on a first century A.D. woolen rug from Mongolia and in felt appliqué on a saddlebag from a burial tomb of the fifth century B.C.

An eagle seizing a serpent or dragon occurs in Persian and Egyptian sculpture and on classical Greek coinage. The Persian designs represent the struggle between good and evil, between the heavenly powers and the powers of darkness, and are based on observations of the daily and annual cycle of light and warmth followed by cold and darkness. In Greece and elsewhere the eagle was an emblem of the sun and was connected with the constellations. Thus Aquila, the eagle, rose in the heavens after the swan and the serpent and could be thought of as pursuing them. In general, from early times to the Christian era, when the eagle became the emblem of resurrection and of Saint John and betokened spirituality, the eagle has stood for the power of good, positive and creative.

Scenes on Babylonian cylinder seals show episodes in a myth concerning a conflict between the storm god Zu, represented as a large bird, and the earth god Enlil. While Enlil was seated on his throne arranging his crown on his head, Zu snatched the destiny tablet of the gods and flew off with it. One seal depicts a large bird in flight, apparently damaging trees, pursued by a weapon-wielding god. Another seal shows a god seated in judgment, with a second god bringing the dead Zu dangling from a pole, and yet a third god is bringing specimens of the damaged vegetation. Zu, as the storm god, was associated with the underworld where the dead wear feathers like birds. This seems to be a version of a common mythological theme—the temporary triumph of the forces of disorder.

Egyptian civilization was able to persist for thousands of years because of the fertility-maintaining Nile and the protection from invasion afforded by the flanking deserts. There, man did not have to fight against aggressive vegetation. Moreover, the dry climate preserved his works of art. Even more important was the Egyptians' concern for the hereafter; this required them to provide Pharaohs and other high officials, in the burial chamber itself, with the paraphernalia of daily life and painted simulations of it. Such tombs, and especially that of Tutankhamen, give us a good

Below *Romanesque sculpture of the eagle of St. John.*
Facing page *Pheasant looking at his reflection in a fountain, in a Franco-Flemish tapestry (c. 1500).*
Overleaf *Birds in a detail of a* mola *(woman's skirt) made by the Cuna Indians of Panama.*

idea of how these people lived. The Egyptian *Book of the Dead* and various inscriptions supply information which helps us to interpret pictorial representations in the tombs. These show us not only city life but what we could call country scenes, especially of hunting, and since birds were numerous and the artists were accurate observers, we have wonderful pictures of some species. Notable are paintings of three species of geese in the tomb of Ne-fer-Maat at Medum, the white-fronted, bean, and red-breasted, dating from no later than 3000 B.C. Among wildfowling scenes is the painting, bustling with vigorous life, from the tomb of the scribe Nebamun (c. 1400 B.C.) in which butterflies mingle with birds and a cat pounces on a duck. Here the hunter uses a throwing stick or boomerang, but on a chest in Tutankhamen's tomb the Pharaoh is seen shooting at the marsh birds with a bow and arrow. Such scenes illustrate the sport of noblemen but they are also found in the graves of commoners from about 2600 B.C. and reappear in temples about 300 B.C. They represent the ritual expulsion of evil. Beside a miniature effigy of the king lying on a bier were set a model of a falcon and a human-headed falcon, two forms the disembodied king might adopt when his soul returned from the other world to visit his mummified body. In other tombs birds representing the soul are pictured hovering over the mummy case. One such tomb contains an inscription stating that the gods granted the deceased power to return as a falcon, swallow, heron, or phoenix. Such feelings of close affinity with the animal world and, indeed, identification with it had evidently persisted from primitive times. The Greek historian Herodotus (c. 484–425 B.C.) indicated how persistent were some Egyptian beliefs, and enables us to see how some art motifs in Greece were inherited from the Nile valley culture. A design on the "Vulci" vase of the mid-sixth century B.C., showing Hercules fighting the flock of Stymphalian birds, which were mainly swan-like but with pointed beaks, is so reminiscent of Egyptian tomb scenes that we may plausibly assume the design was partly inspired by them. From the eighth century the Greeks and Phoenicians were competing for trade in the Mediterranean, and oriental designs certainly influenced Greek artists. Like the Egyptians and some peoples of Iran, the Greeks painted long-necked birds which look like stylized swans.

CLASSICAL AND ORIENTAL BIRD ART
Something, however meager, must be said here concerning bird art in the Far East because many Europeans and Americans tend to ignore the great artistic achievements of the Chinese Middle Kingdom and of Japan. At certain epochs in their history both nations

Facing page (top) *An Egyptian representation of hunters fowling and spearing fish. From the Tomb of Menena, Thebes (c. 1415 B.C.).*
Facing page (bottom) *Captive cranes being herded in Egypt. From a carving in the Tomb of Ti in Saqqara, Egypt.*
Below *Sculptor's model of the Egyptian goddess Nekhebt with her vulture crown, the privilege of a royal female personage or goddess.*

Facing page (top) *Egyptian falcon inlay in faience (c. 600 B.C.).*
Facing page (bottom) *Chinese wine vessel in the form of a goose.*
Below *Owl's head in gold Mixtec style, Mexico. The screech owl was associated with the death god.*

produced superb works of art depicting birds.

Chinese art during two centuries before the birth of Christ reveals the influence of Mesopotamian ideas. Stone carvings in caves dating from about the second century A.D. show winged horses in Mesopotamian style as well as more naturalistic scenes, such as birds in a tree, along with a horse, heron, and monkeys below. Thereafter, up to the Tang dynasty (A.D. 618–907), the art forms are mainly Indian Buddhist. During this epoch, trade was carried on with Arabia and Persia and the influence of Greek art spread as far as Japan. Designs depicting beautiful long-tailed birds perched in trees, and showing ducks confronting each other, have been preserved in a museum at Nara founded by a Japanese emperor in A.D. 749. Landscape art flourished in China during the eleventh century, and lively pictures of tigers and cats were painted. About the fifteenth century birds flying in cloudy landscapes or feeding in marshes became prominent in Japanese art. Imposing portraits of eagles perched on rugged tree branches also survive from this period. The eminent artist Sesshu, who went from Japan to China, painted ducks, hawks, jays, storks, and herons. This tradition was maintained in the Kano school of the sixteenth century and was continued by Chinese and Japanese artists with pictures of flying geese seen from above, graceful herons in trees, and woodland scenes in which birds, perched or in flight, appear among flowers and foliage.

Archaeological evidence confirms that Greek influences, intermingled with Iranian elements, penetrated from the West to the Far East. Human figures with bird wings, indicating superhuman characteristics, appeared in Eastern and Western art, as, for example, Ahura Mazda in Iran, and Nike and the Harpies in Greece. An important Hittite symbol was the double-headed eagle connected with divine or priestly personages. Later this emblem was adopted by Turkish sultans and still later by the Austrian and Russian empires.

The motif of a bird carrying a god or goddess appears in Greek art, as in a beautiful design of Aphrodite riding on a goose, a bird with erotic associations. A similar design appears in Japanese art. A print dating from A.D. 1765 depicts the supernatural being Kosenko borne over the clouds by a goose. A variation on this theme is the myth that Apollo was drawn in a swan chariot to the Hyperborean or northern regions. In India the god of love, Kama, rides a parrot, which has much the same sensual significance as the goose in ancient Greece. The god carried by a bird is also prominent in Brahmanic mythology. Brahma is the soul of the universe, the source, essence, and end of all things;

in the sky of Sassetta's *Procession of the Wise Men* and his *Saint Francis and the Wolf of Gubbio,* or in Bruegel's *Hunters in the Snow.*

Although from early times cranes had figured in legends, it is unlikely that Raphael introduced these birds because of their symbolism—an indication of how much his point of view differed from that of medieval artists. Since they are mentioned in the Biblical books of Isaiah and Jeremiah, Raphael surely knew that cranes might be appropriately depicted by the Lake of Galilee. These birds also nest in northern Italy, so Raphael and Sassetta had probably seen them flying overhead, and Raphael could have sketched semi-domesticated or "winged" specimens in some nobleman's grounds. Cranes used to be much more abundant in Europe and the Middle East before marshes were drained; as one Victorian ornithologist, H. B. Tristam, reports from Beersheba: "The clouds of these enormous birds four feet high and many eight feet from wing to wing, quite darkened the sky towards evening." Actually, Raphael was not especially interested in birds, or indeed in nature. Similarly, that colossus of Italian Renaissance art, Michelangelo, showed little interest in birds apart from one outstanding sculpture, the tondo or round marble bas-relief now at Burlington House, London. This illustrates a theme which occupied artists from the thirteenth century to the seventeenth—the *Virgin and Child with Goldfinch.* Since this bird, in common with the robin redbreast, the crossbill, and the swallow, has a patch of red feathers, it became associated with the Crucifixion and legends were woven relating how the bird had wounded itself when it tried to pick a thorn from the crown of thorns or wrench a nail from the Cross, and so was granted this badge of compassion. The goldfinch was also a fertility symbol. The legend has it that when children brought clay models of birds to the Christ Child, the clay came to life; and this story may have arisen from, and in turn encouraged, the association of the goldfinch with the Madonna and Child in pictures. It was an enormously popular subject and hundreds of paintings were devoted to it. Another historically interesting theme is that of Saint Francis preaching to the birds, which first appeared in the thirteenth century, continued to appear into the fifteenth century, then became popular again in English statuary and church windows in the nineteenth century and has remained so up to the present.

BIRD ART IN BOOKS
The invention of printing caused bird artistry to be increasingly concentrated in book illustration. One of the first books illustrated with pictures of birds was

Facing page *Detail from* Swan and Falcon, *a Chinese painting (c. 1450).*
Below Leda and the Swan *by Paolo Veronese, representing the myth of Zeus, in the shape of a swan, visiting Leda (Italian, sixteenth century.).*

Facing page (*top*) *St. John the Baptist presents a fluttering goldfinch to the Christ Child in a tondo by Michelangelo.*
Facing page (bottom) Madonna and Child *by Donato di Bardi (Italian, fifteenth century).*
Below *Ducks, as depicted in Francis Willughby's* Ornithology (1676), *one of the earliest illustrated books about birds.*

Anser Canadensis
The Canada Goose

Tadorna Bellony
The Sheldrake

Anas niger major
The great black Duck.

TAB. LXX

Part III of the *Hortus sanitatis* (1490–1517), which has over one hundred woodcuts of birds. The frontispiece shows two scholars gesticulating as they engage in a lively discussion while a stork a few feet away seizes a snake and another, on a nest on a housetop, "klappers" at its mate (or rival) on an adjoining housetop. A kite, a cock, and a goose are among other birds illustrated. There were also 160 bird illustrations in Pierre Belon's *Histoire de la nature des oiseaux* (Paris, 1555), and Konrad von Gesner's famous *Historia animalium* contained a number of woodcuts.

The first watercolor paintings of North American birds were made in 1585–86 by John White, better known for his paintings of Indian tribesmen. Apparently they were intended to illustrate Edward Topsell's *Fowles of Heauen* which was not published until recently. Had White's paintings been published when they were made, they would have preceded by more than a century Albin's *A Natural History of Birds,* the first volume on British birds with colored illustrations.

Perhaps the outstanding paintings of birds in the eighteenth century appeared in *The Natural History of Carolina, Florida, and the Bahama Islands* (1731–43) by Mark Catesby. It gave the world a glimpse of the wealth of North American bird life in a splendid series of large color plates by the author, a South Carolinian. Buffon's *Histoire naturelle* (1770) had a large number of colored illustrations. Also in France, several fine works on birds with hand-colored plates appeared at the beginning of the nineteenth century. By this time an Englishman, Thomas Bewick, had achieved a much-improved wood-block technique. His birds are stiff but delicately shaded and accurately delineated with daintily rendered, appropriate backgrounds. Two birds, Bewick's swan and Bewick's wren, were named after him.

One of the most important of all bird illustrators was the French-born American naturalist and painter, John James Audubon (1785–1851). The four volumes of his *Birds of America,* "elephant folio" in size, appeared from 1827 to 1838. A fair-sized table is needed to support one of them, preferably in a well-lit room where the aquatint engravings can be enjoyed to the full. The birds are depicted life size, perched on an appropriate spray of foliage or with sufficient background to indicate the habitat. Because we have now become accustomed to seeing birds portrayed photographically we may consider those shown in some of Audubon's pictures rather stiff and angular, but the people who bought these volumes found them more lifelike than anything they had ever seen—though Chinese and Japanese artists had been painting lively

Facing page Painted Finch, *from* The Natural History of Carolina, Florida, and the Bahama Islands *(1731–43), by Mark Catesby, English naturalist.* Below *Mississippi kite, Tennessee warbler, Kentucky wren, and prairie wren, from* American Ornithology *(1808–1814) by Alexander Wilson (1766–1813), Scottish-born American ornithologist.*

and accurate studies of birds for centuries. Audubon's birds are sometimes depicted in artificially sprightly postures, due, in part, to his effort to use his recollections of the living birds to supplement his working from dead specimens. He was also trying to avoid the static bird profiles favored by previous illustrators. Nowadays the field guides used by bird-watchers are illustrated, like the earliest bird books, with profiles because such pictures are useful in identification, but probably earlier illustrators adopted this practice because it was the easiest to do.

The gun was as essential to early artists as the brush and pencil. Audubon was a crack shot, and in the woods, after attentive observation of the living bird, he would shoot it and study the dead specimen. He and his contemporary, Alexander Wilson (1766–1813), a Scottish-born American who was a competent ornithologist as well as an artist, had to hawk their work around to secure subscribers, a heartbreaking business. Audubon finally succeeded in finding subscribers in England and Scotland as well as in America.

By the time the last of Audubon's volumes appeared (in 1838), photography had become a practical technique, but it was nearly half a century later before successful photographs were made of such lively subjects as birds.

Because they have such brilliant plumage and, as popular cage birds, could be copied from life, parrots have been painted by many artists, notably by J. Barraband, who illustrated François Levaillant's *Histoire naturelle des perroquets* (1801–05), and in England by Edward Lear, who in the 1830s took advantage of lithography to produce a book on parrots with plates colored by hand.

Among bird artists of the Victorian era John Gould stands out. With the help of his wife, who was also an excellent artist, and of Lear and others, he produced some forty volumes illustrating the bird fauna of regions as far apart as the Himalayas and Australia, where he lived from 1838 until 1840. Archibald Thorburn's portraits of birds were also highly esteemed. Two other eminent bird artists were H. Grönvold and J. G. Millais; the former illustrated the four-volume monograph on pheasants (1918–22) by the distinguished American ornithologist William Beebe. In the United States Louis Agassiz Fuertes was probably the most noteworthy painter of birds during his lifetime (1874–1927).

A fine bird artist who was also a great explorer was Edward Wilson (1872–1912). His watercolors of the Antarctic, painted under very difficult conditions, are very beautiful and are, as one might expect of a scientist, accurate in detail.

Althea Floridana.

Avis Tricolor.
The Painted Finch.

Below Mockingbird, *a painting by Mark Catesby.*
Facing page Spur-winged Goose, *a painting by the*
American artist Louis Agassiz Fuertes.

Cornus mas &c.

Turdus minor &c.
The Mock-bird.

-Lake T'sana-
April 4,
1927

So many excellent bird artists have emerged in recent years that any selection of names will seem arbitrary, but it would be a pity not to mention the work in England of such painters as Sir Peter Scott, Winifred Austen, and C. E. Talbot Kelly and wood-engravers such as C. F. Tunnicliffe. Similarly we must name George Miksch Sutton, Don Eckelberry, and Roger Tory Peterson among the outstanding wildlife artists in the United States. In Sweden, B. Liljefors is a fine painter of birds and mammals, and Paul Barruel in France has produced watercolors and illustrations for the *Iconographie des oiseaux de France*. O. Kleinschmidt of Germany has done impressive work and Robert Mainard of Switzerland makes striking woodcuts of insects as well as birds.

The photography of birds in both color and black and white has of course come into its own in the past forty years. Such photographers as Eliot Porter in the United States, Eric Hosking in England, John Warham in Australia, Emil Schulthess in Switzerland, Hans Dossenbach in Germany, Kojo Tanaka in Japan, Loke Wan Tho in Malaysia, and others in Africa and elsewhere have given us brilliant views of both familiar and rare birds. Their works have been reproduced in an ever-increasing number of magazines and books devoted to wildlife.

The advances in the filming of birds have been just as dramatic. Equipped with telescopic lenses and sound-recording apparatus, film-makers have been able to make close-ups of birds and at the same time record their songs. The results are films that show birds more intimately than most viewers are ever likely to see them in life. In the scientific study of birds, moreover, photography has become indispensable in recording what the eye cannot register.

Photography has not yet superseded the special charm of seeing birds through the eyes and sensitivities of a gifted artist-ornithologist, but there is no question that today the majority of people are more familiar with birds as portrayed by the camera than as depicted by art.

Facing page White Pelican, *a painting by the French-born American naturalist and painter John James Audubon (1785–1851).*
Below Red-winged Lory, *a painting by the English artist John Gould.*

10
Birds in
Literature

A writer is the child of his age although he may influence it to greater or lesser extent. The community to which he belongs and its past mold his outlook more subtly than he realizes. Thus ideas about birds in the written and pictorial records of early cultures are nearly always expressed in a religious or magical context.

Among the earliest records of how men regarded birds is a passage in the Sumerian Tilmun myth which describes a time before men and animals had attained their distinctive characteristics; that was a time, the myth relates, when the raven, a bird whose calls have widely been considered ominous, did not utter its croak, and the kite did not give its distinctive cry. This expresses the primitive belief that long ago living things were less differentiated; and there was no clear demarcation between gods and men.

The first great nature poem preserved from antiquity is the "Hymn to the Aten," attributed to the reforming ruler of Egypt in the fourteenth century B.C., Akhenaten. He believed that worship should not be offered to the sun as such but to the vital force which operates through it. So he introduced a new symbol, a disk with descending rays terminating in a number of human hands, representing the bestowal of blessings. Two brief excerpts will illustrate the character of this poem:

Above *Because of his beauty, Ganymede, shown here with a rooster, was carried off by a bird and made cupbearer of the gods. Greek vase (c. 470–460 B.C.).* Facing page *Egyptian hieroglyphics on a coffin lid at Saqqara, Egypt. Birds were common hieroglyphic symbols.*

> All cattle rest upon their pasturage,
> The trees and the plants flourish,
> The birds flutter in their marshes,
> Their wings uplifted in adoration to thee.
> All the sheep dance upon their feet,
> All winged things fly,
> They live when thou hast shone upon them.
>
> When the nestling in the egg chirps in the
>   shell,
> Thou givest him breath therein to preserve
>   him alive
> When thou hast brought him together
> To the point of bursting from the egg,
> He cometh forth from the egg,
> To chirp with all his might.
> He goeth upon his two feet
> When he hath come forth therefrom.

In Tutankhamen's tomb was found a model of a nest containing eggs and a nestling. No doubt it was symbolic of the new life in store for the buried monarch.

Centuries separate the composition of this poem from Psalm 104 of the Bible, but both testify to man's profound appreciation of the Creator and all His work:

Thou dost make springs break out in the gullies,
so that the water runs between the hills.
The wild beasts all drink from them,
the wild asses quench their thirst;
the birds of the air nest on their banks
and sing among the leaves.

The trees of the Lord are green and leafy,
the cedars of Lebanon which He planted;
the birds build their nests in them,
the stork makes her home in their tops.

With Aristotle (384–322 B.C.) we come to the beginnings of scientific biological writing. Not only are factual statements prominent in his *Natural History,* but he sometimes qualifies these when he lacks first-hand knowledge. Thus in his account of the cuckoo he cites different opinions on such questions as whether the young cuckoo takes the food of the other nestlings or kills them. In the eighteenth century, Edward Jenner, the pioneer of vaccination, described the procedure. Even to the scientifically minded naturalist the sight of the newly hatched cuckoo maneuvering the eggs of the foster parent into the hollow in its back and hoisting them overboard suggests a sinister automatism.

PASTORAL POETS AND BIRDS

The scientific approach represented by Aristotle was submerged in later centuries, but the aesthetic appreciation of nature expressed in our quotations from Egyptian and Hebrew verse reappeared in the pastoral poetry of Greece and later European literature. The origins of such poetry may be traced to ancient Middle Eastern ceremonies in which the fading beauty of the year was mourned in elegies on the death of some youth. We have traces of the accompanying myths in the Greek stories of Narcissus and Adonis. The deep human emotions of mourning and rejoicing assured a response for this kind of poetry throughout the centuries. Thus in the "Lament for Bion" by Moschus, Greek poet of about 150 B.C., the nightingales, swallows, and swans wail, but the frog keeps on singing since his song is not beautiful. Among those who contributed to this tradition of idealizing rustic life were Theocritus, Vergil, Petrarch, Boccaccio, Ronsard, Spenser, Milton, and Shelley.

Vergil (70–19 B.C.), the greatest of the Latin poets, who spent his boyhood in rural surroundings, introduced the sights and sounds of the countryside in a way which convinces us that he is writing from experience. His description (in the *Georgics*) of the nesting rock dove taking flight expresses in verse the actual clatter of the bird's wings. He notes the gulls enjoying their bath and the birds among bushes covered with wild berries. He knows the countryman's weather lore, such as the significance of swallows flying low over water and the heron flying high, and speaks of the owl calling at dusk. Although he is careful to state that birds act as they do not because "they have wisdom from on high" but stimulated by their own internal reactions, he also accepts current folklore, such as that a raven observed on one's left is an evil omen.

Pliny was a collector of traditional beliefs rather than a naturalist. He relied uncritically on Aristotle and other writers, though occasionally, as in his unexpected rhapsody on the nightingale's song, he strays from his books into the woods. His *Natural History* was influential for centuries.

During the period of more than a thousand years between Pliny and the great medieval Italian poet Dante, writers continued to allow respect for earlier author-

ities to inhibit their independent observation of nature and animal life. The naturalist today may deplore this cloistered attitude of mind, but without it much earlier learning might have been lost. During the first centuries of the Christian era and into the Middle Ages most scholars, occupied with religious matters, concentrated on things other than the lives of birds and beasts. But this does not mean that interest in nature and compassion for her creatures did not exist. Clement of Alexandria, in the second century, commented on how birds changed their plumage and song according to the season, and he knew that pigeons can be attracted to painted dummies but monkeys are not deceived by girls' dolls. He criticized the treatment of fowl—"crammed with food, fattened in darkness, and reared for death"—and he rebuked self-indulgent "ladies who doted on a parrot, peacock, monkey, or puppy" and used scented make-up "fit to stupefy their husbands."

Saint Basil of Caesarea was a fourth-century bishop and scholar who lived for a time in a hermitage some fifty miles from the Black Sea. His description of the scenery around him is one of the most appreciative in ancient prose literature. Of course he quoted earlier writers, but he included in his book a few of his own observations, such as how flocks of rose-colored pastors (starlings) suddenly appeared during a plague of locusts and devoured them. He also provided one of the earliest descriptions of what we now call "distraction display," the behavior of a parent bird that lures a predator from its nest by dragging itself away as if it had a broken wing. His rapturous description of nature ends with the words: "If things seen are so lovely, what must things unseen be?"

Imagery taken from bird life had a part in the conversion of England to Christianity. According to the Venerable Bede (A.D. 673–735), English historian and theologian, a discussion arose at the court of the pagan King Eadwine of Northumbria as to whether a hearing should be granted to Paulinus, a Christian missionary. A pagan priest expressed his disapproval. Then one of the great nobles arose and said:

> So, methinks is the life of man on earth, as if, while you and your nobles and thegns are feasting on a winter's night, with the fire blazing in the midst of your hall, and the rain and storm raging outside, a sparrow should fly into the hall by one door and fly out by another. For the moment that he is inside he is in warmth and shelter, and then again he goes out into the wintry weather and is seen no more. So, for a short space man's life is before our eyes, but of what is before or follows it, we know nothing. If then this new teacher can enlighten us as to these things, by all means let us hearken to it.

Others agreed and in due course the king and his kingdom accepted Christianity.

THE EUROPEAN TRADITION

It is commonly assumed that we owe to Greece and Rome our heritage of sensitivity to nature, but this neglects the important contribution of Celtic literature which developed apart from the classical tradition and was as a sparkling rivulet entering a placid river. The poetry of these writers is free of the echoes of earlier authors found in even so original a poet as Vergil. It is as if they had suddenly entered the earthly paradise and stood surprised at so much beauty. I remember the reaction of a small boy from city slums on his first outing to the seaside. He stood still for some time, gazing at the sea, and then said in an awed voice: "Is it never still?" So the Celtic poets seem to view nature with the freshness of such a child.

This sensitivity was an Irish characteristic from the earliest times of which we have poetic record. About the eighth or ninth century an unknown Irishman spied a bird singing from a willow twig, golden with pollen-laden blossoms, and jotted down: "The little bird has uttered a whistle from its bright yellow beak; the blackbird from the yellow-tufted bough sends forth his call over loch Loigh." Another unnamed poet of the tenth century wrote delightedly of life in his woodland hermitage:

> The songs of the bright-breasted ring-doves, a beloved movement, the carol of the thrush, pleasant and familiar above my house.
>
> Swarms of bees, beetles, soft music of the world, a gentle humming; wild geese, barnacle geese, shortly before All Hallows, music of the dark torrent.
>
> A nimble singer, the combative brown wren from the hazel bough. . . .
>
> Fair white birds come, cranes, seagulls, the sea sings to them, no mournful music; brown fowl out of the red heather. . . .

This joyous appreciation of nature persisted for centuries. A prose poem by a Welsh poet of the fourteenth century associated the loveliness of birds and bird song with love for his sweetheart:

> The paths of May will be green in the place of April, and the birds will celebrate for me their twittering service. There will come on the highest crest of the oak-trees the songs of young birds, and the cuckoo on the heights in every domain, and the warbling bird and the glad, long day, and white haze after the wind covering the midst of the valley, and bright sky in the gay afternoon, and lovely trees, and grey gossamer, and many birds in the woods, and green leaves on the tree branches; and there will be memories, Morfudd, my golden girl, and a manifold awakening of love.

Having acknowledged the Celtic contribution, we turn back to the continent and to a writer of the highest genius, Dante (1265–1321), steeped in tradition yet an innovator writing in Italian. His indebtedness to the Bible, Vergil, and other classical as well as Christian writers is apparent, endowing his *Divine Comedy* with amazing spaciousness. But his work is also notable for its references to nature. He was Florentine of the Florentines, thoroughly urbanized, but influenced by Vergil, and his references to the loveliness of birds, insects, and flowers glisten with the dew of the morning.

He was a devoted admirer of Saint Francis and like that simple, poor man who preached to the birds,

Facing page *Herring gull on a rock. An unknown Irish poet of the tenth century, reflecting a Celtic sensitivity to nature, wrote, "Fair white birds come, cranes, seagulls, the sea sings to them, no mournful music . . ."*
Below *Birds in a woodcut by a German artist, Jacob Meydenbach (1491).*

235

Dante drew attention to common, natural things by the wayside. In the midst of the majestic measures of his great poem, the *Divine Comedy,* loaded with classical learning and historical references, we come on vivid miniatures from nature: a bird in her nest at dawn taking flight to forage for her nestlings, jackdaws returning to their nests, and a flock of starlings expanding and contracting as the birds wheel in unison, at times a rounded throng, then streaming forth like an elongated cloud.

Dante, like so many later bird-lovers, appreciated the dawn chorus:

And quivering at its touch the branches swayed
All toward that quarter where the holy hill
With the first daylight stretches out its shade.

Yet ne'er swayed from the upright so, but still
The little birds the topmost boughs among
Spared not to practice their tiny skill;

Rather they welcomed with rejoicing song
The dawn-wind to the leaves, which constantly
To their sweet chant the burden bore along.

He is accurate in noting that around dawn birds tend to utter their territorial songs from a high point of vantage. Although Dante must have heard nightingales singing on countless occasions in Italy (for even now they sing close to man's buildings), he does not mention them except in the tragic myth of Procne who, after having her tongue cut out, was transformed into a swallow. It is his familiarity with this story that accounts for the sadness he reads into the swallow's morning twittering.

In the *Inferno* Dante describes the traitors consigned to hell as wedged in ice, "their teeth chattering like the sounds made by storks." He had obviously noticed that these birds, which nested on housetops in Florence, made a "klappering" noise by clashing their mandibles when they greeted one another.

In the *Paradiso* there is an insightful description of the lark's song, emphasizing not the actual utterance but the silence when the bird returns to the ground:

Like the small lark who wantons free in air,
First singing and then silent, as possessed
By the last sweetness that contenteth her.

Centuries later Izaak Walton in *The Compleat Angler* also remarked on this silence: "The lark, when she means to rejoice, to cheer herself and those that hear her, she then quits the earth, and sings as she ascends higher into the air; and having ended her heavenly employment, grows then sad and mute to think she must descend to the dull earth, which she would not touch but for necessity."

Apart from Petrarch (1304–1374), who managed to combine a love of wild places with a love of high society, there is in Italian literature little of the devotion to nature found in British writers. Nor is French literature notable in this respect.

Ronsard (1524–1585) refers to the skylark and nightingale singing love songs and pleads with the former, in spite of unfavorable folktales about it, to continue nesting in the furrows. Jean Antoine de Baïf (1532–1589) in his poem "Springtime" alludes to the shepherd's flageolet stimulating the nightingale to sing. This is not merely a poetic conceit; by whistling to a bird in full song it is easy to draw it into competition. The great seventeenth-century French writers Corneille, Molière, and Racine show a negligible interest in birds, but the famous seventeenth-century naturalist Buffon (1707–1788) devoted nine of the twenty-six volumes of his *Histoire naturelle* to them.

In spite of his "back to nature" ideas, Rousseau

(1712–1778) had little sympathy for birds, but his ideas may have influenced later writers, such as Lamartine, who introduces birds nostalgically into his verse, motivated by recollections of his childhood in the countryside.

Although Alfred de Vigny (1797–1863) hardly ever mentions a bird he manifests some feeling for nature.

Victor-Marie Hugo (1802–1885) introduces occasional references to birds.

Perhaps Alphonse Daudet (1840–1897) comes nearest to British countryside writers in his attitude to birds, introducing them appropriately in word-pictures of the landscape. Anatole France made use of birds satirically in his *Island of Penguins*. As one ornithologist well acquainted with French literature, Miss Winwood Reade, says, "The average French poet knew that a skylark and nightingale sing beautifully, and that swallows/swifts (*'hirondelles'*) nest around houses and church towers—and little else."

Geoffrey Chaucer (1340–1400), the greatest English writer before Shakespeare, took delight in being out of doors. From his references in *The Parlement of Foules* and elsewhere, we may safely infer that he was a falconer:

> There was the tiraunt with his fetheres donne
> And grey, I mene the goshauk, that doth pyne
> To bryddes for his outrageous ravyne.
> The gentyl faucoun, that with his feet distrayneth
> The kynges hand; the hardy sperhauk eke,
> The quayles too; the merlioun, that payneth
> Hymself ful ofte the larke for to seke.

In *Troilus and Criseyde,* he shows that he knew that the nightingale ordinarily sings tentatively but will burst out into full song if there is some disturbance in the bushes around it.

In general, Chaucer retains the moralistic attitude of the medieval *Physiologus* and the bestiaries, regarding animals as symbolizing human characteristics. Birds gave him pleasure, but he accepted the tradition that attributed various human frailties to them; thus the sparrow is lecherous, the lapwing deceitful, the cuckoo murderous, the cormorant gluttonous, and ravens, crows, and owls are ominous. His "Saint Valentine's Day" includes a list of birds, each mentioned with the characteristic conventionally attributed to it.

This mode of introducing birds into poetry originated in the "Bird Mass," in which various species were represented as taking part. The Welsh poet Dafydd ap Gwilym wrote the following lines in this tradition:

> The Chief Priest was the nightingale: the lark
> And thrush assisted him: and some small bird
> (I do not weet his name) acted as clerk.

Facing page *King vulture. Accepting the view of vultures as sinister, Milton characterized Satan as a vulture.*

Below *Heron, a detail from a late fifteenth century Franco-Flemish tapestry. With the coming of the Renaissance, both art and literature portrayed birds more realistically.*

Facing page *Robins. Shakespeare echoes ancient folklore when he writes of a robin covering an unburied body with moss.*
Below *Birds appeared as a detail in the work that heralded the dawn of the Renaissance, the bronze doors on the baptistery in Florence by Lorenzo Ghiberti (1378–1465).*

THE RENAISSANCE ATTITUDE

The Renaissance and England's Elizabethan Age inaugurated a change in man's attitude to life and nature. The known world had become much larger and the cloistered outlook was no longer adequate. Nevertheless, William Shakespeare (1564–1616) inherited and used some of the strange menagerie of creatures found in the books of his time. Friar Bartholomew's *Liber de proprietatibus rerum* (1485) was the standard authority during Shakespeare's youth and it influenced thought and literature for centuries in spite of being crammed with what we now regard as absurdities. From this or similar books Shakespeare borrowed such ideas as that a turtledove mourns a lost mate forever, the kingfisher faces into the wind even after it is killed and hung up, the ostrich eats iron, the cry of an owl is a warning of death, and parrots are noisy before rain. A good example of how effectively he used bird legend occurs in *Cymbeline* when, introducing the notion that a robin will cover the dead body of a man or woman with moss, he writes:

> The raddock would,
> With charitable bill (O, bill, sore shaming
> Those rich-left heirs that let their fathers lie
> Without a monument!), bring thee all this,
> Yea, and furr'd moss besides. When flow'rs are
>   none,
> To winter-ground thy corse.

Shakespeare did not believe all the ancient lore he introduced; he used much of it because it supplied him with vivid imagery. But some of his references to nature, and especially to plants and wild flowers, reflect the appreciative experiences of one who had spent his boyhood in lovely Stratford-on-Avon with its placid river and neighboring woods. His delight in birds as well as his interest in rural folklore appear in a song in *A Midsummer Night's Dream*:

> The ousel cock so black of hue,
>   With orange-tawny bill,
> The throstle with his note so true,
>   The wren with little quill—
>
> The finch, the sparrow, and the lark,
>   The plain-song cuckoo grey,
> Whose note full many a man doth mark,
>   And dares not answer nay.

So, too, in the famous song in *Cymbeline,* he mingles his joy in singing birds, a reference to Phoebus, the ancient god of the sun, and a countryman's name for marigolds:

> Hark, hark, the lark at heaven's gate sings,
>   And Phoebus 'gins arise,

His steeds to water at those springs
   On chalic'd flow'rs that lies;
And winking Mary-buds begin to ope
   their golden eyes;
With every thing that pretty is, my lady
   sweet, arise:
      Arise, arise!

The tradition of using birds symbolically was maintained by John Milton (1608–1674). In his verse they serve to illustrate human vices. His general lack of sympathy for animals is revealed in his imagery, much of which refers to snared creatures. The devil and types of people whom he disliked are given avian characteristics. Thus Satan is a vulture, bishops are ravens, and his critics are owls and cuckoos. Although his genius enabled him to write elegantly of a few birds, such as the nightingale, he was seldom able to forget his books when writing of birds. He knew his Dante and must have read the Italian poet's description of the lark's song with its emphasis on the silence after the bird's descent. He may have recalled that passage when, referring to the nightingale's song at eventide in *Paradise Lost,* he used the magical words: "Silence was pleased."

Milton's animal imagery echoes Saint Basil's, and thus he revived ideas more than a thousand years old. The church father had written, "Proud is the peacock, adorned, a lover of elegance is the peacock"; and in *Paradise Lost,* Milton uses almost the same words. He is also echoing Basil when he describes migrating cranes—a sight he himself had never seen:

   Part loosly wing the Region, part more wise
   In common, rang'd in figure wedge their way,
   Intelligent of seasons, and set forth
   Their Aierie Caravan high over Seas
   Flying, and over lands with mutual wing

   Easing their flight; so stears the prudent Crane
   Her annual voiage, born on Windes. . . .

Similarly, where Basil speaks of the female nightingale as "never ceasing to sing throughout the night," Milton follows suit with:

   Nor then the solemn Nightingale
   Ceas'd warbling, but all night tun'd her layers.

Milton continued to revive such fantastic lore even after his contemporaries John Ray and Francis Willughby had written scientifically about birds. The foundation of the Royal Society (ten years before Milton died) may be regarded as a milestone after which it was hardly excusable for a serious writer to make use of zoological old wives' tales.

ADVENT OF THE SCIENTIFIC ATTITUDE

As we have noted, early writers referring to birds and their behavior relied almost entirely on ancient sources and traditions. In the encyclopedic works which Isidore of Seville compiled in the seventh century, he relied on Aristotle for most of his zoology. He wrote of the sentinel crane's holding a stone in its claws so that if it dozed off, the falling stone would awaken it, and of how cuckoos on migration took rides on kites—at that time common birds of prey.

One of the first books to include firsthand observations of birds other than hawks was *The Art of Falconry,* by Emperor Frederick II (1194–1250). Ignoring the statements of earlier authorities, he wrote of the cuckoo:

The cuckoo does not build a nest but lays its eggs in the nests of other birds, such as blackbirds and others of this type. These foster-parents hatch the cuckoo's eggs and feed the young until they reach maturity. We have verified this fact from actual experience. A nest of the small bird known as *praeneus* [perhaps a hedge sparrow or pipit] was

once brought to us for inspection. In the nest were the young of this bird together with a diminutive creature of dreadful, misshapen aspect that offered no resemblance to any avian species. This featherless mite had an immense mouth and was covered with long, thick hair-like down over its whole head, obscuring its eyes and beak. That we might eventually establish the identity of this strange nestling we fed it carefully along with the other young birds; and, behold, on maturity, we saw that it was a young cuckoo.

Frederick also questioned other received beliefs, such as the notion that barnacle geese were generated from shellfish.

In 1544 in Cologne, William Turner, Dean of Wells, published his *Avium praecipuarum,* a book that the distinguished Cambridge ornithologist, Alfred Newton, described as "the first commentary . . . conceived in anything like the spirit which moves modern naturalists." Turner's account of the robbing of gannets' nests may have been based on firsthand observation. The bird, he says, "looks to its young with so much loving care that it will fight gallantly with lads that are let down in baskets by a rope to carry them away, not without danger of life. Nor must we fail to mention that a salve, most valuable for many a disease, is made by Scots from the fat of this goose, for it is wonderfully full of fat. . . ." He also declared that he had often seen marsh hawks attacking coots, and he wrote of kites that they dared to "snatch bread from children, fish from women, and handkerchiefs from off hedges and out of men's hands. They are accustomed to carry off caps from men's heads when they are building their nests." Shakespeare was echoing this when he says in *A Winter's Tale:* "When the kite builds, look to lesser linen." Now, unhappily, the

British kite population is reduced to a few pairs in Wales.

Turner was on good terms with the Swiss naturalist Konrad Gesner and the latter—in his work on birds, a section of his *Historia animalium* (1551–1558)—made use of Turner's observations on geese (both brent and barnacle), the nightjar, night heron, and pelican.

The next major work on this subject, the sixteen-volume *Historia naturalium* (1599–1603) by Ulysses Aldrovandus of Bologna, contained little that was new about birds, but he does provide a link with two English naturalists, John Ray (1628–1705) and Francis Willughby (1635–1672), who visited him in 1664 and saw his collections, including six volumes of bird pictures. Ray was lecturer in Greek and mathematics at Cambridge as well as an ornithologist. He and his friend Willughby made a "grand tour" of the Continent, noting many species new to them. After his friend's death at the early age of thirty-seven, Willughby completed the *Ornithologia,* which has been called "the first standard, illustrated textbook of the birds of the British Isles."

The greatest field naturalist of the eighteenth century, so far as influence is concerned, was an observant, retiring English clergyman, Gilbert White. The work for which he is famous is his *Natural History and Antiquities of Selborne,* which has had nearly 150 editions since it appeared in 1789. White's book is a record of his observations of birds and nature generally in the environs of Selborne, a Hampshire village that has changed little since his time. A discovery which particularly pleased White was his establishing that there were three species of what he calls "willow wren" —the willow wren, the wood wren, and the chiffchaff. He was musical—a flute player—and it was by listening to their songs that he distinguished the three

Facing page *A huge young cuckoo being fed by its much smaller "foster parent," a lesser whitethroat. Emperor Frederick II recorded such behavior in* The Art of Falconry (1248). *This book was an early example of the adoption of a scientific attitude in studying birds.*
Left *Robbing gannets' nests in the Orkney Islands, as shown in an eighteenth century engraving.*

species. This village parson's book is read today when the works of the zoologists of his day are forgotten. It is a landmark in the massive contribution to ornithology made by the English clergy—a tradition that has continued from Turner to the present day but, sadly, there are no successors in sight.

After White, who in his unpretentious way united the scientific and the literary, we return to the poets and other writers who have contributed to both our knowledge and appreciation of birds.

THE POETS' COMPASSION FOR BIRDS

Chaucer in "The Cage" declared that a caged bird would be twenty thousand times happier living in freedom in "a forest, that is nude and cold." And the Elizabethan playwright John Webster wrote: "We think caged birds sing when indeed they cry." Regardless of the accuracy of such sentiments—the opposite extreme of the poets who project into the birds' experience their own pleasure in listening to them—they remind us that whatever joy a caged bird may bring to its owner is at the cost of subjection to unnatural conditions. A Cambridge poet, Christopher Smart (1722–1771), rebuked a scholar who kept an eagle in the court of one of the colleges:

> The stream of love ne'er from his heart
> Flows out to act fair pity's part,
> But stinks and stagnates there.

Pope (1688–1744) is not generally associated with a love of birds, yet sympathy suffuses lines in "Windsor Forest" in which he refers to the victims of a wildfowler:

> Oft, as in airy rings they skim the heath,
> The clamorous lapwings feel the leaden death:
> Oft as the mounting larks their notes prepare,
> They fall, and leave their little lives in air.

And in his "Essay on Man" he questions an assumption of his time which still warps our thinking:

> Has God, thou fool! work'd solely for thy good,
> Thy joy, thy pastime, thy attire, thy food,
> Is it for thee the lark ascends and sings,
> Joy tunes his voice, joy elevates his wings?
> Is it for thee the linnet pours his throat,
> Loves of his own and raptures swell the note?
> Is thine alone the seed that strews the plain?
> The birds of heaven shall vindicate their grain.

The most forthright of poets in condemning cruelty to birds was Blake (1757–1827). A precursor of Romanticism, a movement which emphasized affinity with nature, Blake expostulated in "Auguries of Innocence":

> A robin redbreast in a cage
> Puts all heaven in a rage.
> A dove-house fill'd with doves and pigeons
> Shudders Hell thro' all its regions.
>
> Each outcry of the hunted hare
> A fibre from the brain does tear.
> A skylark wounded in the wing,
> A cherubim does cease to sing.
> The game-cock clipt and arm'd for fight
> Does the rising sun affright.

Blake's contemporary, Shelley (1792–1822), also sympathized with caged birds:

> Poor captive bird! who, from thy narrow cage,
> Pourest such music, that it might assuage
> The rugged hearts of those who prisoned thee,
> Were they not deaf to all sweet melody.

It is difficult to believe that up to the beginning of this century birds were blinded with a red-hot needle in the belief that their songfulness would thus be improved. Thomas Hardy, his mind suffused with the

tragedy of life but also with anthropomorphism, wrote poignantly in "The Blinded Bird":

> Who hath charity? this bird.
> Who suffereth long and is kind,
> Is not provoked, though blind
> And alive ensepulchred?
> Who hopeth, endureth all things?
> Who thinketh no evil, but sings?
> Who is divine? This bird.

In compassion for birds the poets indeed have a fine record.

The grand scenery in which William Wordsworth lived in the Lake District of northern England is reflected in his verse. Relating how he first became a poet, he said: "I date from it my consciousness of the infinite variety of natural appearances which had been unnoticed by the poets of any age or country . . . and I made a resolution to supply in some degree the deficiency." Like Ruskin and a number of other English writers he was something of a nature mystic. All his life he was a roamer in the countryside, walking, his friend De Quincey reckoned, about 180,000 miles in his lifetime. His contribution lay in his expression of the profound joy that intimacy with nature can bring. However, considering the number of interesting and beautiful birds in the wild region where he spent his life, his bird poetry is rather meager and sometimes his observation is at fault. In "The Green Linnet" (greenfinch) he overpraises the bird's song and plumage and calls it solitary, whereas it is social. For Wordsworth "the least motion which [birds] made . . . seemed a thrill of pleasure."

The nature poet John Clare's criticism of Keats was that as a city man "he often described nature as she appeared to his fancies." But as a work of beauty Keats's "Ode to a Nightingale" is unsurpassed in English poetry. It was inspired by an experience in which he sat under a plum tree and spent hours listening to the nightingale's song in the garden of his biographer, C. A. Brown. What it describes is not the bird's song—which is indescribable—but the visions aroused by the song:

> Thou wast not born for death, immortal Bird!
>   No hungry generations tread thee down;
> The voice I hear this passing night was heard
>   In ancient days by emperor and clown:
> Perhaps the self-same song that found a path
>   Through the sad heart of Ruth, when, sick for home,
> She stood in tears amid the alien corn;
>   The same that oft-times hath
> Charm'd magic casements, opening on the foam
>   Of perilous seas, in faery lands forlorn.

Facing page and below *Details from* Don Manuel Osorio de Zuniga *by the Spanish painter Francisco de Goya, showing a sympathetic response to a caged bird similar to that found in the poetry of Chaucer, Blake, and Shelley.*

Facing page *Swans taking flight, just such a scene as that described in "Wild Swans at Coole," a poem by William Butler Yeats.*

Like Keats, Shelley was not interested in birds from an ornithological point of view. He would not have been much concerned by the charge that he displayed ornithological ignorance in his "Kingfishers" when he wrote:

I cannot tell my joy, when o'er a lake
Upon a drooping bough with nightshade twined,
I saw two azure halcyons clinging downward
And thinning one bright bunch of amber berries,
With quick long beaks, and in the deep there lay
Those lovely forms imaged as in a sky.

Kingfishers do not "cling downward" on boughs twined with nightshade, nor do they feed on berries. But Shelley was describing an ideal world. That he was exercising poetic license is apparent in his choice of birds—esoteric halcyons rather than actual kingfishers.

In his "To a Skylark" he proclaimed that his lark was not the bird of the scientist:

Hail to thee, blithe spirit!
Bird thou never wert,
That from Heaven, or near it,
Pourest thy full heart
In profuse strains of unpremeditated art.

It could be argued that the analytical attitude of the present day renders it difficult for many of us ever to experience the joy that a wholehearted emotional response to nature makes possible.

It is not surprising, though worth pointing out, that most poets writing about birds have concentrated on songbirds, and even when they refer to other species, such as the raven, the birds' utterances have received prominence, as in Edgar Allan Poe's "The Raven" with its premonitions of evil. Not until this century, with the realization that most bird song is territorial, was it understood that birds' songs are defensive rather than amatory—although, as we have already noted, a number of species utter courtship songs. Coleridge objected to poets' reading their own sad sentiments into the nightingale's song, but he himself answered a child's query thus:

Do you ask what the birds say? The sparrow, the dove,
The linnet and thrush say, "I love and I love!"

Coleridge immortalized another bird, the albatross, in his famous poem *The Rime of the Ancient Mariner*.

Burns (1759–1796) said that he responded to the call of a curlew and the cries of a flock of plover with "an elevation of soul like the enthusiasm of devotion or poetry."

Tennyson (1809–1892) mentions as many as sixty birds, and some of his lines about them are memorable, such as, "The music of the moon sleeps in the plain eggs of the nightingale," and, in "The Eagle":

He clasps the crag with crooked hands;
Close to the sun in lonely lands,
Ring'd with the azure world he stands.
The wrinkled sea beneath him crawls;
He watches from his mountain walls,
And like a thunderbolt he falls.

Imitating the repetitive notes of the song thrush, he wrote:

Summer is coming, summer is coming,
I know it, I know it, I know it,
Light again, leaf again, love again,
Yes, my wild poet.

Browning (1812–1889) also noted this reiteration:

That's the wise thrush, he sings each song twice over,
Lest you should think he never could recapture
The first fine careless rapture!

His remarks on the song of "the merry nightingale" were that "he crowds and hurries," and "precipitates with fast thick warble his delicious notes." It was long a convention, derived from Greek mythology, that the female nightingale sings mournfully; here, at least, the male bird receives his due.

To do justice to more recent poets who mention birds would require more space than is available here. However, to withhold reference to W. B. Yeats would be to omit a singer who caught the spirit of the Irish countryside in a way reminiscent of the earlier poets who wrote in Gaelic. Among his most memorable lines are these from "The Lake Isle of Innisfree":

> There midnight's all a-glimmer, and noon a purple
>   glow,
> And evening full of the linnet's wings.

In "The Wild Swans at Coole" he wrote:

> I have looked upon these brilliant creatures,
> And now my heart is sore.
> All's changed since I, hearing at twilight,
> The first time on this shore,
> The bell-beat of their wings above my head,
> Trod with a lighter tread.

Among American poets, Longfellow in "Hiawatha" harked back to ancient folklore, depicting Keneu, "the great war-eagle," attacking "the Kenabeek, the great serpents." In "The Birds of Killingworth" he described the terrible visitation of caterpillars which followed the heedless destruction of the region's birds:

> Think of your woods and orchards without birds!
> Of empty nests, that cling to boughs and beams
> As in an idiot's brain remembered words
> Hang empty 'mid the cobwebs of his dreams!

He goes on to tell how numbers of songbirds were reintroduced to the area:

> From all the country round these birds were brought,
> By order of the town, with anxious quest,
> And, loosened from their wicker prisons sought
> In woods and fields the places they loved best.

When Longfellow retired from the Smith Professorship of Modern Languages at Harvard, he was succeeded by James Russell Lowell (1819–1891), a man of many parts and a bird-lover. Such a poem as his "Indian Summer Reverie" contains numerous references to birds. The oriole was a favorite of his and he mentions it in "The Nest" and in "Auf Wiedersehen," and in "Under the Willows" he writes:

>   Hush! 'tis he!
> My oriole, my glance of summer fire,
> Is come at last, and, ever on the watch,
> Twitches the pack-thread I had lightly wound
> About the bough to help his housekeeping—
> Twitches and scouts by turns, blessing his luck,
> Yet fearing me who laid it in his way,
> Nor, more than wiser we in our affairs,
> Divines the providence that hides and helps.
> *Heave ho! heave ho!* he whistles as the twine
> Slackens its hold; *once more now,* and a flash
> Lightens across the sunlight to the elm,
> Where his mate dangles at her cup of felt.

Walt Whitman (1819–1892), almost exactly Lowell's contemporary, in his very fine "Out of the Cradle Endlessly Rocking" mingles exultation and pathos as mirrored in the life of man and bird. In "The Dalliance of the Eagles" he vividly captures an aerial encounter:

> The rushing amorous contact high in space together
> The clinching interlocking claws, a living, fierce,
>   gyrating wheel,
> Four beating wings, two beaks, a swirling mass tight
>   grappling,
> In tumbling turning clustering loops, straight down-
>   ward falling.

Facing page *Nesting albatross in New Zealand. This large bird was immortalized as a symbol of guilt by Samuel Coleridge in "The Rime of the Ancient Mariner," and it is still constantly referred to in this sense.*

Below *The quaint appearance of the puffin has made it the subject of several well-known children's poems.*

Robert Frost in our century has written some effective and touching bird poems, such as "On a Bird Singing in Its Sleep."

Although Thoreau (1817–1862) was not an ornithologist, he has a secure place in American literary history as one of those who identified themselves with nature. There seem to be all gradations between almost overwhelming mystical experiences in the presence of nature, such as the American psychologist William James described, and rapt appreciation of the wonders of the natural world, which comes in some degree to many folk. Thoreau belonged to a time when the American wilderness had immense attractions for the naturalist-recluse type. In his hut in the woods at Walden Pond, among birds which came at his call, he cultivated his thoughts much as Eastern sadhus are said to do. John Burroughs, who wrote at the end of the nineteenth century, was more of a naturalist than a philosopher and did much to alert his countrymen to the attractions of wildlife. A society named after him awards its medal annually to outstanding writers on natural history. His *Fresh Fields,* describing his reactions to the English countryside, is of interest to naturalists on both sides of the Atlantic.

One of the finest writers in English on nature was W. H. Hudson (1841–1922). He was brought up in the Argentine but took root in England and portrayed its natural beauties with a delicate pen and in so natural a way that Joseph Conrad said: "He writes as the grass grows." Although an essayist rather than an ornithologist, he had an appreciative ear for bird song. From the scientific point of view, the most influential of the nineteenth-century English literary writers on ornithology was the naturalist Edmund Selous (1858–1933), who has only recently come into his own. He set an example by painstakingly watching, noting, and describing details of bird behavior, and was a pioneer of the now fully established science of ethology. Like Thoreau and Hudson, he was a "loner." To some extent so was Eliot Howard, whose book *Territory in Bird Life* (1920) marked an epoch in the scientific observation of birds.

Nowadays poets, perhaps fearful of being charged with sentimentality, or too timid to tread where science reigns, are wary of writing verse in which birds are mentioned more than incidentally. The "countryside essay" kind of bird book has given place to more purely ornithological writing. But the spread of enlightened interest in birds and the eagerness of city-dwellers to escape whenever possible to field and forest, mountain and seacoast, guarantee that poet and scientist alike will continue to share their experiences with those who find in nature their solace and their joy.

Appendix:
A Selection of
Great Writings
About Birds

Alexander von Humboldt   *Cavern of the Guacharo*

Alexander Wilson   *The Ivory-Billed Woodpecker*

John James Audubon   *Slaughter of the Passenger Pigeons*

Charles Darwin   *On the Galapagos*

Henry David Thoreau   *The Loons*

Henry Walter Bates   *Taming a Parrot*

Charles Kingsley   *The Fens*

John Muir   *The Water-Ouzel*

Louis Agassiz Fuertes   *Trogons and Motmots*

W.H. Hudson   *Jackdaws*

William Beebe   *A Hoatzin Chick Meets a Challenge*

Gustav Eckstein   *The Canaries' Singing Lesson*

Marjorie Kinnan Rawlings   *The Dance of the Cranes*

Aldo Leopold   *Geese and the Unity of Nations*

Paul A. Zahl   *Flamingo Hunt in the West Indies*

Konrad Z. Lorenz   *Foster Mother to Mallard Ducklings*

Sigurd F. Olson   *Wild Geese*

CAVERN OF THE GUACHARO
by Alexander von Humboldt

Berlin-born Baron Alexander von Humboldt (1769–1859) was undoubtedly the most versatile of the eminent men of his time. He began as a diplomat but his greatest fame came from his work as an explorer-scientist, mainly in South America and Central Asia. The passage below comes from his monumental Travels in the Equinoctial Regions of the New World, *first published in France in 1807. In the page preceding this excerpt, Humboldt describes the jungle around the cavern in which the guacharos nest and, as seen by the light of torches, the awesome interior of the cave itself and the throng of birds in it.*

The guacharo is of the size of our fowls. It has the mouth of the goatsuckers and procnias, and a port like those vultures whose crooked beaks are surrounded with stiff silky hairs. . . . It forms a new genus, very different from the goatsucker, in the loudness of its voice, in the vast strength of its beak (containing a double tooth), and in feet without the membranes which join the anterior phalanges of the claws. It is the first example of a nocturnal bird among the *Passeres dentirostrati*. Its habits present analogies both with those of the goatsuckers and the alpine crow. The plumage of the guacharo is of a dark bluish grey mixed with small streaks and specks of black. Large white spots in the form of a heart, and bordered with black, mark the head, wings, and tail. The eyes of the bird, which are dazzled by the light of day, are blue, and smaller than those of the goatsucker.

The guacharo quits the cavern at nightfall, especially when the moon shines. It is almost the only fruit-eating nocturnal bird yet known; the conformation of its feet sufficiently shows that it does not hunt like our owls. It feeds on very hard fruits, like the nutcracker and the pyrrhocorax. . . . It would be difficult to form an idea of the horrible noise occasioned by thousands of these birds in the dark part of the cavern. Their shrill and piercing cries strike the vaults of the rocks, and are repeated by the subterranean echoes. The Indians showed us the nests of the guacharos by fixing a torch to the end of a long pole. These nests were fifty or sixty feet above our heads, in holes in the shape of funnels, with which the roof of the grotto is pierced like a sieve. The noise increased as we advanced, and the birds were scared by the light of the torches of copal. . . .

The Indians enter the Cueva del Guacharo once a year, near midsummer. They go armed with poles, with which they destroy the greater part of the nests. At that season several thousand birds are killed; and the old ones, as if to defend their brood, hover over the heads of the Indians, uttering terrible cries. The young, which fall to the ground, are opened on the spot. Their peritoneum is found loaded with fat, and a layer of fat reaches from the abdomen to the anus, forming a kind of cushion between the legs of the bird. This quantity of fat in frugivorous animals, not exposed to the light and exerting very little muscular motion, reminds us of what has been observed in the fattening of geese and oxen. It is well known how greatly darkness and repose favour this process. The nocturnal birds of Europe are lean, because, instead of feeding on fruits, like the guacharo, they live on the scanty produce of their prey. At the period called the oil harvest, the Indians build huts with palm leaves, near the entrance, and even in the porch of the cavern. There, with a fire of brushwood, they melt in pots of clay the fat of the young birds just killed. This fat is known by the name of butter or oil (*manteca,* or *aceite*) of the guacharo. It is half liquid, transparent, without smell and so pure that it may be kept above a year without becoming rancid. At the convent of Caripe no other oil is used in the kitchen of the monks; and we never observed that it gave the food a disagreeable taste or smell.

The race of the guacharos would have been long ago extinct had not several circumstances contributed to its preservation. The natives, restrained by their superstitious ideas, seldom have the courage to penetrate far into the grotto. It also appears that birds of the same species dwell in neighbouring caverns which are too narrow to be accessible to man. Perhaps the great cavern is repeopled by colonies which forsake the small grottoes; for the missionaries assured us that hitherto no sensible diminution of the birds has been observed.

THE IVORY-BILLED WOODPECKER
by Alexander Wilson

Alexander Wilson (1766–1813) was born in Glasgow and worked in the mills there until he decided in 1794 (as Audubon did a few years later) to come to America. In the States he became a teacher but, loving nature, he began to study and draw birds, and was soon an excellent ornithologist and bird artist. His American Ornithology, *from which our selection comes, began to appear in 1808 but was still not finished when he died.*

This majestic and formidable species, in strength and magnitude, stands at the head of the whole class of woodpeckers hitherto discovered. He may be called the king or chief of his tribe; and nature seems to have designed him a distinguished characteristic in the superb carmine crest and bill of polished ivory with which she has ornamented him. His eye is brilliant and daring; and his whole frame so admirably adapted for his mode of life, and method of procuring subsistence, as to impress on the mind of the examiner the most reverential ideas of the Creator. His manners have also a dignity in them superior to the common herd of woodpeckers. Trees, shrubbery, orchards, rails, fence posts, and old prostrate logs, are alike interesting to those, in their humble and indefatigable search for prey; but the royal hunter now before us, scorns the humility of such situations, and seeks the most towering trees of the forest; seeming particularly attached to those prodigious cypress swamps, whose crowded giant sons stretch their bare and blasted or moss-hung arms mid-way to the skies. In these almost inaccessible recesses, amid ruinous piles of impending timber, his trumpet-like note and loud strokes resound through the solitary savage wilds, of which he seems the sole lord and inhabitant. Wherever he frequents he leaves numerous monuments of his industry behind him. We there see enormous pine trees with cartloads of bark lying around their roots, and chips of the trunk itself in such quantities as to suggest the idea that half a dozen of axe-men had been at work there for the whole morning. The body of the tree is also disfigured with such numerous and so large excavations, that one can hardly conceive it possible for the whole to be the work of a woodpecker. With such strength, and an apparatus so powerful, what havoc might he not commit, if numerous, on the most useful of our forest trees! and yet with all these appearances, and much of vulgar prejudice against him, it may fairly be questioned whether he is at all injurious; or, at least, whether his exertions do not contribute most powerfully to the protection of our timber. Examine closely the tree where he has been at work, and you will soon perceive, that it is neither from motives of mischief nor amusement that he slices off the bark, or digs his way into the trunk.—For the sound and healthy tree is the least object of his attention. The diseased, infested with insects, and hastening to putrefaction, are *his* favourites; there the deadly crawling enemy have formed a lodgement between the bark and tender wood, to drink up the very vital part of the tree. It is the ravages of these vermin which the intelligent proprietor of the forest deplores, as the sole perpetrators of the destruction of his timber. Would it be believed that the larvae of an insect, or fly, no larger than a grain of rice, should silently, and in one season, destroy some twenty thousand acres of pine trees, many of them from two to three feet in diameter, and a hundred and fifty feet high! Yet whoever passes along the high road from Georgetown to Charleston, in South Carolina, about twenty miles from the former place, can have striking and melancholy proofs of this fact.

The first place I observed this bird at, when on my way to the south, was about twelve miles north of Wilmington in North Carolina. Having wounded it slightly in the wing, on being caught, it uttered a loudly reiterated, and most piteous note, exactly resembling the violent crying of a young child; which terrified my horse so, as nearly to have cost me my life. It was distressing to hear it. I carried it with me in the chair, under cover, to Wilmington. In passing through the streets, its affecting cries surprised every one within hearing, particularly the females, who hurried to the doors and windows with looks of alarm and anxiety. I drove on, and, on arriving at the piazza of the hotel, where I intended to put up, the landlord came forward, and a number of other persons who happened to be there, all equally alarmed at what they heard; this was greatly increased by my asking, whether he could furnish me with accommodations for myself and my baby. The man looked blank and foolish, while the others stared with still greater astonishment. After diverting myself for a minute or two at their expense, I drew my woodpecker from under the cover, and a general laugh took place. I took him up stairs and locked him up in my room, while I went to see my horse taken care of. In less than an hour I returned, and, on opening the door, he set up the same distressing shout, which now appeared to proceed from grief that he had been discovered in his attempts at escape. He had mounted along the side of the window, nearly as high as the ceiling, a little below which he had begun to break through. The bed was covered with large pieces of plaster, the lath was exposed for at least fifteen inches square, and a hole, large enough to admit the fist, opened to the weather-boards; so that in less than another hour he would certainly have succeeded in making his way through. I now tied a string round his leg, and, fastening it to the table, again left him. I wished to preserve his life, and had gone off in search of suitable food for him. As I reascended the stairs, I heard him again hard at work, and on entering had the mortification to perceive that he had almost entirely ruined the mahogany table to which he was fastened, and on which he had wreaked his whole vengeance. While engaged in taking a drawing, he cut me severely in several places, and, on the whole, displayed such a noble and unconquerable spirit, that I was frequently tempted to restore him to his native woods. He lived with me nearly three days, but refused all sustenance, and I witnessed his death with regret.

SLAUGHTER OF THE PASSENGER PIGEONS
by John James Audubon

Born in Haiti and educated in Paris, Audubon (1785–1851) came to America in 1805. He tried being a storekeeper, then turned to tramping the wilderness areas, painting birds as he went. His work is among the most magnificent bird painting ever done. He also wrote vividly about his experiences, as in this famous passage from The Birds of North America *(1839).*

The multitudes of Wild Pigeons in our woods are astonishing. Indeed, after having viewed them so often, and under so many circumstances, I even now feel inclined to pause, and assure myself that what I am going to relate is fact. Yet I have seen it all, and that too in the company of persons who, like myself, were struck with amazement.

In the autumn of 1813, I left my house at Henderson, on the banks of the Ohio, on my way to Louisville. In passing over the Barrens a few miles beyond Hardensburgh, I observed the Pigeons flying from northeast to southwest, in greater numbers than I thought I had ever seen them before, and feeling an inclination to count the flocks that might pass within the reach of my eye in one hour, I dismounted, seated myself on an eminence, and began to mark with my pencil, making a dot for every flock that passed. In a short time finding the task which I had undertaken impracticable, as the birds poured in in countless multitudes, I rose, and counting the dots then put down, found that 163 had been made in twenty-one minutes. I travelled on, and still met more the farther I proceeded. The air was literally filled with Pigeons; the light of noon-day was obscured as by an eclipse; the dung fell in spots, not unlike melting flakes of snow; and the continued buzz of wings had a tendency to lull my senses to repose.

Whilst waiting for dinner at Young's inn at the confluence of Salt river with the Ohio, I saw, at my leisure, immense legions still going by, with a front reaching far beyond the Ohio on the west, and the beech-wood forests directly on the east of me. Not a single bird alighted; for not a nut or acorn was that year to be seen in the neighbourhood. They consequently flew so high, that different trials to reach them with a capital rifle proved ineffectual; nor did the reports disturb them in the least. I cannot describe to you the extreme beauty of their aerial evolutions, when a Hawk chanced to press upon the rear of a flock. At once, like a torrent, and with a noise like thunder, they rushed into a compact mass, pressing upon each other towards the centre. In these almost solid masses, they darted forward in undulating and angular lines, descended and swept close over the earth with inconceivable velocity, mounted perpendicularly so as to resemble a vast column, and, when high, were seen wheeling and twisting within their continued lines, which then resembled the coils of a gigantic serpent.

Before sunset I reached Louisville, distant from Hardensburgh fifty-five miles. The Pigeons were still passing in undiminished numbers, and continued to do so for three days in succession. The people were all in arms. The banks of the Ohio were crowded with men and boys, incessantly shooting at the pilgrims, which there flew lower as they passed the river. Multitudes were thus destroyed. For a week or more, the population fed on no other flesh than that of Pigeons, and talked of nothing but Pigeons.

It is extremely interesting to see flock after flock performing exactly the same evolutions which had been traced as it were in the air by a preceding flock. Thus, should a Hawk have charged on a group at a certain spot, the angles, curves, and undulations that have been described by the birds, in their efforts to escape from the dreaded talons of the plunderer, are undeviatingly followed by the next group that comes up. Should the bystander happen to witness one of these affrays, and, struck with the rapidity and elegance of the motions exhibited, feel desirous of seeing them repeated, his wishes will be gratified if he only remains in the place until the next group comes up.

As soon as the Pigeons discover a sufficiency of food to entice them to alight, they fly around in circles, reviewing the country below. During their evolutions, on such occasions, the dense mass which they form exhibits a beautiful appearance, as it changes its direction, now displaying a glistening sheet of azure, when the backs of the birds come simultaneously into view, and anon, suddenly presenting a mass of rich deep purple. They then pass lower, over the woods, and for a moment are lost among the foliage, but again emerge, and are seen gliding aloft. They now alight, but the next moment, as if suddenly alarmed, they take to wing, producing by the flappings of their wings a noise like the roar of distant thunder, and sweep through the forests to see if danger is near. Hunger, however, soon brings them to the ground. When alighted, they are seen industriously throwing up the withered leaves in quest of the fallen mast. The rear ranks are continually rising, passing over the main-body, and alighted in front, in such rapid succession, that the whole flock seems still on wing. The quantity of ground thus swept is astonishing, and so completely has it been cleared, that the gleaner who might follow in their rear would find his labour completely lost. Whilst feeding, their avidity is at times so great that in attempting to swallow a large acorn or nut, they are seen gasping for a long while, as if in the agonies of suffocation.

On such occasions, when the woods are filled with these Pigeons, they are killed in immense numbers, although no apparent diminution ensues. About the middle of the day, after their repast is finished, they settle on the trees, to enjoy rest, and digest their food. On the ground they walk with ease, as well as on the branches, frequently jerking their beautiful tail, and moving the neck backwards and forwards in the most graceful manner. As the sun begins to sink beneath the horizon, they depart en masse for the roosting-place, which not unfrequently is hundreds of miles distant, as has been ascertained by persons who have kept an account of their arrivals and departures.

Let us now, kind reader, inspect their place of nightly rendezvous. One of these curious roosting-places, on the banks of the Green river in Kentucky, I repeatedly visited. It was, as is always the case, in a portion of the forest where the trees were of great magnitude, and where there was little underwood. I rode through it upwards of forty miles, and, crossing it in different parts, found its average breadth to be rather more than three miles. My first view of it was about a fortnight subsequent to the period when they had made choice of it, and I arrived there nearly two hours before sunset. Few Pigeons were then to be seen, but a great number of persons, with horses and wagons, guns and ammunition, had already established encampments on the borders. Two farmers from the vicinity of Russelsville, distant more than a hundred miles, had driven upwards of three hundred hogs to be fattened on the pigeons which were to be slaughtered. Here and there, the people employed in plucking and salting what had already been procured, were seen sitting in the midst of large piles of these birds. The dung lay several inches deep, covering the whole extent of the roosting-place. Many trees two feet in diameter, I observed, were broken off at no great distance from the ground; and the branches of many of the largest and tallest had given way, as if the forest had been swept by a tornado. Everything proved to me that the number of birds resorting to this part of the forest must be immense beyond conception. As the period of their arrival approached, their foes anxiously prepared to receive them. Some were furnished with iron-pots containing sulphur, others with torches of pine-knots, many with poles, and the rest with guns. The sun was lost to our view, yet not a Pigeon had arrived. Every thing was ready, and all eyes were gazing on the clear sky, which appeared in glimpses amidst the tall trees. Suddenly there burst forth a general cry of "Here they come!" The noise which they made, though yet distant, reminded me of a hard gale at sea, passing through the rigging of a close-reefed vessel. As the birds arrived and passed over me, I felt a current of air that surprised me. Thousands were soon knocked down by the pole-men. The birds continued to pour in. The fires were lighted, and a magnificent, as well as wonderful and almost terrifying, sight presented itself. The Pigeons, arriving by thousands, alighted everywhere, one above another, until solid masses were formed on the branches all round. Here and there the perches gave way under the weight with a crash, and, falling to the ground, destroyed hundreds of the birds beneath, forcing down the dense groups with which every stick was loaded. It was a scene of uproar and confusion. I found it quite useless to speak, or even to shout to those persons who were nearest to me. Even the reports of the guns were seldom heard, and I was made aware of the firing only by seeing the shooters reloading.

No one dared venture within the line of devastation. The hogs had been penned up in due time, the picking up of the dead and wounded being left for the next morning's employment. The Pigeons were constantly coming, and it was past midnight before I perceived a decrease in the number of those that arrived. The uproar continued the whole night; and as I was anxious to know to what distance the sound reached, I sent off a man, accustomed to perambulate the forest, who, returning two hours afterwards, informed me he had heard it distinctly when three miles distant from the spot. Towards the approach of day, the noise in some measure subsided; long before objects were distinguishable, the Pigeons began to move off in a direction quite different from that in which they had arrived the evening before, and at sunrise all that were able to fly had disappeared. The howlings of the wolves now reached our ears, and the foxes, lynxes, cougars, bears, raccoons, opossums and pole-cats were seen sneaking off, whilst eagles and hawks of different species, accompanied by a crowd of vultures, came to supplant them, and enjoy their share of the spoil.

It was then that the authors of all this devastation began their entry amongst the dead, and dying, and the mangled. The Pigeons were picked up and piled in heaps, until each had as many as he could possibly dispose of, when the hogs were let loose to feed on the remainder.

Persons unacquainted with these birds might naturally conclude that such dreadful havoc would soon put an end to the species. But I have satisfied myself, by long observation, that nothing but the gradual diminution of our forests can accomplish their decrease, as they not unfrequently quadruple their numbers yearly, and always at least double it. In 1805 I saw schooners loaded in bulk with Pigeons caught up the Hudson river, coming in to the wharf at New York, when the birds sold for a cent a piece. I knew a man in Pennsylvania, who caught and killed upwards of 500 dozens in a clap-net in one day, sweeping sometimes twenty dozens or more at a single haul. In the month of March 1830, they were so abundant in the markets of New York, that piles of them met the eye in every direction. I have seen the Negroes at the United States' Salines or Saltworks of Shawnee Town, wearied with killing Pigeons, as they alighted to drink the water issuing from the leading pipes, for weeks at a time; and yet in 1826, in Louisiana, I saw congregated flocks of these birds as numerous as ever I had seen them before, during a residence of nearly thirty years in the United States.

ON THE GALAPAGOS
by Charles Darwin

One of the giants of science, Darwin (1809–1882) based his historic theories of evolution and natural selection on his observations of animal life. Among the most important of his studies were those he made of birds on the Galapagos Islands, which he recorded in The Voyage of H.M.S. Beagle, 1831–36.

I will conclude my description of the natural history of these islands by giving an account of the extreme tameness of the birds.

This disposition is common to all the terrestrial species —namely, to the mocking-thrushes, the finches, wrens, tyrant flycatchers, the dove, and carrion-buzzard. All of them often approached sufficiently near to be killed with a switch, and sometimes, as I myself tried, with a cap or hat. A gun is here almost superfluous, for with the muzzle I pushed a hawk off the branch of a tree. One day, whilst lying down, a mocking-thrush alighted on the edge of a pitcher made of the shell of a tortoise, which I held in my hand, and began very quietly to sip the water. It allowed me to lift it from the ground whilst seated on the vessel. I often tried, and very nearly succeeded, in catching these birds by their legs. Formerly the birds appear to have been even tamer than at present. Cowley (in the year 1684) says that the "turtle-doves were so tame that they would often alight upon our hats and arms, so that we could take them alive; they not fearing man, until such time as some of our company did fire at them, whereby they were rendered more shy." Dampier also, in the same year, says that a man in a morning's walk might kill six or seven dozen of these doves. At present, although certainly very tame, they do not alight on people's

arms, nor do they suffer themselves to be killed in such large numbers. It is surprising that they have not become wilder; for these islands during the last hundred and fifty years have been frequently visited by buccaneers and whalers, and the sailors, wandering through the woods in search of tortoises, always take cruel delight in knocking down the little birds.

These birds, although now still more persecuted, do not readily become wild. In Charles Island, which had then been colonized about six years, I saw a boy sitting by a well with a switch in his hand, with which he killed the doves and finches as they came to drink. He had already procured a little heap of them for his dinner; and he said that he had constantly been in the habit of waiting by this well for the same purpose. It would appear that the birds of this archipelago, not having as yet learned that man is a more dangerous animal than the tortoise or the amblyrhynchus, disregard him, in the same manner as in England shy birds, such as magpies, disregard the cows and horses grazing in our fields.

THE LOONS
by Henry David Thoreau

Although not a professional naturalist and most famous for a highly personal book on the relationship of man and nature, Walden, *Thoreau (1817–1862) was a masterly reporter of nature's ways, as he demonstrates in this excerpt from his* Journal.

1845–47 (no exact date). The loon comes in the fall to sail and bathe in the pond, making the woods ring with its wild laughter in the early morning, at rumor of whose arrival all Concord sportsmen are on the alert, in gigs, on foot, two by two, three by three, with patent rifles, patches, conical balls, spy-glass or open hole over the barrel. They seem already to hear the loon laugh; come rustling through the woods like October leaves, these on this side, those on that, for the poor loon cannot be omnipresent; if he dive here, must come up somewhere. The October wind rises, rustling the leaves, ruffling the pond water, so that no loon can be seen rippling the surface. Our sportsmen scour, sweep the pond with spy-glass in vain, making the woods ring with rude[?] charges of powder, for the loon went off in that morning rain with one loud, long, hearty laugh, and our sportsmen must beat a retreat to town and stable and daily routine, shop work, unfinished jobs again.

Or in the gray dawn the sleeper hears the long ducking gun explode over toward Goose Pond, and, hastening to the door, sees the remnant of a flock, black duck or teal, go whistling by with outstretched neck, with broken ranks, but in ranger order. And the silent hunter emerges into the carriage road with ruffled feathers at his belt, from the dark pond-side where he has lain in his bower since the stars went out.

And for a week you hear the circling clamor, clangor, of some solitary goose through the fog, seeking its mate, peopling the woods with a larger life than they can hold.

For hours in fall days you shall watch the ducks cunningly tack and veer and hold the middle of the pond, far from the sportsmen on the shore,—tricks they have learned and practiced in far Canada lakes or in Louisiana bayous.

The waves rise and dash, taking sides with all waterfowl.

Oct. 8, 1852. P.M.—Walden. As I was paddling along the north shore, after having looked in vain over the pond for a loon, suddenly a loon, sailing toward the middle, a few rods in front, set up his wild laugh, and betrayed himself. I pursued with a paddle and he dived, but when he came up I was nearer than before. He dived again, but I miscalculated the direction he would take, and we were fifty rods apart when he came up, and again he laughed long and loud. He managed very cunningly, and I could not get within half a dozen rods of him. Sometimes he would come up unexpectedly on the opposite side of me, as if he had passed directly under the boat. So long-winded was he, so unweariable, that he would immediately plunge again, and then no wit could divine where in the deep pond, beneath the smooth surface, he might be speeding his way like a fish. He had time and ability to visit the bottom of the pond in its deepest part. It was as well for me to rest on my oars and await his reappearing as to endeavor to calculate where he would come up. When I was straining my eyes over the surface, I would suddenly be startled by his unearthly laugh behind me. It was commonly a demoniac laughter, yet somewhat like a water-bird, but occasionally, when he had balked me most successfully and come up a long way off, he uttered a long-drawn unearthly howl, probably more like a wolf than any other bird. This was his looning. As when a beast puts his muzzle to the ground and deliberately howls; perhaps the wildest sound I ever heard, making the woods ring; and I concluded that he laughed in derision of my efforts, confident of his own resources. Though the sky was overcast, the pond was so smooth that I could see where he broke the surface if I did not hear him. His white breast, the stillness of the air, the smoothness of the water, were all against him. At length, having come up fifty rods off, he uttered one of those prolonged unearthly howls, as

if calling on the god of loons to aid him, and immediately there came a wind from the east and rippled the surface, and filled the whole air with misty rain. I was impressed as if it were the prayer of the loon and his god was angry with me. How surprised must be the fishes to see this ungainly visitant from another sphere speeding his way amid their schools!

TAMING A PARROT
by Henry Walter Bates

In 1848, Bates (1825–1892) joined another young naturalist, Alfred Russel Wallace, on a specimen-collecting expedition to South America. Bates stayed eleven years, collected 8000 insects and established his reputation as a scientist and explorer. Here is one of the experiences he recorded in his delightful book, The Naturalist on the River Amazon (1863).

On recrossing the river to Aveyros in the evening, a pretty little parrot fell from a great height headlong into the water near the boat, having dropped from a flock which seemed to be fighting in the air. One of the Indians secured it for me and I was surprised to find the bird uninjured. There had probably been a quarrel about mates, resulting in our little stranger being temporarily stunned by a blow on the head from the beak of a jealous comrade. The species was the *Conurus guianensis,* called by the natives Maracana; the plumage was green, with a patch of scarlet under the wings. I wished to keep the bird alive and tame it, but all our efforts to reconcile it to captivity were vain; it refused food, bit every one who went near it, and damaged its plumage in its exertions to free itself. My friends in Aveyros said that this kind of parrot never became domesticated. After trying nearly a week I was recommended to lend the intractable creature to an old Indian woman, living in the village, who was said to be a skillful bird-tamer.

In two days she brought it back almost as tame as the familiar love-birds of our aviaries. I kept my little pet for upwards of two years; it learned to talk pretty well and was considered quite a wonder as being a bird usually so difficult of domestication. I do not know what arts the old woman used: Captain Antonio said that she fed it with her saliva. The chief reason why almost all animals become so wonderfully tame in the houses of the natives is, I believe, their being treated with uniform gentleness and being allowed to run at large about the rooms. Our Maracana used to accompany us sometimes in our rambles, one of the lads carrying it on his head. One day, in the middle of a long forest road, it was missed, having clung probably to an overhanging bough and escaped into the thicket without the boy perceiving it. Three hours afterwards, on our return by the same path, a voice greeted us in a colloquial tone as we passed—"Maracana!" We looked about for some time, but could not see anything until the word was repeated with emphasis—"Maracana!" when we espied the little truant half concealed in the foliage of a tree. He came down and delivered himself up, evidently as much rejoiced at the meeting as we were.

THE FENS
by Charles Kingsley

Although best known as an author of historical novels, Kingsley (1819–1875) was also a clergyman, a professor of history, and an active Christian Socialist. One of his most beautiful essays, which appeared in his Prose Idylls (1873), *deals with the fen country in which he was brought up.*

A certain sadness is pardonable to one who watches the destruction of a grand natural phenomenon, even though its destruction bring blessings to the human race. Reason and conscience tell us, that it is right and good that the Great Fen should have become, instead of a waste and howling wilderness, a garden of the Lord, where

> All the land in flowery squares,
> Beneath a broad and equal-blowing wind,
> Smells of the coming summer.

And yet the fancy may linger, without blame, over the shining meres, the golden reed-beds, the countless water-fowl, the strange and gaudy insects, the wild nature, the mystery, the majesty—for mystery and majesty there were—which haunted the deep fens for many a hundred years. Little thinks the Scotsman, whirled down by the Great Northern Railway from Peterborough to Huntingdon, what a grand place, even twenty years ago, was that Holme and Whittlesea, which is now but a black, unsightly, steaming flat, from which the meres and reed-beds of the old world are gone, while the corn and roots of the new world have not as yet taken their place.

But grand enough it was, that black ugly place, when backed by Caistor Hanglands and Holme Wood, and the patches of the primæval forest; while dark-green alders, and pale-green reeds, stretched for miles round the broad lagoon, where the coot clanked, and the bittern boomed, and the sedge-bird, not content with its own sweet song, mocked the notes of all the birds around; while high overhead hung, motionless, hawk beyond hawk, buzzard beyond buzzard, kite beyond kite, as far as eye could see. Far off, upon the silver mere, would rise a puff of smoke from a punt, invisible from its flatness and its white paint. Then down the wind came the boom of the great stanchion-gun; and after that sound another sound, louder as it neared; a cry as of all the bells of Cambridge, and all the hounds of Cottesmore; and overhead rushed and whirled the skein of terrified wild-fowl, screaming, piping, clacking, croaking, filling the air with the hoarse rattle of their wings, while clear above all sounded the wild whistle of the curlew, and the trumpet note of the great wild swan.

They are all gone now. No longer do the ruffs trample the sedge into a hard floor in their fighting-rings, while the sober reeves stand round, admiring the tournament of their lovers, gay with ears and tippets, no two of them alike. Gone are ruffs and reeves, spoonbills, bitterns, avocets; the very snipe, one hears, disdains to breed.

THE WATER-OUZEL
by John Muir

Brought from Scotland to Wisconsin in 1849, Muir (1838–1914) fell in love with the wild world of nineteenth century America. After training as a geologist he began his extraordinary "walks" through the mountains of western America from California to Alaska. His enchanting essay on the ouzel comes from The Mountains of California (1894), *one of his many books.*

The waterfalls of the Sierra are frequented by only one bird—the Ouzel or Water Thrush (*Cinclus Mexicanus*). He is a singularly joyous and lovable little fellow, about the size of a robin, clad in a plain waterproof suit of bluish gray, with a tinge of chocolate on the head and shoulders. In form he is about as smoothly plump and compact as a pebble that has been whirled in a pot-hole, the flowing contour of his body being interrupted only by his strong feet and bill, the crisp wing-tips, and the up-slanted wren-like tail.

Among all the countless waterfalls I have met in the course of ten years' exploration in the Sierra, whether among the icy peaks, or warm foot-hills, or in the profound yosemitic cañons of the middle region, not one was found without its Ouzel. No cañon is too cold for this little bird, none too lonely, provided it be rich in falling water. Find a fall, or cascade, or rushing rapid, anywhere upon a clear stream, and there you will surely find its complementary Ouzel, flitting about in the spray, diving in foaming eddies, whirling like a leaf among beaten foam-bells; ever vigorous and enthusiastic, yet self-contained, and neither seeking nor shunning your company.

If disturbed while dipping about in the margin shallows, he either sets off with a rapid whir to some other feeding-ground up or down the stream, or alights on some half-submerged rock or snag out in the current, and immediately begins to nod and courtesy like a wren, turning his head from side to side with many other odd dainty movements that never fail to fix the attention of the observer.

He is the mountain streams' own darling, the hummingbird of blooming waters, loving rocky ripple-slopes and sheets of foam as a bee loves flowers, as a lark loves sunshine and meadows. Among all the mountain birds, none has cheered me so much in my lonely wanderings,—none so unfailingly. For both in winter and summer he sings, sweetly, cheerily, independent alike of sunshine and of love, requiring no other inspiration than the stream on which he dwells. While water sings, so must he, in heat or cold, calm or storm, ever attuning his voice in sure accord; low in the drought of summer and the drought of winter, but never silent.

What may be regarded as the separate songs of the Ouzel are exceedingly difficult of description, because they are so variable and at the same time so confluent. Though I have been acquainted with my favorite ten years, and during most of this time have heard him sing nearly every day, I still detect notes and strains that seem new to me. Nearly all of his music is sweet and tender, lapsing from his round breast like water over the smooth lip of a pool, then breaking farther on into a sparkling foam of melodious notes, which glow with subdued enthusiasm, yet without expressing much of the strong, gushing ecstasy of the bobolink or skylark.

The more striking strains are perfect arabesques of melody, composed of a few full, round, mellow notes, embroidered with delicate trills which fade and melt in long slender cadences. In a general way his music is that of the streams refined and spiritualized. The deep booming notes of the falls are in it, the trills of rapids, the gurgling of margin eddies, the low whispering of level reaches, and the sweet tinkle of separate drops oozing from the ends of mosses and falling into tranquil pools.

The Ouzel never sings in chorus with other birds, nor with his kind, but only with the streams. And like flowers that bloom beneath the surface of the ground, some of our favorite's best song-blossoms never rise above the surface of the heavier music of the water. I have often observed him singing in the midst of beaten spray, his music completely buried beneath the water's roar; yet I knew he was surely singing by his gestures and the movements of his bill.

His food, as far as I have noticed, consists of all kinds of water insects, which in summer are chiefly procured along shallow margins. Here he wades about ducking his head under water and deftly turning over pebbles and fallen leaves with his bill, seldom choosing to go into deep water where he has to use his wings in diving.

He seems to be especially fond of the larvæ of mosquitoes, found in abundance attached to the bottom of smooth rock channels where the current is shallow. When feeding in such places he wades up-stream, and often while his head is underwater the swift current is deflected upward along the glossy curves of his neck and shoulders, in the form of a clear, crystalline shell, which fairly incloses him like a bell-glass, the shell being broken and re-formed as he lifts and dips his head; while ever and anon he sidles out to where the too powerful current carries him off his feet; then he dexterously rises on the wing and goes gleaning again in shallower places.

The Ouzel is usually found singly; rarely in pairs, excepting during the breeding season, and *very* rarely in threes or fours. I once observed three thus spending a winter morning in company, upon a small glacier lake, on the Upper Merced, about 7,500 feet above the level of the sea. A storm had occurred during the night, but the morning sun shone unclouded, and the shadowy lake, gleaming darkly in its setting of fresh snow, lay smooth and motionless as a mirror. My camp chanced to be within a few feet of the water's edge, opposite a fallen pine, some of the branches of which leaned out over the lake. Here my three dearly welcome visitors took up their station, and at once began to embroider the frosty air with their delicious melody, doubly delightful to me that particular morning, as I had been somewhat apprehensive of danger in breaking my way down through the snow-choked cañons of the lowlands.

The portion of the lake bottom selected for a feeding-ground lies at a depth of fifteen or twenty feet below the surface, and is covered with a short growth of algæ and other aquatic plants—facts I had previously determined while sailing over it on a raft. After alighting on the glassy surface, they occasionally indulged in a little play, chasing one another round about in small circles; then all three would suddenly dive together, and then come ashore and sing.

The Ouzel seldom swims more than a few yards on the surface, for, not being web-footed, he makes rather slow progress, but by means of his strong, crisp wings he swims, or rather flies, with celerity under the surface, often to considerable distances. But it is in withstanding the force of heavy rapids that his strength of wing in this respect is most strikingly manifested. The following may be regarded as a fair illustration of his power of sub-aquatic flight. One stormy morning in winter when the Merced River was blue and green with unmelted snow, I observed one of my Ouzels perched on a snag out in the midst of a swift-rushing rapid, singing cheerily, as if everything was just to his mind; and while I stood on the bank admiring him, he suddenly plunged into the sludgy current, leaving his song abruptly broken off. After feeding a minute or two at the bottom, and when one would suppose that he must inevitably be swept far downstream, he emerged just where he went down, alighted on the same snag, showered the water-beads from his feathers, and continued his unfinished song, seemingly in tranquil ease as if it had suffered no interruption.

The Ouzel alone of all birds dares to enter a white torrent. And though strictly terrestrial in structure, no other is so inseparably related to water, not even the duck, or the bold ocean albatross, or the stormy-petrel. For ducks go ashore as soon as they finish feeding in undisturbed places, and very often make long flights overland from lake to lake or field to field. The same is true of most other aquatic birds. But the Ouzel, born on the brink of a stream, or on a snag or boulder in the midst of it, seldom leaves it for a single moment. For, notwithstanding he is often on the wing, he never flies overland, but whirs with rapid, quail-like beat above the stream, tracing all its windings. Even when the stream is quite small, say from five to ten feet wide, he seldom shortens his flight by crossing a bend, however abrupt it may be; and even when disturbed by meeting some one on the bank, he prefers to fly over one's head, to dodging out over the ground. When, therefore, his flight along a crooked stream is viewed endwise, it appears most strikingly wavered—a description on the air of every curve with lightning-like rapidity. . . .

His flight is solid and impetuous, without any intermission of wing-beats,—one homogeneous buzz like that of a laden bee on its way home. And while thus buzzing freely from fall to fall, he is frequently heard giving utterance to a long outdrawn train of unmodulated notes, in no way connected with his song, but corresponding closely with his flight in sustained vigor.

The Ouzel's nest is one of the most extraordinary pieces of bird architecture I ever saw, odd and novel in design, perfectly fresh and beautiful, and in every way worthy of the genius of the little builder. It is about a foot in diameter, round and bossy in outline,

with a neatly arched opening near the bottom, somewhat like an old-fashioned brick oven, or Hottentot's hut. It is built almost exclusively of green and yellow mosses, chiefly the beautiful fronded hypnum that covers the rocks and old drift-logs in the vicinity of waterfalls. These are deftly interwoven, and felted together into a charming little hut; and so situated that many of the outer mosses continue to flourish as if they had not been plucked. A few fine, silky-stemmed grasses are occasionally found interwoven with the mosses, but, with the exception of a thin layer lining the floor, their presence seems accidental, as they are of a species found growing with the mosses and are probably plucked with them. The site chosen for this curious mansion is usually some little rock-shelf within reach of the lighter particles of the spray of a waterfall, so that its walls are kept green and growing, at least during the time of high water. . . .

Furthermore, at certain hours of the day, when the sunshine is poured down at the required angle, the whole mass of the spray enveloping the fairy establishment is brilliantly irised; and it is through so glorious a rainbow atmosphere as this that some of our blessed Ouzels obtain their first peep at the world.

In these moss huts three or four eggs are laid, white like foam-bubbles; and well may the little birds hatched from them sing water songs, for they hear them all their lives, and even before they are born. . . .

Such, then, is our little cinclus, beloved of every one who is so fortunate as to know him. Tracing on strong wing every curve of the most precipitous torrents from one extremity of the Sierra to the other; not fearing to follow them through their darkest gorges and coldest snow-tunnels; acquainted with every waterfall, echoing their divine music; and throughout the whole of their beautiful lives interpreting all that we in our unbelief call terrible in the utterances of torrents and storms, as only varied expressions of God's eternal love.

TROGONS AND MOTMOTS
by Louis Agassiz Fuertes

Fuertes (1874–1927) was, like his famous predecessors, Alexander Wilson and John James Audubon, not only an excellent painter of birds but also an able reporter of their behavior. Born in the United States in 1874, he published many books on birds. The following description of two striking tropical species appeared in the periodical Bird-Lore *in 1915.*

Every student in the tropics hopes he may soon meet with Trogons, at once the most beautiful and the most mysterious of all the varied tropical birds. Nothing could exceed the richness of their contrasting blood-red underparts, white and black tails, and resplendent emerald-green heads and backs. The large *Pharomacrus* Trogons, of which the famed Quetzal is a type, with their delicate yet richly gorgeous and pendulous mantle of feathers, are, for sheer beauty, among Nature's truly great triumphs, and cannot fail to force deep appreciation from the most calloused or mercenary collector. *P. antisianus* has a loud, rolling call, which I put in my notes as *Whee oo, corre o,* done in a round, velvety whistle. When, after quite a long time spent in imitating the unknown note, in the soggy tree-fern forest at the ridge of the coast Andes, this magnificent ruby and emerald creature came swinging toward me in deeply undulating waves and perched alertly in full sight not far away, I found it hard to breathe, so great was my excitement and joy. We never found it a common bird and only three were seen in all our travel in Colombia. . . .

The curious racket-tailed Motmots have what I call the most velvety of all bird notes. It is usually a single short *oot,* pitched about five tones below where one can whistle. This note is very gentle, though fairly loud, and I think that some persons who do not hear low vibrations very well would often fail to notice it at a short distance. Most of the natives have sound-names for Motmots, and the Maya Indians of Yucatan call the brilliant little *Eumomota* "Toh," and, as an appreciation of the interest, he has come to nest and roost familiarly in the age-long deserted ruins of their former glory.

Indeed, these mysterious, gentle, shy, little birds came to me, at least, to be the living symbol of this great lost magnificence; for the present-day Mayas know naught of the art and history of their great forefathers, whose temples and beautiful buildings are now in utter oblivion and disuse, except as the shelters and dwellings of little "Toh," the Motmot, and his soft *hoot* is the only sound that ever issues from their carved portals.

JACKDAWS
by W. H. Hudson

Although he was born in Buenos Aires of American parents and lived on the pampas until 1868, Hudson (1841–1922) spent the rest of his life in England and is famous as a British naturalist. Of his charming books about wildlife in South America and England, the best known is probably his romantic novel, Green Mansions. *Our excerpt comes from* Bird and Man (1901).

The cathedral daws, on account of their numbers, are the most important of the feathered inhabitants of Wells. These city birds are familiarly called "Bishop's Jacks," to distinguish them from the "Ebor Jacks," the daws that in large numbers have their home and breeding-place in the neighbouring cliffs, called the Ebor Rocks. . . .

At Wells most of the cathedral birds—a hundred couples at least—breed in the cavities behind the stone statues, standing, each in its niche, in rows, tier above tier, on the west front. In April, when the daws are busiest at their nest-building, I have amused myself early every morning watching them flying to the front in a constant procession, every bird bringing his stick. This work is all done in the early morning, and about half-past eight o'clock a man comes with a barrow to gather up the fallen sticks—there is always a big barrowful, heaped high, of them; and if not thus removed the accumulated material would in a few days form a rampart or zareba, which would prevent access to the cathedral on that side.

It has often been observed that the daw, albeit so clever a bird, shows a curious deficiency of judgment when building, in his persistent efforts to carry in sticks too big for the cavity. Here, for instance, each morning in turning over the litter of fallen material I picked up sticks measuring from four or five to seven feet in length. These very long sticks were so slender and dry that the bird was able to lift and to fly with them; therefore to his corvine mind they were suitable for his purpose. It comes to this: the daw knows a stick when he sees one, but the only way of testing its usefulness to him is to pick it up in his beak, then to try to fly with it. If the stick is six feet long and the cavity will only admit one of not more than eighteen inches, he discovers his mistake only on getting home. The question arises: Does he continue all his life long repeating this egregious blunder? One can hardly believe that an old, experienced bird can go on from day to day and year to year wasting his energies in gathering and carrying building materials that will have to be thrown away in the end—that he is, in fact, mentally on a level with the great mass of meaner beings who forget nothing and learn nothing. It is not to be doubted that the daw was once a builder in trees, like all his relations, with the exception of the cliff-breeding chough. He is even capable of reverting to the original habit, as I know from an instance which has quite recently come to my knowledge. In this case a small colony of daws have been noticed for several years past breeding in stick nests placed among the clustering foliage of a group of Scotch firs. This colony may have sprung from a bird hatched and reared in the nest of a carrion crow or magpie. Still, the habit of breeding in holes must be very ancient, and considering that the jackdaw is one of the most intelligent of our birds, one cannot but be astonished at the rude, primitive, blundering way in which the nest-building work is generally performed. The most we can see by carefully watching a number of birds at work is that there appears to be some difference with regard to intelligence between bird and bird. Some individuals blunder less than others; it is possible that these have learned something from experience; but if that be so, their better way is theirs only, and their young will not inherit it.

One morning at Wells as I stood on the cathedral green watching the birds at their work, I witnessed a rare and curious scene—one amazing to an ornithologist. A bird dropped a stick—an incident that occurred a dozen times or oftener any minute at that busy time; but in this instance the bird had no sooner let the stick fall than he rushed down after it to attempt its recovery, just as one may see a sparrow drop a feather or straw, and then dart down after it and often recover it before it touches the ground. The heavy stick fell straight and fast on to the pile of sticks already lying on the pavement, and instantly the daw was down and had it in his beak, and thereupon laboriously flew up to his nesting-place, which was forty to fifty feet high. At the moment that he rushed down after the falling stick two other daws that happened to be standing on ledges above dropped down after him, and copied his action by each picking up a stick and flying with it to their nests. Others daws followed suit, and in a few minutes there was a stream of descending and ascending daws at that spot, every ascending bird with a stick in his beak. It was curious to see that although sticks were lying in hundreds on the pavement along the entire breadth of the west front, the daws continued coming down only at that spot where the first bird had picked up the stick he had dropped. By-and-by, to my regret, the birds suddenly took alarm at something and rose up, and from that moment not one descended.

Presently the man came round with his rake and broom and barrow to tidy up the place. Before beginning his work he solemnly made the following remark: "Is it not curious, sir, considering the distance the birds go to get their sticks, and the work of carrying them, that they never, by any chance, think to come down and pick up what they have dropped!" I replied that I had heard the same thing said before, and that it was in all the books; and then I told him of the scene I had just witnessed. He was very much surprised, and said that such a thing had never been witnessed before at that place. It had a disturbing

effect on him, and he appeared to me to resent this departure from their old ancient conservative ways on the part of the cathedral birds.

For many mornings after I continued to watch the daws until the nest-building was finished, without witnessing any fresh outbreak of intelligence in the colony: they had once more shaken down into the old inconvenient traditional groove, to the manifest relief of the man with the broom and barrow.

A HOATZIN CHICK MEETS A CHALLENGE
by William Beebe

One of the best-known naturalists of his day, Dr. Beebe (1877–1962) was Curator of Birds at the New York Zoological Garden (the Bronx Zoo). He was famous not only for his field work, especially in Central and South America, but also for his descents by bathysphere into the ocean depths. Our excerpt comes from his popular book, Jungle Peace (1918).

But the heart of our interest in the hoatzins centered in the nestlings. Some kind Providence directed the time of our visit, which I chose against the advice of some of the very inhabitants of New Amsterdam. It turned out that we were on the scene exactly at the right time. A week either way would have yielded much poorer results. The nestlings, in seven occupied nests, observed as we drifted along shore, or landed and climbed among the thorns, were in an almost identical stage of development. In fact, the greatest difference in size occurred between two nestlings of the same brood. Their down was a thin, scanty, fuzzy covering, and the flight feathers were less than a half-inch in length. No age would have showed to better advantage every movement of wings or head.

When a mother hoatzin took reluctant flight from her nest, the young bird at once stood upright and looked curiously in every direction. No slacker he, crouching flat or awaiting his mother's directing cries. From the moment he was left alone he began to depend upon the warnings and signs which his great beady eyes and skinny ears conveyed to him. Hawks and vultures had swept low over his nest and mother unheeded. Coolies in their boats had paddled underneath with no more than a glance upward. Throughout his week of life, as through his parents' and their parents' parents' lives, no danger had disturbed their peaceful existence. Only for a sudden windstorm such as that which the week before had upset nests and blown out eggs, it might be said that for the little hoatzin chicks life held nothing but siestas and munchings of pimpler leaves.

But one little hoatzin, if he had any thoughts such as these, failed to count on the invariable exceptions to every rule, for this day the totally unexpected happened. Fate, in the shape of enthusiastic scientists, descended upon him. He was not for a second nonplussed. If we had concentrated upon him a thousand strong, by boats and by land, he would have fought the good fight for freedom and life as calmly as he waged it against us. And we found him no mean antagonist, and far from reptilian in his ability to meet new and unforeseen conditions.

His mother, who a moment before had been packing his capacious little crop with predigested pimpler leaves, had now flown off to an adjoining group of mangroves, where she and his father croaked to him hoarse encouragement. His flight feathers hardly reached beyond his finger-tips, and his body was covered with a sparse coating of sooty black down. So there could be no resort to flight. He must defend himself, bound to earth like his assailants.

Hardly had his mother left when his comical head, with thick, blunt beak and large intelligent eyes, appeared over the rim of the nest. His alert expression was increased by the suspicion of a crest on his crown where the down was slightly longer. Higher and higher rose his head, supported on a neck of extraordinary length and thinness. No more than this was needed to mark his absurd resemblance to some strange, extinct reptile. A young dinosaur must have looked much like this, while for all that my glance revealed, I might have been looking at a diminutive Galapagos tortoise. Indeed this simile came to mind often when I became more intimate with nestling hoatzins.

Sam, my black tree-climber, kicked off his shoes and began creeping along the horizontal limbs of the pimplers. At every step he felt carefully with a calloused sole in order to avoid the longer of the cruel thorns, and punctuated every yard with some gasp of pain or muttered personal prayer, "Pleas' doan' stick me, Thorns!"

At last his hand touched the branch, and it shook slightly. The young bird stretched his mittened hands high above his head and waved them a moment. With similar intent a boxer or wrestler flexes his muscles and bends his body. One or two uncertain, forward steps brought the bird to the edge of the nest at the base of a small branch. There he stood, and raising one wing leaned heavily against the stem, bracing himself. My man climbed higher and the nest swayed violently.

Now the brave little hoatzin reached up to some tiny side twigs and, aided by the projecting ends of dead sticks from the nest, he climbed with facility, his thumbs and forefingers apparently being of more aid than his feet. It was fascinating to see him ascend, stopping now and then to crane his head and neck far out, turtle-wise. He met every difficulty with some new contortion of body or limbs, often with so quick or so subtle a shifting as to escape my scrutiny. The branch ended in a tiny crotch and here perforce, ended his attempt at escape by climbing. He stood on the swaying twig, one wing clutched tight, and braced himself with both feet.

Nearer and nearer crept Sam. Not a quiver on the part of the little hoatzin.

A black hand grasped the thorny branch six feet from his perch, and like a flash he played his next trick— the only remaining one he knew, one that set him apart from all modern land birds, as the frog is set apart from the swallow.

The young hoatzin stood erect for an instant, and then both wings of the little bird were stretched straight back, not folded, bird-wise, but dangling loosely and reaching well beyond the body. For a considerable fraction of time he leaned forward. Then without effort, without apparent leap or jump he dived straight downward, as beautifully as a seal, direct as a plummet and very swiftly. There was a scarcely-noticeable splash, and as I gazed with real awe, I watched the widening ripples which undulated over the muddy water—the only trace of the whereabouts of the young bird.

It seemed as if no one, whether ornithologist, evolutionist, poet or philosopher could fail to be profoundly impressed at the sight we had seen. Here I was in a very real, a very modern boat, with the honk of motor horns sounding from the river road a few yards away through the bushes, in the shade of this tropical vegetation in the year nineteen hundred and sixteen; and yet the curtain of the past had been lifted and I had been permitted a glimpse of what must have been common in the millions of years ago. It was a tremendous thing, a wonderful thing to have seen, and it seemed to dwarf all the strange sights which had come to me in all other parts of the earth's wilderness. I had read of these habits and had expected them, but like one's first sight of a volcano in eruption, no reading or description prepares one for the actual phenomenon.

I sat silently watching for the re-appearance of the young bird. We tallied five pairs of eyes and yet many minutes passed before I saw the same little head and emaciated neck sticking out of the water alongside a bit of drift rubbish. The only visible thing was the protruding spikes of the bedraggled tail feathers. I worked the boat in toward the bird, half-heartedly, for I had made up my mind that this particular brave little bit of atavism deserved his freedom, so splendidly had he fought for it among the pimplers. Soon he ducked forward, dived out of sight and came up twenty feet away among an inextricable tangle of vines. I sent a little cheer of well wishing after him and we salvaged Sam.

Then we shoved out the boat and watched from a distance. Five or six minutes passed and a skinny, crooked, two-fingered mitten of an arm reared upward out of the muddy flood and the nestling, black and glistening, hauled itself out of water.

Thus must the first amphibian have climbed into the thin air. But the young hoatzin neither gasped nor shivered, and seemed as self-possessed as if this was a common occurrence in its life. There was not the slightest doubt however, that this was its first introduction to water. Yet it had dived from a height of fifteen feet, about fifty times its own length, as cleanly as a seal leaps from a berg. It was as if a human child should dive two hundred feet!

In fifteen minutes more it had climbed high above the water, and with unerring accuracy directly toward its natal bundle of sticks overhead. The mother now came close, and with hoarse rasping notes and frantic heaves of tail and wings lent encouragement. Just before we paddled from sight, when the little fellow had reached his last rung, he partly opened his beak and gave a little falsetto cry,—a clear, high tone, tailing off into a guttural rasp. His splendid courage had broken at last; he had nearly reached the nest and he was aching to put aside all this terrible responsibility, this pitting of his tiny might against such fearful odds. He wanted to be a helpless nestling again, to crouch on the springy bed of twigs with a feather comforter over him and be stuffed at will with delectable pimpler pap. Such is the normal right destiny of a hoatzin chick, and the whee-og! wrung from him by the reaction of safety seemed to voice all this.

THE CANARIES' SINGING LESSON
by Gustav Eckstein

Gustav Eckstein, born in Cincinnati, Ohio, in 1890, was a physician and a professor of physiology. But he also became increasingly interested in the behavior of birds, rats, apes and other animals, some of which he kept as pets and about which he wrote a number of charming books. Especially perceptive are his descriptions of the ways of his pet canaries in Canary: The History of a Family, *from which a section is printed below.*

Through all this Striped Male's voice still had not changed. The worst was, from my point of view, it was affecting the other voices. Canary voices are affected by anything. In the parts of the year when I am using the typewriter most, all the voices go up.

And for his private concerts Striped Male continued to mount to the heights of the book-closet, as he did that first night. The book-closet stuck like a platform out over the laboratory, and I had noticed long before this that when a male was feeling particularly male he was apt to go up there to sing. Striped Male might give eight to ten to twenty performances a day.

This was a matinee.

The program was already part over when I noticed Hinge fly to the fishpole. That put Hinge higher than Striped Male because the fishpole was higher. After a while Striped Male came to a rest in the music. He stopped, as if to clear his throat. Then he began again— and instantly Hinge began. This in itself was not unusual except for how Hinge's trill came right on top of Striped Male's trill, and except—and this was the amazing—how Hinge's exactly reproduced Striped Male's own harsh high-pitched quality. And Hinge's kept up. It kept up for as long as Striped Male's kept up, and when Striped Male's couldn't any longer, still kept up. This Hinge could do because he had big lungs by nature, and because for all his laziness I suspected he had learned considerable from Father. Then, with great skill, Hinge dropped from Striped Male's quality down to his own, lingered on that a while too. Thumbed his nose, it seemed.

This was only the sample. In fact, had it occurred but once I would not have believed it. Every time now that Striped Male began to sing Hinge began to sing. I think there can be no question what it meant. Whoever in those days visited the laboratory thought the scene farce. I too, and I was happy besides because I believed I could once more detect a change in the Community singing—as though Hinge's lessons were bringing back a courage for the singing of the old days. But even had it only been that I was wanting this to be true, and therefore made myself think I saw signs that it was, what clinched it for me was the effect on Striped Male. That anyone could see. He had lost his dominance. He was very changed. He was as quiet as the quietest. He worried me. I tried to think it was his time for moulting, but it was not. You could see the change in his walk. His head feathers scarce ever rose up now.

All this transpired less than a year after the birth of Junior, Penguin, and Candy. Junior began to look more drum-major than his father. From Striped Male the drum-major was faded out. He would even, like one of the duller birds, go up on the window-sash and stand long periods in the sun—a sick old man taking his constitutional. His long legs looked longer. Anybody could eat egg when he ate egg. Anybody could eat banana.

THE DANCE OF THE CRANES
by Marjorie Kinnan Rawlings

Marjorie Kinnan Rawlings, born in 1896, is a well-known American novelist and this description of two children captivated by the courtship ritual of cranes comes from her most popular novel, The Yearling *(1938).*

Jody saw the great white birds in the distance. His father's eye, he thought, was like an eagle's. They crouched on all fours and crept forward slowly. Now and then Penny dropped flat on his stomach and Jody dropped behind him. They reached a clump of high saw-grass and Penny motioned for concealment behind it. The birds were so close that it seemed to Jody he might touch them with his long fishing pole. Penny squatted on his haunches and Jody followed. His eyes were wide. He made a count of the whooping cranes. There were sixteen.

The cranes were dancing a cotillion as surely as it was danced at Volusia. Two stood apart, erect and white, making a strange music that was part cry and part singing. The rhythm was irregular, like the dance. The other birds were in a circle. In the heart of the circle, several moved counter-clock-wise. The musicians made their music. The dancers raised their wings and lifted their feet, first one and then the other. They sunk their heads deep in their snowy breasts, lifted them and sunk again. They moved soundlessly, part awkwardness, part grace. The dance was solemn. Wings fluttered, rising and falling like out-stretched arms. The outer circle shuffled around and around. The group in the center attained a slow frenzy.

Suddenly all motion ceased. Jody thought the dance was over, or that the intruders had been discovered. Then the two musicians joined the circle. Two others took their places. There was a pause. The dance was resumed. The birds were reflected in the clear marsh water. Sixteen white shadows reflected the motions. The evening breeze moved across the saw-grass. It bowed and fluttered. The water rippled. The setting sun lay rosy on the white bodies. Magic birds were dancing in a mystic marsh. The grass swayed with them, and the shallow waters, and the earth fluttered under them. The earth was dancing with the cranes, and the low sun, and the wind and sky.

Jody found his own arms lifting and falling with his breath, as the cranes' wings lifted. The sun was sinking into the saw-grass. The marsh was golden. The whooping cranes were washed with gold. The far hammocks were black. Darkness came to the lily pads, and the water blackened. The cranes were whiter than any clouds, or any white bloom of oleander or of lily. With-out warning, they took flight. Whether the hour-long dance was, simply, done, or whether the long nose of an alligator had lifted above the water to alarm them, Jody could not tell, but they were gone. They made a great circle against the sunset, whooping their strange rusty cry that sounded only in their flight. Then they flew in a long line into the west, and vanished.

GEESE AND THE UNITY OF NATIONS
by Aldo Leopold

The distinguished career of Aldo Leopold (1887–1948) as conservationist began in the U.S. Forest Service in 1909 and led to a chair in game management at the University of Wisconsin in 1933. But he is best known for his profound identification with wildlife in its confrontations with man, as in his famous A Sand County Almanac and Sketches Here and There *(1949), from which this passage is taken.*

It is an irony of history that the great powers should have discovered the unity of nations at Cairo in 1943. The geese of the world have had that notion for a longer time, and each March they stake their lives on its essential truth.

In the beginning there was only the unity of the Ice Sheet. Then followed the unity of the March thaw, and the northward hegira of the international geese. Every March since the Pleistocene, the geese have honked unity from China Sea to Siberian Steppe, from Euphrates to Volga, from Nile to Murmansk, from Lincolnshire to Spitsbergen. Every March since the Pleistocene, the geese have honked unity from Currituck to Labrador, Matamuskeet to Ungava, Horseshoe Lake to Hudson's Bay, Avery Island to Baffin Land, Panhandle to Mackenzie, Sacramento to Yukon.

By this international commerce of geese, the waste corn of Illinois is carried through the clouds to the Arctic tundras, there to combine with the waste sunlight of a nightless June to grow goslings for all the lands between. And in this annual barter of food for light, and winter warmth for summer solitude, the whole continent receives as net profit a wild poem dropped from the murky skies upon the muds of March.

FLAMINGO HUNT IN THE WEST INDIES
by Paul A. Zahl

Paul A. Zahl, widely travelled research biologist, author and photographer, has published many articles and books based on his expeditions (generally sponsored by the National Geographic Society) in the South American jungles, the Caribbean and elsewhere.

Among his best known books are Coro-Coro: The World of the Scarlet Ibis *and* Flamingo Hunt in the West Indies (1952), *from which our excerpt was taken.*

By ten o'clock next morning we were two thirds of the way down the lake. John and I had separated and were proceeding parallel 100 yards apart. The idea was that of a two-man broadfront piston—as yet at a considerable distance, to be sure—forcing the pink line ahead of it. In my pocket was a pair of pliers, and over my shoulder hung a small camera. In John's pocket was the ball of cord, and over his shoulder was a necklace of bird bands. The latter flashed in the sunlight, and he carried them as though never once doubting that we'd soon have plenty of flamingo legs in hand for banding. I wasn't quite sure of the plan, but John had everything figured out. We must concentrate the birds against the far end of the lake, he had said, then drive them along the north shore and into a bay there that tapered off like a funnel. How we'd actually catch the birds, once funneled, was still a mystery to me. . . .

As we closed in, the herd dumbly crowded into the bay's mangrove-walled V. It had been my vague impression that John's plan involved thus kraaling the herd tightly into that V and there somehow fencing them in with the cord. Then we could catch them singly for banding and release. But when John came over, handed me one end of the cord and began giving instructions I realized I was wrong. It was evident now that he was up to one of the oldest tricks in the flamingo hunter's book, long since described to me by Robbie Ferguson and others. The classic technique is for two or more men to corner a group of preflight waders, then, with each man holding the end of a fishline or facsimile, force the birds to stampede out across it. The birds rush blindly through the space between the two men, who then pull the cord taut and begin sweeping it powerfully forward. Under the right conditions two good huntsmen can break the legs of dozens of flamingos within a few seconds and stun many more. These drop out of the stampede and float helplessly on the water. Once the rush for freedom has begun, there is no stopping it. The birds will keep hurtling into the cord trap—some successfully hopping over, some successfully darting under, but many intercepting it squarely.

This plan is fine for native hunters in quest of fresh meat, but cruelly unsuited to a bird-banding mission. We'd have caught twenty or thirty birds, certainly, but half of them—legs or necks fractured—flapping great mortal flaps on the water . . . No, that was definitely not for us. Already I'd come to suspect that these adolescent birds were too wild and too nearly grown to be caught by any humane means. In bringing my 1,000 bands to Inagua I had envisioned a rookery with nestlings small enough to make their capture easy and harmless. That period had long since passed. Also, at the time of the first break I had been within close-up view of the fleeing birds. I had looked well at those tall pink toothpicks; their fragility had struck at the heart of me.

Unaware of my thoughts, John was unrolling the cord and preparing for the advance on the herd, which cowered, restlessly trapped, a couple of hundred yards before us. I called him back and, opening my camera case, said we'd go closer to take some pictures, but to forget about the banding. As best I could I explained that to band ten or twenty birds would be of no value whatever; and, even if it were, the capture would involve mortal injury to a prohibitively large number of others. These birds were definitely too old. It would be like trying to brand a herd of nearly grown range cattle.

John gave me an uncomprehending look: here after strenuous herding we finally had got a thousand of the quarry nicely bottled up; we had these lovely shiny rings and a pair of pliers with which to apply them; certainly no man in his right mind would pass up this wonderful opportunity.

But I wasn't to be persuaded; we were going in closer with only a camera. . . .

Closer and closer. Now I was within good range and had the camera to my eye. I hoped to take pictures fast, then retreat. But just as I snapped the shutter it happened. The dam broke.

They came at us like the front of a tidal wave—heads down, necks stretched out in front, wings beating wildly. Those horizontally held heads and necks resembled the downspear charge of an ancient army, and it was this more than anything else that put the fear of God into me. To be trampled underfoot by birds seems like a silly thing, hardly possessing any element of danger. But these thousand wild creatures were nearly as tall as I and as dense as a solid wall.

John was about twenty feet to my left. I hastily glanced at him for a cue as to what to do. But just at that instant the tide hit us, obliterating John from sight. We were stones now on the shores of a raging pink sea. Suddenly my world was one of wings beating down and across my head and face, flamingo eyes and mouths inches from my own, necks spearing past. The first impact knocked me over, and I was knees-down on the ten-inch-deep bottom. Reflexively I turned my back on the stream and crouched with my head low. On and on they came, their webbed wet feet stamping up over my back, water from those alongside splashing up into my face. Out of the corner of my eye I could see only a speeding forest of pink bamboo.

The feeling swept over me that this could not be reality. It was so wholly removed from any other experience of my lifetime that for a moment I suspected my senses of deceit. Its duration was a year ten seconds long. Then it was over. I raised my head and saw the rear end of the herd tearing away in front of me. There was no lessening in speed until they were all across the bay and back into the primary lake.

Only then did I remember John and turn to where he had last stood. He was still there and most remarkably so. He too had stooped and turned his back to the flood. But, instead of being mentally stunned as I had been, he had worked. As the birds swept by he had reached and plucked one after another by its neck or its legs or even its wings. Now he stood there with a grin on his face and with nine flamingos somehow stuck to him. He held the necks of three in each hand, had another couple tucked under his arms, was holding one between his legs. They were quiet, beaten, subdued by his grasp.

I had managed somehow to keep my camera above water during the charge, and the first thing I can remember doing was snapping John's picture. Then I walked over. Several of the birds whose necks he was gripping in his big strong hands seemed limp and dead. I repeated that there'd be no banding, and why not release his catch? He saw I was serious and dropped the load. Six of the nine immediately galloped off. Three slumped into the water, stunned or half choked. I picked their heads up and held them above the surface. They were still breathing and would recover.

John stood awkwardly by. His fine banding plan had been vetoed, and he was still wondering why. On an impulse I told him to untie his necklace and remove three bands. Then I reached into my wet pocket and handed him the pliers. I lifted the leg of one of the flamingos and held it above the water. John's gloom evaporated. He quickly pliered open one of the aluminum rings. Then with the uncertain sureness of a bridegroom he placed the metal on the finger-thick flamingo leg and bent it back into circular shape. We did this to all three birds, which soon revived, stood up and loped away in the direction of the main flock. With each lope we could see the sparkle of something shiny.

There were at least eight birds stuck in the mangrove. We made our way to each of these and got them extricated. Placed back in the water, they too hurried along.

Three banded birds can have no scientific significance. But, should you ever run across a flamingo wearing a serial-numbered ankle bracelet, I'd certainly like to know.

FOSTER MOTHER TO MALLARD DUCKLINGS
by Konrad Z. Lorenz

Born in Vienna in 1903, Lorenz studied medicine and zoology but soon turned to the field of animal behavior and became an outstanding authority on the psychology of such animals as geese, cats and dogs. His most beguiling experiment is described in King Solomon's Ring *(1952),* a classic in its field.

I was experimenting at one time with young mallards to find out why artificially incubated and freshly hatched ducklings of this species, in contrast to similarly treated greylag goslings, are unapproachable and shy. Greylag goslings unquestioning accept the first living being whom they meet as their mother, and run confidently after him. Mallards, on the contrary, always refused to do this. If I took from the incubator freshly hatched mallards, they invariably ran away from me and pressed themselves in the nearest dark corner. Why? I remembered that I had once let a muscovy duck hatch a clutch of mallard eggs and that the tiny mallards had also failed to accept this foster-mother. As soon as they were dry, they had simply run away from her and I had trouble enough to catch these crying, erring children. On the other hand, I once let a fat white farmyard duck hatch out mallards and the little wild things ran just as happily after her as if she had been their real mother. The secret must have lain in her call note, for, in external appearance, the domestic duck was quite as different from a mallard as was the muscovy; but what she had in common with the mallard (which, of course, is the wild progenitor of our farmyard duck) were her vocal expressions. Though, in the process of domestication, the duck has altered considerably in colour pattern and body form, its voice has remained practically the same. The inference was clear: I must quack like a mother mallard in order to make the little ducks run after me. No sooner said than done. When, one Whit-Saturday, a brood of purebred young mallards was due to hatch, I put the eggs in the incubator, took the babies, as soon as they were dry, under my personal care, and quacked for them the mother's call-note in my best Mallardese. For hours on end I kept it up, for half the day. The quacking was successful. The little ducks lifted their gaze confidently towards me, obviously had no fear of me this time, and as, still quacking, I drew slowly away from them, they also set themselves obediently in motion and scuttled after me in a tightly huddled group, just as ducklings follow their mother. My theory was indisputably proved. The freshly hatched ducklings have an inborn reaction to the call-note, but not to the optical picture of the mother. Anything that emits the right quack note will be considered as mother, whether it is a fat white Pekin duck or a still fatter man. However, the substituted object must not exceed a certain height. At the beginning of these experiments, I had sat myself down in the grass amongst the ducklings and, in order to make them follow me, had dragged myself, sitting, away from them. As soon, however, as I stood up and tried, in a standing posture, to lead them on, they gave up, peered searchingly on all sides, but not upwards towards me and it was not long before they began that penetrating piping of abandoned ducklings that we are accustomed simply to call "crying." They were unable to adapt themselves to the fact that their foster-mother had become so tall. So I was forced to move along, squatting low, if I wished them to follow me. This was not very comfortable; still less comfortable was the fact that the mallard mother quacks unintermittently. If I ceased for even the space of half a minute from my melodious "Quahg, gegegegeg, Quahg, gegegegeg," the necks of the ducklings became longer and longer corresponding exactly to "long faces" in human children—and did I then not immediately recommence quacking, the shrill weeping began anew. As soon as I was silent, they seemed to think that I had died, or perhaps that I loved them no more: cause enough for crying! The ducklings, in contrast to the greylag goslings, were most demanding and tiring charges, for, imagine a two-hour walk with such children, all the time squatting low and quacking without interruption! In the interests of science I submitted myself literally for hours on end to this ordeal.

So it came about, on a certain Whit-Sunday, that, in company with my ducklings, I was wandering about, squatting and quacking, in a May-green meadow at the upper part of our garden. I was congratulating myself on the obedience and exactitude with which my ducklings came waddling after me, when I suddenly looked up and saw the garden fence framed by a row of dead-white faces: a group of tourists was standing at the fence and staring horrified in my direction. Forgivable! For all they could see was a big man with a beard dragging himself, crouching, round the meadow, in figures of eight, glancing constantly over his shoulder and quacking—but the ducklings, the all-revealing and all-explaining ducklings were hidden in the tall spring grass from the view of the astonished crowd.

WILD GEESE
by Sigurd F. Olson

Sigurd F. Olson, born in Chicago in 1899, was a university professor until he began devoting himself to the establishment and defense of wilderness areas. He has achieved a wide reputation for his sensitive books on the life and legends of the north country, including The Lonely Land, Runes of the North, *and* The Singing Wilderness *(1956), from which this excerpt has been taken.*

It was November and I was on top of a high, birch-covered ridge. The air was rich with the smell of down leaves and the ground was covered with bronze and tarnished gold. Far below was a blue lake with a rice-filled river flowing into it. Where the river met the open water, the rice fanned out like a golden apron, solidly colored at the gathered waist, flecked with blue toward its fringes.

Suddenly out of the north came the sound I had been waiting for, a soft, melodious gabbling that swelled and died and increased in volume until all other sounds were engulfed by its clamor. Far in the blue I saw them, a long skein of dots undulating like a floating ribbon pulled toward the south by an invisible cord tied to the point of its V.

I have never killed a goose and now I never intend to; the sight and the sound of them is enough. But there was a time when, more than anything else in the world, I wanted to bring one of those high wanderers down to earth. The sound of wild geese on the move haunted me and I felt that somehow I must capture some of their mystery, some of their freedom and of the blue distances into which they disappeared. The idea grew into an obsession, and I used to lie awake at night, dreaming and planning how I would bring it about. I never went hunting without a handful of shells loaded with buckshot, never heard the grand music without praying that the birds would come close. I do not believe that there was ever a boy who wanted a goose as badly as I did. It was not just a case of being able to say: "I killed a goose," though in my country, well out of the main flyways, that would have been something to boast about. It was far more than that; it was involved with the way I felt and with the wonder of listening to them as they came year after year and wove their way into space.

There was a time when a flock of them alighted in an open field and I crawled on my belly for a mile, praying every foot of the way that the birds would not see the waving of the stubble, that they would keep on feeding until I was within range. That day there were other flocks in the air and the wind was alive with their calling. I can still hear those geese gabbling softly to themselves as they fed on the down grain, still see the long necks, the outstretched heads of the sentinels as I drew near. Then just when I was at the limit of range, a crow flew over, cawing its find to the world. They took to the air with a thunder of wings and I lay there a bare hundred yards away, watching them disappear over the horizon.

Another time, when the sun was setting over the marshes of Totogatik Lake, the wild gabbling came out of the north and the birds were silhouetted against a flaming sky. That time they caught me in the open between the rice and the tall grass near shore, but it was dusk and the canoe blended into its background. That instant is burned into my memory: the water like wine, the approaching flock, black spruce etched against the sky. Then they came, down—down—down out of the gloom until I could feel the measured beat of their wings. As they swung to land, a hunter fired from the far shore. They swerved and went out the way they had come.

A third time, in the hills during deer season, I heard a flock circling and circling, looking for a spot of open water. I knew a man who had shot one with a rifle; I had talked to him and wondered enviously if I would ever have such luck. The birds were big, their flight slow, and if you held right, your chances were good; but when the flock finally swung over that day in the hills, though they were well within range, nothing happened. Only a lone wing feather floated down, spiraling lazily out of the cold November sky.

Then one year my great chance came. I had been following a trail through a black spruce swamp on my way to the river, where I hoped to find a few last mallards feeding in the rice. It was in the very center of the bog that I heard them—just the merest hint of melody, but enough to stop me in my tracks. The flock was far away and almost instantly the sound was gone. Mallards were forgotten, everything else in the world but the geese circling the bend in the river. I reloaded my gun with buckshot, checked and rechecked my safety, placed the duck loads where I could not possibly make a mistake. Nothing must go wrong now. This was the time I had been praying for.

I stood there straining to catch the music again, but the moss-hung spruces and the soft cushion of muskeg seemed to absorb it. Suddenly the sound grew louder, changed in a moment from a vague, blended harmony to the clear, joyous clamor of birds coming in to feed. As yet I could see nothing, but the music rose and fell as the flock dipped between the hills and valleys looking for a place to land. Then they were overhead and their bugling filled the trees, and I ran madly for the closest ridge where I might have a chance of seeing them as they came by. I plunged through the tangle of heather and sphagnum beneath the spruces, scrambled up the rocks to the crest of the ridge. They had seen the patch of rice in the river, had spotted the blue open water, and would have to circle close to the ledge in order to land. Wild, impossible thoughts were mine that day, but nothing was impossible then.

I was breathless when I reached the top. From where I stood, I commanded a clear view of the swamp, the winding blue of the river, the golden spot of rice in the mallard hole. The din of their calling grew louder and at last was so deafening that the rocks themselves seemed to bounce back the sound. Then they were directly above and I could see the outstretched necks with their white chin straps, the snowy undersides of the wings.

Straight overhead now in a wavering V, still just out of range. I crouched against a boulder and prayed that they would swing back. For a moment they disappeared behind a ridge, and as the calling died I was sick at heart, knowing I should have taken my chance and fired.

Then they were back, and as they sailed over the spruce tops I knew this was the moment I had been waiting for. They were much bigger than I had ever imagined. I could not only hear the beat of their wings and the rush of air through them, but could actually feel it. At that moment they seemed almost close enough to touch and I could see their eyes, the wary turning of their heads, their outstretched feet. Then they saw me there against the rock and pandemonium broke loose. The flock climbed into the sky, beat the air desperately to escape. Not until then did I remember my gun and what I had come for, and now it was too late. The birds were out of range.

After that boyhood experience I never tried to kill a goose, and now that I am older and a little wiser, I think I know the reason why. As I look back, I could comfort the boy I was. I could tell him that one should never try to capture something as wild and beautiful as the calling of geese, that it is better to wait and listen as they go by and wonder where they have gone. But, knowing that boy, I realize that he would not believe me. Only many years could heal the wound of that October day.

The long skein of dots was fading into the horizon and the calling grew fainter and fainter. Then for a moment it was gone and I heard it almost as a remembered sound. Once more it came and I caught the lift of the flock just before it was swallowed in the blue.

INDEX
Italic numbers refer to illustrations.

Aepyornis titan, 18, 94
Aesop, 99
African myths, 65, 68, *144, 163*
albatrosses, 28, 166, 246, *249;* Laysan, 33, *45*
American Indian myths: North, *52–53, 55, 61,* 68, *69,* 74, 76, *78, 78,* 79, 89, 91, *91, 93,* 247; South, *51, 58,* 73, 74
anatomy of birds, 14–16, *26–27, 28, 28, 29, 31*
anhingas, 25
ankas (mythical), 79, 99
anthropomorphism, 239–241, 245
Arabian myths, 78, 79, 93, 98, 99
Archaeopteryx lithographica 14–17, *14, 15,* 26, 28
Aristophanes, 78, 144–148
Aristotle, 8, 232, 241
Asian myths, 65, 74, 75, 78, 93, 98, 162, 202, 204
Assyrian myths, 77, 89, 202
Audubon, John James, *180–181,* 222–224, *228,* 253–255, 259
Audubon Society, 179–187
auks: great, 16, 25, 172, 176–178, *177,* 179; little, 87
Australian myths, 74, 91
Austrian myths, 89, 212
avocets, 182, 257

Babylonian myths, 89, 102, 128, 202, 204
banding birds, 33, 127, *186, 187,* 264–266
bantams, Belgian Mille Fleurs, *146–147*
Basil of Caesarea, St., 233, 241
Baskin, Leonard, 202
Bates, Henry Walter, 256–257
bee-eaters, 41
Beebe, William, 224, 261–263
behavior, 22, 34, *40,* 41–49, *42, 43, 45, 48, 49,* 74, 128, *140,* 158
bestiaries, *54, 82, 86, 86,* 239
Bewick, Thomas, 222
Bible, 8, 50, 65, 79, 84, 93, 102, 131, 140, 221, 230–232, 235
bird-headed or bird-winged men, 6, *92,* 200–202, *200, 203,* 212–215
birdmen, 8, 93, 162, 216
birds, human-headed, 88, 91, 211
birds of paradise, 45, 157, 171; Emperor of Germany's, *48;* greater, 17, 150, *150,* 157,

187–188; king, 45; Princess Stephanie, *70–71;* Salvadori's red, *189*
birds of prey, 76, 127, 193, 241
bird-watching, 124–127, *126,* 224
bitterns, 197, 257
blackbirds, *12,* 25, *34,* 188, 190, 235, 241
blackcocks, 75
Blake, William, 243
bobolinks, 42–45
Boccaccio, Giovanni, 232
boobies, Peruvian, 144
Bosch, Hieronymus, 202
Boucher, Francois, *133*
British Forestry Commission, 182
Browning, Robert, 246
Bruegel, Pieter, 221
Buddha, Dialogues of the, 65
budgerigars, 128, 139, *139*
Buffon, Georges, 222, 239
buntings: house, 128; snow, 136–139, 197; Townsend's, 179
Burns, Robert, 246
Burroughs, John, 248
bustards, 18
buzzards, 128, 193, 255, 257

caladrius (mythical), *50, 54*
calls, bird; 17, 33, 36, 260; *see also* songs
Cambrensis, Giraldus, 83–84, 87
canaries, 139, 263
capercaillies, *43*
Carson, Rachel, 193
cassowaries, 21, *22*
Catesby, Mark, 222, *225, 226*
chaffinches, 139
Chaucer, Geoffrey, 81, 239, 243
chickens, domestic, *see* fowl
chickens, prairie, 127, 179
Chinese myths, 78, *80,* 87–89, *87, 88,* 94, 99, 162, 215
Christian symbols, *50, 54, 58, 60, 62, 62, 63,* 76, 79–81, *82,* 84–86, 99, 131, 140, 143, 148, 204, *204,* 215–221, *216, 223,* 233
Clare, John, 245
clothing: bird designs, *9, 75, 206–207;* feather, *156,* 161–162, *162, 164, 170, 172,* 202
cocks: fights, 105–108, *106–108;* shys, 105; three-legged (mythical), 89
coins, bird-design, 8, 68, 73, 91, 150
Coleridge, Samuel Taylor, 246
Columbus, Christopher, 66,

135, 158
condors, 25, *51;* Andean, 124, *125;* California, 124, 182, *182*
conservation, 100–102, 161, 172, 187–198
continental drift, 21–22, 23
coots, 242, 257
coraquenques, 160–161
cormorants, 16, 121–124, *122,* 144, 166, 239; flightless, *121;* proto-, 7
corncrakes, 41
courtship: displays, 22, *40,* 42–49, *42, 43, 45, 48, 49,* 74, *140,* 158, 264; grounds, *49,* 74, 127; songs or calls, 34, 42, 158
cranes, 18, 36, 61, 65, *69,* 115, *142, 210,* 216–221, *218,* 235, 241; greater sandhill, *184–185;* sentinel, 241; whooping, 179, 182, *183,* 264
crossbills, *65,* 68, 221
crows, 62, 73, 196, 239; hooded, 136
cuckoos, 36, 61, 232, 235, 239–241, *242*
curlews, *27,* 246
Cuyp, Albert, 111

dances: bird, 45–49, *46–47,* 264; mimicked by man, *69, 70–71,* 74–75, 78, *96,* 162, 202
Dante, 232, 235–236, 241
Darwin, Charles, 26, 74, 128, 150, 255
Daudet, Alphonse, 239
DDT, 121, 193
defense: displays, 42, 242; songs, 34
dialects, birdsong, 42
Diatryma 18, *19*
displays: visual, 41, 42–49, 233, 242 (*see also* courtship; defense; distraction; territorial; threat); vocal, 41 (*see also* calls; songs)
distraction displays, 233
dodos, 16, 25, 174–176, *174*
domesticated birds, 8, 128–149, 256–257
doves, 8, 50, *58,* 65, 84, *123,* 131, *131, 138,* 144, 202–204, 246, 255; collared, 176, 182, 188; ring, 235; rock, 131, 232; *see also* turtledoves
ducks, 16, 18, *100,* 115, *123, 136,* 211, 212, 215, *216,* 222; domestic, 8, 266; eider, 165–166; Labrador, 179; mallard, 266–267; mandarin, 143, *208;* Muscovy, 143, 266; wood, 143, *186*

eagles, 25, *31,* 94, 98, 110, 115, 158, *159,* 161, 193, 212, 243; bald, *175,* 179, 196; double-headed (mythical), *90,* 212; golden, 197; harpy, 160; imperial, 197; martial, 114; monkey-eating, *194;* white-headed, *27;* symbolism, 8, 58, 61–62, *62,* 69, 72, 73, *73,* 74, 76, 77, 78, *81,* 89–93, *90–91,* 94, 102, 202–204, *204, 209,* 246, 247
ecological niches, 18–21, 26, *26–27,* 176, 182
Eckstein, Gustav, 263
eggs, 6, 18, *21,* 22, 94, 143, 148–149; Easter, 143
egrets, 79, *127,* 157, *171,* 172; snowy, *173*
Egyptian myths, 75, *75,* 79, 88, 89–91, *91–93,* 98, 131, 144, 160, 202, 204–211, *211,* 230
eiderdown, 165–166
elephant birds, 18, 22
emus, 21, 74
endangered species, 124, 172, 174, 175, 179–182, *180–185,* 188–198, *189,* 242
English myths, 50, 61, 62, 76, 79, 91
Erasmus, 105
Etruscan myths, 73
European myths, 50–61, *57,* 65, 75, 76, 89–91, 99, 131, 140, 148, 202, 212
Evelyn, John, 107
evolution, 14–26, *26–27,* 42
extinct species, 7, 16, 22, 25, *25,* 172, *174,* 174–179, *177–181,* 188, 253–255

falconry, 13, 107, 110–121, *110–119*
falcons, 89, 91, *92,* 110, *110,* 115, *118, 119,* 121, 135, 211, *213,* 215, *216, 220,* 239; hooded, *111;* merlin, 115, 116–121, 239; peregrine, 115, 116, 193; prairie, *61; see also* gyrfalcons
feathers, 16–17, 75, 160, 165–166, 168; *see also* clothing; headdresses; hats; ornaments
fêng huang (mythical), 87–88, 150
fertility symbols, 56, 78, 131–132, 140, 150, 158, 212, 221
finches, 240; Bengalese, 139; Darwin's, 26, 255; painted, *255;* weaver, 61; woodpecker, 26; zebra, 139; *see also* chaffinches; goldfinches; greenfinches; linnets

firecrests, 182

fishing, with birds, 121–124, *122*

flamingoes, *16*, 18, 127, 197, 198, 264–266; American, *27*; lesser, *199*

flight, 16–17, 28, *29*, *31*, *32*, *37*, 73

flightless birds, 16, 21, 22, *22*, 28, 178; *see also* ostriches

flycatchers, 128, 239, 255

food-getting, 18–21, 26, *26–27*, 36–41, 116–121, 258–259

fossils, 14–18, *14*, *15*, *17*, *19*, 25–26, 28

fowl, domestic, 8, 73, 89, 124, 143, *143*, 144–149, *144*, 146–148, 162, 165, 215, 216, 222, *230*, 233

fowl, jungle, 107, 143, 144

fowl, wild, *6*, 102

Francis of Assisi, St., 13, 216, *216*, 221, 235

Frederick II, Holy Roman Emperor, 13, 115, 241–242

Frost, Robert, 248

Fuertes, Louis Agassiz, *26–27*, 224, *227*, 259–260

gallinules, common, *26*

gannets, 65, 177, 242, *243*

Garuda (Hindu myth), 93, *96*, *97*, 98

geese, 18, 25, 36, 65, 75, 115, *123*, 128, 165, 212, *213*, 215, 222, 264, 267–268; barnacle, 86–87, 235, 242; brent, 242; Canada, 143; Chinese, *129*, 131, 143; domestic, 8, 128–131, *130*, 143, 144, greylag (bean), *32*, *128*, 211, *266*; Hawaiian, 188; red-breasted, 128, 211; spur-winged, *277*; white-fronted, 128, 211

gerahavs (mythical), 86

Gerda (Malayan myth), 93

German myths, 61, 65, 75, 89

Gesner, Konrad von, 222, 242

Ghiberti, Lorenzo, *240*

Giotto, 13

goatsuckers, 251

godwits, black-tailed, 182

goldfinches, 188, 211, *223*

Goldsmith, Oliver, 139

goshawks, 239

Gould, John, 139, 224, *229*

Goya, Francisco de, *244*

grebes, 16, 18, *123*, 166; horned, *26*; great crested, 45, 166; short-winged, 166; western, 45, *46–47*

Greek myths, 61, 66, 68, *68*, 73–74, 76–79, *79*, 81–83, 91, 131, 132, 140–143, 148, 149, 204, *209*, 211, 212, *215*, 216, *221*, *230*, 232, 236, 240, 247

greenfinches, 188, 245

griffins (mythical), 94, *98*, 99

grosbeaks, rose-breasted, 49

grouse, *49*, 100, 116, 196; ruffed, 34, *101*; sharp-tailed, *49*; *see also* caper-caillies

guacharos, 251

guano, 144

guillemots, 177, 193, *193*; black, 45

guinea fowl, 143, 149

gulls, 18, 41, 216, 232, 235; herring, *234*

gyrfalcons, *59*, 115, 116

habitats, 36–41, 42, 190–193, 197–198

Hakluyt, Richard, 177–178

halcyons (mythical), 81–84, *82*, 246

hansas (mythical), 131

Hardy, Thomas, 243–245

Harpies, 212

hats, feathered, *161*, 168–172, *169–171*

hawks, 110, *112–113*, 115, 116, *117*, 121, 158, 196, 212, *214*, 255; Cooper's, *26*; duck, 190; eagle, 91; kestrel, 28, 115, 190; marsh, 193, 197, 242; sparrow, 115, 121; *see also* goshawks

headdresses, feather, 6, *70–71*, *151–153*, 157–162, *158*, *160*, *163*, 172

"healing" birds, 50, 68

heath hens, 178–179

Herodotus, 79, 211

herons, 18, 79, *110*, 211, 212, 232, *239*; night, 242; purple, 197

Hesiod, 61, 79

Hesperornis, 17

Heyerdahl, Thor, 162, 193

Hindu symbols, 78, 91–93, *96*, *97*, *98*, 168, 212–215

hippogriffs (mythical), 99

Hittite myths, 212

hoatzins, 17, 261–263

Hogarth, William, 105, *106*

Homer, 131, 132

homing pigeons, 132–135, *132*, *133*

Hondecoeter, Melchior de, *143*

honeycreepers, 198; Hawaiian, 25

honey eaters, 161

honey guides, 33, 65

hoopoes, *123*, *135*, 216

hornbills: helmeted, 161; rhinoceros, 94, 161

Hudson, W. H., 248, 260–261

Humboldt, Alexander von, 136, 157, 251

hummingbirds, 21, *21*, 28, *37*, 171; ruby-throated, *187*; scintillating, 21

hunting: of birds, *6*, 8, *10–11*, 100–102, *100*, *104*, *105*, 136–139, 187–188, *201*, *210*, 211, 251, 254–255, 267–268; *see also* falconry

ibises, *218*

Icelandic myths, 65

Icthyornis, 17

imprinting, 128, 266

Indian myths, 62–63, 98, 99, 140, 212

International Council for Bird Preservation, 187

International Union for the Conservation of Nature and Natural Resources, 187

introduced species, 188–190, 193

Irish myths, 8, *56*, 86–87, 140

Islamic symbols, 131, 202–204

jacanas, pheasant-tailed, *188*

jackdaws, 236, 260–261

Japanese myths, 99, 212, 215, *215*

jays, *12*, 17, 212

Jewish symbols, 91, 131

Kano Tsuneobu, 214

Keats, John, 245–246

kingfishers, 75, 81–84, 240, 246; *see also* halcyons

Kingsley, Charles, 257

kites, 62, 193, 222, 230, 241, 242, 257; Everglades, 174; Mississippi, *224*

kiwis, 28

Lamartine, Alphonse de, 239

lammergeirs, African, 182

lapwings, *239*, *243*

larks, 22, 236, 239–241, 243; prairie horned, 42; *see also* skylarks

League of American Sportsmen, 182–187

learning, 41–42

Leopold, Aldo, 264

linnets, 102, 139, 246, 247

Longfellow, Henry, 247

Longhi, Pietro, *100*

loons, 17, 127, 197, 255–256

Lorenz, Konrad, 136, 266–267

lories, red-winged, *229*

lyre birds, *177*

macaws, 135–136; great red, 157

magpies, 50–61, 62, 196

Malayan myths, 93

manakins, 157

Marco Polo, 94, 115, 148, 149

martins, 41; house, 190; purple, *190*; sand, 190

masks, bird, *69*, 74, 77, *78*, 89, 91, *154–155*, 157, *202*

messenger birds, 132–135, *132*, *133*

Mexican myths, *72*, *73*, 74, 91

Michelangelo, 221, *223*

Middle Eastern myths, 77, 79, *79*, 89, *89*, *90*, 93, 131, 202, 204, 212, 230

migration, 28–33, *32*, 36, 45, 50, 65, 127, 182, 187

Millais, J. G., 224

Milton, John, 121, 232, 241

mimicry of speech, 42, 128, 136

moas, 22, 25, *25*

mockingbirds, *36*, 128, *226*

Molière, Jean Baptiste, 239

Mongolian myths, 78, 204

motmots, 259–260

Muir, John, 257–259

mynas, Indian, 136, 139

mythical birds, 18, 50, *52–54*, 76–99, *76*, *78–80*, *87*, *88*, *95*, *98*, 150, 161, 211, 212, *219*

nestbuilding, *6*, 65, 75, 259, 260–261

nesting colonies, *6*, *35*, 41, 42, 65, *199*

Newton, Alfred, 177, 242

nightingales, 41, 139, 196, 232, 236, 239, 241, 245–247

nightjars, 242

Norse myths, 61, 76–78, 93, 162

nutcrackers, 17

nuthatches, 22

Olson, Sigurd, 267–268

omens: bad, 61–74, *68*, 102, 230, 232, 236, 240, 246; good, 61–74, *68*, *72*, 87, 204

orioles, 247

ornaments, feather, *61*, 89, 140, 150–158, *152*, 161, *165*, 168, *168*

ornithological societies, 13, 179–187

ospreys, 182

Osteodontornis, 18

ostriches, 7, 18, *20–21*, 21–22, 102–103, *103–104*, 197, 198; feathers, 160, *161*, 162, 168–172, *169*

ouzels, 240, 257–259

owls, 25, 33, *64*, 65, *68*, 73, 212, 232, 239–241; barn, *33*; eagle, 162, 188; great horned, *36*, *64*; snowy, 182, *182*, 200

oxpeckers, 197

oystercatchers, 193

Pacific Islands myths, 61, *70–71*, 74, 202, *203*

pair bonding, 41, 42

parakeets, 161, 176; blossom-headed, 136; Carolina (extinct), 179, *180–181*

parks, national, 124, 194–198

parrots, 16, *134*, *135*, 136, 137, 212, 224, 233, 240, 256–257;

gray, 136
partridges, 17, 116; red-legged, *12*
pastors, rose-colored, 233
peace symbols, 84
peacocks, 140–143, *140–142*, 149, 168, 215, 233, 241
pelicans, 21, *35*, 84–86, *84–86*, 115, 127, 242; brown, 144; white, *31*, 196, *228*
penguins, 16, 178; yellow-eyed, *40*
Persian myths, *95*, 98–99, *99*, 204, 212, *217*
Peterson, Roger Tory, 229
Petrarch, 232, 236
petrels, giant, *197*
pets, 108–110, 135–139, *138*, *139, 141*, 233, 243–245
phalaropes, red-necked, 34
pheasants, 76, 78, *102*, 196, *205, 216*; crested love (mythical), 87–88, 150; golden, 143; silver, 143
phangs (mythical), 99
phengs (mythical), 99
Phoenician myths, 131
phoenixes (mythical), 79–81, *79, 80*, 83, *87, 88*, 99, 161, 211, *219*
Phororhacos, 18
photography, bird, 127, 224–229, 265–266
pi fangs (mythical), *88, 89*
pigeons, 74, 131, *132, 133*, 135, *198*; passenger, 172, 178–179, *178–179*, 188, 253–255; pink, 176; wood, 100, 176, 188; Torres Strait, 74
pipits, 241–242; meadow, 121
Pliny, 13, 68, 83, 132, 136, 165, 232
plovers, 246; American golden, 33, little ringed, 182; ringed, 128, 193; upland, 45
Plutarch, 66, 73–74, 78, 108
Poe, Edgar Allan, 246
pollution, 193–194
Pope, Alexander, 243
prehistoric birds, 14–26, *14, 15, 19*, 28, 94, 182
"prophetic" birds, 36, 50–51, 73, 75, 78, 91, 148
ptarmigans, 165
pterodactyls, 14
pterosaurs, 14, *17*, 18
puffins, 248; Atlantic, *27*

quails, 16, 108–110, *109*, 144, 239
quetzals, 260

Racine, Jean, 239
rails, 18
"rainmaking" birds, 36, 74, 76–78, 98, 140
Raphael, 216–221

ratites (flightless), 16
ravens, *60, 62, 63, 65*, 66, *67*, 68, 73, 74, 215, 230, 232, 239, 241, 246
Rawlings, Marjorie, 264
Ray, John, 241, 242
razorbills, 192, 193
Red Data Book, 187
redshanks, spotted, 45
redstarts, *123*; black, 182
Resurrection symbols, 81, 140, 143, 204
Rhamphorynchus, 17
rheas, 21, 22, *22*
Rig-Veda, 91, 168
robins, 36, *45*, 50, 221, 240, *241, 243*
rocs (mythical), 18, 93–94, *95, 99*
Roman myths, 68–73, 78, 79, 81, 91, *102*, 131, 140, 204, 215, 216, 232
Ronsard, Pierre de, 232, 236
rooks, 190
Rousseau, Jean-Jacques, 239
Royal Society for the Protection of Birds, 187
ruffs, *42*, 74, 75, 179, 182, 257
Russian myths, 89, 212

sacred birds, 73, 93, 131–132, 144, 202–204, 215
sacrificial birds, 6, 131, 148
sandpipers, 18; Cooper's, 179
Sassetta, Stefano, 221
Satan, 121, 241
Scott, Sir Peter, 229
sedge-birds, 257
Shakespeare, William, 61–62, 66, 81, 83, 86, *102*, 107, 108, 115–116, 240–242
Shelley, Percy, 232, 243, 246
shrikes, *123*, boubou, *198*; red-backed, 65
Siberian Indian myths, 65, 74, 75, 78
simurghs (mythical), 79, 98–99, *99*
skimmers, *38–39*
skylarks, 42, 188, 196, 236, 239, 243, 246
snipe, 257; Wilson's, 34
solitares, 128, 176
songs, bird, 33–49, 158, 236, 258, 263; recorded, 13, 127; *see also* calls
Spanish myths, 57
sparrows, 233, 239, 240, 246; hedge, 241–242; house, 188, 190; Java, 139
Spenser, Edmund, 115, 232
spontaneous generation, 79, 87
spoonbills, *197*, 257; roseate, 27
sports, 102–110, 124, 135
starlings, 136, 187, 188, 190, 198, 233, 236, *237*
storks, 18, 25, 50, *191*, 212,

222, 232, 236; whale-headed, 18, *18*; white, 33, 34
Stymphalian birds (mythical), *201*, 211
Sumerian myths, 89, 230
"sun" birds, 74, 76, 89, 91, 93, 148, 204, 215
swallows, 33, 50, 66–68, *66*, 74, 131, *142*, 190, 211, 221, 232, *236*, 239; barn, 66; fairy, *see* pigeons
swans, 8, *8, 30*, 78, 115, 204, 215, 216, *220, 221*, 232, 247, *247*; Bewick's 222; mute, 143; trumpeter, 166
swifts, 28, *32*, 41, 50, 190, 239; chimney, 190

Tennyson, Alfred, 246
teratorns: incredible, 25, 182; Merriam's, 25
terns, 28, 42; Arctic, *32*, 33; black, 197; little, 193
territorialism, 41; displays, 42; songs or calls, 34, 42, 236
Theocritus, 232
Thoreau, Henry, 248, 255–256
thrashers, 41
thrushes, 22, 41, 121, 187, 235, 239, 246; mocking, 255; song, 188, 190, 240, 246; *see also* ouzels
thunderbirds (mythical), *52–53, 76, 78, 78*
titmice, 128
toucans, *27*, 157
touracos, Hartlaub's, 158
trogons, 259–260
tropic birds, 161
turkeys: domestic, 25, 74, *142*, 143, 149, *149*; wild, 143, *195*, 197
Turkish myths, 89, *89*, 212
Turner, William, 242, 243
turtledoves, 131, 240, 255

U.S. Bureau of Sport Fisheries and Wildlife, 187
U.S. Fish and Wildlife Service, 187

varieties, bird (manmade), 135, 139, 148
Vergil, 232, 233, 235
Veronese, Paolo, 216, *221*
Vinci, Leonardo da, 216
vultures, 18, 25, *44*, 74, 75, *75*, 86, 89, 98, 197, *211*, 241; black, 74; king, 74, 238

wagtails, yellow, 61
Wallace, Alfred, 157, 256
Walton, Izaak, 236
warblers, 121, 190; great reed, 197; sedge, *41*; Tennessee, *224*; willow, 196; wood, 196
water hens, 158
waxwings, 61

"weather-forecasting" birds, 36, 50–61, 66, 76, 83, 140, 148, 232, 240
whimbrels, 116
whippoorwills, 36
White, Gilbert, 140, 242–243
whitethroats, lesser, *242*
Whitman, Walt, 247
Willughby, Francis, 222, 241, 242
Wilson, Alexander, *224*, 251–252, 259
Wilson, Edward, 224
Wood, John, 123–124
woodcocks, 36
woodpeckers, 26, 34, 68–73, 76–78, 84; black, 76; green, 76; ivory-billed, 179, *180–181*, 251–252
Wordsworth, William, 196, 245
wrens, 75, 127, 128, 240, 255; Bewick's, 222; chiffchaff, 242; house, 190; Kentucky, *224*; prairie, 224; willow, 242; winter (European), 34, 42, 158, 235; wood, 242
wrynecks, 33, 50

Yeats, William Butler, 247

Zahl, Paul A., 264–266

CREDITS

The sources for the illustrations in this book are shown below. Abbreviations used: AMNH—American Museum of Natural History, MMA—Metropolitan Museum of Art, NAS—National Audubon Society, NYPL—New York Public Library

6, British Museum
7, Emil Schulthess from Black Star
8, Chase Manhattan Bank
9, Harald Schultz
10–11, George Holton
12, Museo delle Terme, Rome
13, British Museum
14, AMNH
15, AMNH
16, A. W. Ambler from NAS
17, AMNH
18, Arthur Christiansen
19, AMNH
20, Leonard Lee Rue III from NAS
21, AMNH
22, Leonard Lee Rue III from NAS
23, Howard S. Friedman
24, Alan Rokach
25, AMNH
26, *top and center* Mrs. Mary Fuertes Boyton
bottom Laboratory of Ornithology, Cornell University
27, AMNH
28, H. R. Duncker
29, Andreas Feininger
30, Arthur Christiansen
31, *top* Andreas Feininger
bottom E. Bry
32, *both* Arthur Christiansen
bottom Dave Repp from NAS
33, Eric Hosking
34, Arthur Christiansen
35, Guido Cregor
36, *top and bottom* Ronald Austing from NAS
37, Bruce Coleman
38–39, Hans D. Dossenbach
40, Francisco Erize
41, Arthur Christiansen
42, Arthur Christiansen
43, Arthur Christiansen
44, Arthur Christiansen
45, *left* Phillip Strobridge from NAS
right O. S. Pettingill, Jr. from NAS
46–47, Ed Bry
48, New York Zoological Society
49, *left and right* Ed Bry
50, Blackader Library, McGill University
51, Walter Aguiar
52–53, AMNH
54, NYPL
55, *top* AMNH
bottom British Museum
56, Musée de l'homme, Paris
57, Ampliaciones NAS
58, *top* Walter Aguiar
bottom MMA
59, MMA
60, Badia Fiorentina, Florence
61, AMNH

62, Nelson Gallery-Atkins Museum, Kansas City
63, George Holton
64, Lynwood M. Chace
65, Ed Bry
66, Ed Bry
67, Robert J. Erwin from NAS
68, Chase Manhattan Bank
69, *top and bottom* Museum of the American Indian, New York
70–71, George Holton
72, AMNH
73, Walter Aguiar
75, MMA
76, AMNH
77, MMA
78, AMNH
79, Giraudon
80, MMA
81, NYPL
82, NYPL
84, Jessie Gibbs
85, MMA
86, NYPL
87, British Museum
88, MMA
89, Musée de l'homme, Paris
90, MMA
91, *left* Chase Manhattan Bank
right New York State Historical Association
92, MMA
93, George Holton
94, MMA
95, The British Library
96, Indonesian Consulate General
97, The Brooklyn Museum
98, The Brooklyn Museum
99, The Pierpont Morgan Library, New York
100, Galleria Querini Stampalia, Venice
101, The Bettmann Archive
102, Bibliothèque Nationale
103, The Pierpont Morgan Library, New York
104, AMNH
105, NYPL
106, NYPL
107, Free Lance Photographers Guild
108, NYPL
109, NYPL
110, The Bettmann Archive
111, MMA
112–113, MMA
114, Shelly Grossman from Alpha Photo Associates
115, The Bettmann Archive
117, Victoria and Albert Museum
118, Foto Claus, Fulda, Germany
119, *both* Akademischer Druck, Graz, Austria
120, Bibliothèque de l'Arsenal, Paris
121, Walter Aguiar
122, Japan National Tourist Organization
123, MMA
125, A. W. Ambler from NAS
126, Allan D. Cruickshank from NAS
127, Willis Peterson

128, Ronald Thompson from Annan Photo Features
129, Jane J. Miller
130, George Holton
131, MMA
132, U.S. Army
133, MMA
134, Harald Schultz
135, *left* William T. Hoff
right Pictorial Parade
136, MMA
137, The Pierpont Morgan Library, New York
138, Pictorial Parade
139, John Carnemolla from Free Lance Photographers Guild
140, Jack Dermid
141, Victoria and Albert Museum
142, MMA
143, Synagogue of Ma'on, Nirim, Israel
144, MMA
145, Jane J. Miller
146–147, Jane J. Miller
148, Paul Popper
149, Victoria and Albert Museum
150, Chase Manhattan Bank
151, Rodman Wanamaker from AMNH
152, Harald Schultz
153, George Holton
154–155, George Holton
156, George Holton
157, AMNH
158, Museum of the American Indian, New York
159, Museum of the American Indian, New York
160, AMNH
161, Free Lance Photographers Guild
162, MMA
163, Pictorial Parade
164, AMNH
165, AMNH
166, NAS
167, Harald Schultz
168, MMA
169, *top* Culver Pictures
bottom Photo World
170, The Bettmann Archive
171, The Bettmann Archive
172, The Bettmann Archive
173, S. A. Grimes
174, AMNH
175, Willis Peterson
177, *top* Blau Pix
bottom Eric Hosking
178, The Bettmann Archive
179, Smithsonian Institution
180, NAS
181, NAS
182, *top* Wilford L. Miller from NAS
bottom Carl Koford from NAS
183, F. W. Lahrman from NAS
184–185, Lovett Williams from NAS
186, Jack Dermid
187, Ronald Austing from NAS
188, Loke Wan Tho
189, R. Van Nostrand from NAS
190, Jack Dermid

191, French Government Tourist Office
192, Alvin E. Staffan from NAS
193, Arthur Christiansen
194, Free Lance Photographers Guild
195, Duryea Morton from NAS
197, John Warham
198, George Holton
199, Mark Boulton from NAS
200, Photo Windels
201, British Museum
202, University Museum, Philadelphia
203, *top* Sovfoto
bottom George Holton
204, Musée de l'Unterlinden, Colmar, France
205, MMA
206–207, George Holton
208, MMA
209, Louvre
210, *top* MMA
bottom George Holton
211, MMA
212, AMNH
213, *top* MMA
bottom Brooklyn Museum
214, MMA
215, *both* British Museum
216, *top* Niedersachsische Landesgalerie, Hanover
bottom British Museum
217, MMA
218, *top* Royal Ontario Museum
bottom George Holton
219, George Holton
220, Nelson Gallery-Atkins Museum, Kansas City
221, Alinari
222, Blacker-Wood Library, McGill University
223, *top* Royal Academy of Arts, London
bottom MMA
224, NYPL
225, James Valentine courtesy Emory University Library
226, James Valentine courtesy Emory University Library
227, Field Museum
228, New York Historical Society
229, Blacker-Wood Library, McGill University
230, MMA
231, George Holton
233, George Holton
234, Arthur Christiansen
235, The Pierpont Morgan Library, New York
236, Eric Hosking
237, *top* NYPL
bottom Arthur Christiansen
238, A. W. Ambler from NAS
239, MMA
240, Alinari
241, Eric Hosking from NAS
242, Arthur Christiansen
243, NYPL
244, Prado
245, MMA
247, Arthur Christiansen
248, Leonard Lee Rue III
249, George Holton